De-
ath
life

De

HIP HOP AND THANATOLOGICAL
NARRATIONS OF BLACKNESS

ANTHONY B. PINN

ath—
life

DUKE UNIVERSITY PRESS
Durham and London   2024

Printed in the United States of America on acid-free paper ∞
Project Editor: Livia Tenzer
Designed by Courtney Leigh Richardson
Typeset in Warnock Pro with Raginy and Knockout
by Westchester Publishing Services

Library of Congress Cataloging-in-Publication Data
Names: Pinn, Anthony B., author.
Title: Deathlife : Hip Hop and thanatological narrations of
blackness / Anthony B. Pinn.
Description: Durham : Duke University Press, 2024. | Includes
bibliographical references and index.
Identifiers: LCCN 2023015283 (print)
LCCN 2023015284 (ebook)
ISBN 9781478025412 (paperback)
ISBN 9781478020608 (hardcover)
ISBN 9781478027485 (ebook)
ISBN 9781478093824 (ebook other)
Subjects: LCSH: Rap (Music)—Religious aspects. | Rap
(Music)—Social aspects. | Hip-hop—Influence. | African
Americans—Songs and music—Social aspects. | African
Americans—Race identity. | Death in music. | Life. | BISAC:
SOCIAL SCIENCE / Ethnic Studies / American / African
American & Black Studies | MUSIC / Genres & Styles /
Rap & Hip Hop
Classification: LCC ML3921.8.R36 P56 2024 (print) | LCC
ML3921.8.R36 (ebook) | DDC 782.421649—dc23/eng/20231023
LC record available at https://lccn.loc.gov/2023015283
LC ebook record available at https://lccn.loc.gov/2023015284

Cover art: Antoine Williams, *You Thirsty!?*, 2017. Ink on vellum.
Courtesy of the artist.

This book is freely available in an open access edition thanks to TOME
(Toward an Open Monograph Ecosystem)—a collaboration of the
Association of American Universities, the Association of University
Presses, and the Association of Research Libraries—and the generous
support of Rice University. Learn more at the TOME website, available
at: openmonographs.org.

Dedicated to

those who can imagine
Sisyphus happy

CONTENTS

PART I

Signifying Deathlife

PART II

Consuming Deathlife

ACKNOWLEDGMENTS

This book was a long time coming—delayed in numerous ways by the trauma of COVID. Despite many difficulties, the project was finished and you now hold the book in your hands (or see it on your screen). Getting to this point took the hard work and dedication of many, and I want to thank them. First, I must thank my editor, Miriam Angress, for her confidence in this project and her energy and insights resulting in moving it from files on my computer to finished book. I must also thank the Duke University Press team—thank you! In addition, the external reviewers offered comments, critiques, and suggestions that made the book much better. I appreciate the time they put into reading my manuscript, and I'm grateful for the ways in which they helped me refine my argument.

My friend and colleague Maya Reine worked in record time to address formatting and stylistic issues related to preparing the final manuscript for submission. Other friends like Corey Garrett, Pastor Rudy Rasmus, Bun B, Philip Butler, Terrence Johnson, Juan Floyd-Thomas, Erika Gault, and a host of others helped me think through the ideas presented here. I'm also appreciative for the opportunity to present some of these ideas at a variety of institutions—including Hannover Institute for Philosophical Research (Hannover, Germany), St. Lawrence University, College of Charleston, Paris Lodron University (Salzburg), Bucknell University, and University of Southern Mississippi. I extend my appreciation to my students—undergraduate and graduate—whose appreciation for hip hop and its implications has been an inspiration. Finally, as always, I'm grateful to my family for love, support, encouragement, and perfectly timed text messages!

PARADIGMS OF DEATH (OR LIFE)
AND *DEATHLIFE*

Perhaps the whole root of our trouble, the human trouble, is that we will sacrifice all the beauty of our lives, will imprison ourselves in totems, taboos, crosses, blood sacrifices, steeples, mosques, races, armies, flags, nations, in order to deny the fact of death, the only fact we have. It seems to me that one ought to rejoice in the fact of death—ought to decide, indeed, to earn one's death by confronting with passion the conundrum of life.
—JAMES BALDWIN, *The Fire Next Time*

In light of ongoing existential circumstances, Black expressive culture naturally has interrogated and wrestled with the constitution of existence—its beginning, its present, and its end. Why would it be otherwise when, as the above epigraph makes clear, denial of the realness of death is futile and unproductive in that it deforms both the nature and the meaning of death and life?

Death and life: while some, as is the American way, seek to sever the connection between the two, social circumstances contain language and practices (e.g., cultural depictions of Black bodies as dangerous, "law and order," geographic confinement as something like a grave) that serve to reinforce their relationship despite objections. To avoid this discussion is to misunderstand history and deform aesthetic framing of the social world. They—death and life—are thought together to the extent that being for Black bodies involves the simultaneous potentiality of both, and this generates a geography of speculation both reasonable (drawn from interrogation of sociopolitical, economic, and cultural conditions) and affective. One way to describe this relationship of death and life is through the image of dying. And, so, what Victor Brombert says concerning Franz Kafka's take on death—one whose poor health kept death always a consideration—is applicable here. "Death for Kafka means not an end," Brombert writes, "nor a passing (or passage) located in a time soon to come, but an everlasting reality of pain in the present; not in fact death, but a permanent dying."[1]

Pushing forward, Blackness attached to certain bodies has long functioned as a trope, a graphic sign, of this dying—housing at once the terror of death and the longing for life. In a sense, Blackness within the context of the United States has served as a frame for decay, a relationship to social chaos constituted by and monitored in terms of the counterdynamics of whiteness. And in this narration, in this performance against (Black) death and for the sake of (white) life, Black bodies are always and already representative of a perceived dangerous intersection. To think and perform Blackness is, within the context of our social world, to negotiate death and life. In fact, Blackness is constituted by the coherence, the coterminous relationship, of death and life as this is projected onto certain weight-carrying communities. As a consequence, in terms of physical exposure and metaphysical restriction, the history of the United States in relationship to Blackness is a history of demise—an often-denied performance of what I call *deathlife*. One of the more graphic narrations of this configuration comes from hip hop culture. In certain ways, hip hop culture—and I am particularly concerned with the lyrical content of rap music—offers a language, an alternate grammar and vocabulary, for articulating the nature and meaning of *deathlife*.

In what follows here, I position *deathlife* against another paradigm—life distinctive from death—in order to set the stage for its application vis-à-vis rap music.[2] The examination of these two paradigms isn't intended to suggest a distinction between death and *deathlife*. Rather, my aim is to isolate for discussion the intent behind *deathlife* as a structuring of the Other. Whites, by means of whiteness, don't "see" *deathlife*—privilege involves not having to. Instead, they feel its meaning and name its impact using the language of death *or* life.[3] The distinction (death *or* life versus *deathlife*) is a matter of orientation (whiteness or Blackness), not substance. In making this claim, in the following section, I mean to highlight, from the vantage point of whiteness's logic, a cartographical presentation of *deathlife* cast as death *or* life. The goal is to provide a sense of how embodied Blacks are positioned within US social arrangements related to *deathlife* (or what whiteness projects as death *or* life) and the discourse of anxiety marking this positioning of Blackness.[4] The aim of whiteness in so doing is to position Blacks in relationship to death and life—and in this way ratify the social world. In making this argument, I begin to contextualize and offer pretext for narrations of *deathlife* that are presented in the remaining chapters.

Paradigm I: Life or/and Death

How does it feel to be a problem?
—**W. E. B. DU BOIS**, *The Souls of Black Folk*

By considering the manner in which Blackness has been constructed as the meaning of death for whites, and publicly performed as the "technology" of *deathlife*, I want to extend the notion of Blacks as a problem presented by W. E. B. Du Bois early in *The Souls of Black Folk*.[5] And I do this by recognizing that the "Veil"—his term for what is not only a material source of division and exclusion but also a type of hermeneutical device, or tool of perception—hampers the manner in which Black people are viewed and understood by whites, but affords a clear presentation of whites.[6] Hence, Blacks as a problem is tied to the production of whiteness (by white people) and its aims. Mindful of this, I want to note the flip side of that formulation (i.e., Blacks as a problem) by briefly considering Du Bois's later formulation of whiteness as presented in the essay "The Souls of White Folks." For Du Bois, something about the second sight of Blacks allows them to "see" and to know whites—to view them from a place of familiarity in that he, like all Black people, is "bone of their thought and flesh of their language." This is a deep familiarity informing Black people, but one that troubles and angers whites, resulting in white denial of Black people's substance and place within the social world; instead, as Du Bois writes, "They deny my right to live and be and call me misbirth! My word is to them mere bitterness and my soul, pessimism."[7]

Undergirding this is a modern development: the creation of white people as unique and special, the measure of humanity, the standard, ontology's conclusion, with Blacks as a failed ontology in that they are defined by a radical status as "not like whites." This is a modern logic, which serves to shape the expanse of the social world and all its resources—and which is summed up by the category of whiteness. Or, as Du Bois expresses the predicament, "There must come the necessary despisings and hatreds of these savage half-men, this unclean canaille of the world—these dogs of men. All through the world this gospel is preaching. It has its literature, it has its priests, it has its secret propaganda and above all—it pays!"[8]

Whiteness is a justification for total consumption, for unbridled expression of desire; it frames a system of thought combined with diabolical practice that is sanctioned through violence and disregard of any (and all) who pose a threat to this logic of superiority and its grand claims. Or, in Du Bois's words, "Whiteness is the ownership of the earth forever and ever, Amen!"[9] According to the grand narrative, without the presence of whiteness and white people to maintain it, the world would lack substance and meaning—and instead would devolve into chaos. Du Bois sees the trick here, knows the falseness of such claims, and names what whiteness puts in place to manage such exposure. This barbarity isn't a misrepresentation of white people, not a misnaming of whiteness; rather, it is the very nature of white culture. Maintenance of this falsehood is intense and bloody. It is rabid in its moralizing and championing of a white world through condemnation of Blackness vis-à-vis Black people: "Say to a people: 'The one virtue is to be white,' and the people rush to the inevitable conclusion, 'Kill the "nigger"!'"[10]

Here, one begins to see the manner (and means) by which whiteness captures the idea of Blacks through a discourse of anxiety, with Blackness constructed as a corrective narration of *deathlife* distinct from the experience of whiteness as a relationship of life *over against* death. In other words, the construction of Blackness carried through Black bodies is meant to isolate death for the white population in something other than themselves. By so doing, Blackness through Black bodies takes on death so that others (i.e., white members of the social world) are able to operate through a controlled encounter with death. Put another way, I am suggesting that whites (through the development and operation of whiteness) work to construct existential arrangements and ontological structures that make death visible and "manageable" by projecting it onto Black bodies.

White bodies do experience death, but whites are able to "attach"—a type of projection—their worst fears about death (as the taking of life), the most grotesque dimensions of their anxiety of death, to Black bodies. This happens with respect to two geographies: (1) physical demise and (2) irrelevance—as an ontological and epistemological rupture in its most graphic form.

The nature and meaning of death have changed; the locations for death and the framing of death have altered due to various socioeconomic, political, and cultural shifts in collective life over the centuries. Yet something related to the awareness of death remains in place and undergirds reflective awareness of life's vulnerability. Whites live with an understanding of and fear regarding the end of physical existence. This is such a strong component of individual and collective life that physical death loses its distinctiveness and becomes less easily distinguished from what is called life. In this regard, one might think in terms of material, physical life/death as opposed to a much clearer distinction such as life . . . death.[11] There have been efforts, of course, to control, monitor, and ritualize material death (the end of vital biological functions), or to privatize it so as to make it manageable, to make it fit within a particular sociocultural understanding.

Death experienced in this form gives whites time, resource, and opportunity to work out arrangements in a way consistent with individual need/ want and in light of communal assumptions and priorities. It might involve arrangement of resources, nurturing relationships, and so on. This is an economy of death that is manageable and to some extent "owned" by whites. The opposite of this, the type of death avoided, involves a hard death, entailing death that is untimely (outside the socially assumed chronological frame for human life), death that is violent or in some other way outside the pattern of life or death desired by the person, or death that for any other reason is outside the dominant narrative of life or death. Such death disrupts sociocultural arrangements that mark out life or physical being within a given community. In this way, physical death produces *dis*-ease within a community and fosters a certain type of anxiety within individuals.

While there may be cultural nuance and difference in the practices of marking off and discussing death, whites and Blacks use similar structuring(s) of physical death; laws, for instance, determine how any body can be disposed of or stored.[12] The physical body, the biochemical reality whose biological functions end, can be ritually addressed after death.[13] It can be mourned, represented in a variety of ways, and then set apart from living in a clear and "final" manner. It can be presented and available to the living in cemeteries and urns but still at a safe distance from the living, confined, managed, epistemologically docile. Not so with irrelevance premised on a certain epistemology. It, the body, must be apparent, in place, and exposed to life so as to differentiate it from that which isn't meaninglessness. In this regard, the practices related to the material body are fairly set across cultures and social dynamics. For example, whites and Blacks both use professionals who prepare bodies for presentation and ritualized goodbyes, and so on. Yet there are limits to this connection, in that death as presented here grabs at Blacks in certain ways and casts Blacks in a particular relationship to demise. The challenge is this: contacts, or communities, nurture structures of connection that ease the reality of death, but they also involve the production of circumstances (e.g., diseases and violence) that undercut the offerings of relationship. There is the movement through the world aware that life is framed by death, and death by life.[14] This, of course, is true for those who are considered human in ways that have fundamental mattering—who are socioeconomically, politically, religiously, and culturally human—that is, whites.[15]

The arts have recognized and faced this dilemma over and over again. Particular social developments and challenges have prompted this recognition and the need to aesthetically present it. Karla FC Holloway's insight is worth noting: there is an intimate link between "color and death." And this connection guides much of what she, and others who hold to this opinion, says about the nature and meaning of the rituals and processes of addressing physical demise within Black communities. In addition, Holloway argues, this connection between color and death shaped cultural production, as the arts became a way to express the nature and meaning of this tragic relationship.[16] But regardless of the motivation, the arts have marked out deep awareness of this limitation. On this point I share a question with Sharon Patricia Holland: "What if some subjects never achieve, in the eyes of others, the status of the 'living'?" Our answers are different. Holland frames the question in light of Toni Morrison's brilliant *Beloved* and raises the specter of existing with the dead, being "at one with the dead."[17] For Holland, Blacks are perceived as ghosts.[18] Not so for me—and this is where we begin to move away from the physicality of death. I suggest Blacks do not achieve the status of the "living" not because they are categorized with the dead—the ancestors, for instance—but because they are neither fully objects nor fully subjects. Put another way, they have a particular materiality—an embodiedness that produces discomfort and anxiety in the general non-Black population—but they have limited metaphysical importance, in that their presence is without deep epistemological and ontological significance because they have no will that matters. They, through socioeconomic and political arrangements, for example, are put in place and monitored by the dominant population; in this way, they occupy an in-between space of sorts.

The dead must also be "alive"—present, ever-present—if the meaning of whiteness is to have meaning. But the dead can't be so present as to cause epistemological and ontological discomfort on a fundamental level for those (advocates of white supremacy, among others) depending on this particular arrangement of the dead. Put differently, Blacks must be recognizable— "human" enough to be visible, or regarded—but not able to demand so much attention, or significance in time and space, as to threaten those who advocate modalities of white advantage. One might think of the deaths of Michael Brown, George Floyd, Breonna Taylor, and Trayvon Martin as representing this visceral desire to maintain the placement of Black bodies.[19] To talk about death—to understand it on some level within and beyond its most superficial dimensions as confrontation of the senses in the form of physical demise—is to talk about life. This, nonetheless, is a reality fought on a variety of fronts. The logic of life, in fact, is death.

ONTOLOGICAL DEATH

There are ways in which the very presence of Blacks in North America entails a certain type of death. Slavery, as the sociologist Orlando Patterson has aptly noted, involves social death: the surrender of will or authority for the sake of physical life.[20] This arrangement has certainly shaped the context and content of Blacks' existence in the Americas, but I have in mind a different dimension of this situation, related, but to be wrestled with in its own right. What Patterson describes so vividly entails the existential arrangements of "life," the experience of living within a context of race-based discrimination. The embodied Black body is confined in time and space in ways felt through the flesh and in relationship to other bodies. Yet there are also ontological considerations of note, meaning ways in which the very being of Blacks is defined by the presence of demise. Indeed, the Black body as social construct is the language of demise, in that it was meant to signify and speak of and tame the end of being as a subject. This ontological death is not the end of vital functions such as heart activity or brain activity. Nor do I mean the end of spiritual vitality in a traditional religious-theological sense. This is not death as a physical or "spiritual" condition, but rather death more fully as an ontological positioning and an epistemological rupture regarding knowledge of being, of life integrity, of dignity, and so on. It is the loss of meaning more generally as opposed to the particular ending of a particular person's mattering.[21]

This ontological and epistemological situation means the "identity" of Blacks isn't simply marked by stigma. That is to say, Erving Goffman's keen work on the nature and meaning of the stigma as marking a person who is "re-duced in our minds from a whole and usual person to a tainted, discounted one" doesn't fully capture the construction—epistemologically and ontologically—of Blacks.[22] For Blacks aren't simply human with both "virtual" *and* "actual" social identity as less than—as somehow and in some way impure. It isn't a matter of a Black person, a complex human being understood or stereo-typed in a way that renders them problematic or deficient in some way.[23] No, the Black person means something more fundamentally different, and perceived as a necessary danger. Stigma has too limited a range of influence and form, in that any given attribute can render an individual "usual" or "un-usual."[24] Such is not the case for Blacks, for whom the challenge is always and already deeply ontological-epistemological and expressed existentially. Even the idea that some "attributes" are always a problem doesn't fully capture the situation. Furthermore, the "not quite human" sense, as Goffman outlines it, the sense of race as a stigma, doesn't recognize sufficiently the nature of the ontological *dis*-ease (not simply social understandings and arrangements, that is, social identity) assumed to be constituted by Blackness. In some re-spects, what Goffman points out as stigma involves a type of social and/or physical symmetry lacking in some persons. For the Black person, however, it is more than this lack of symmetry.[25]

What Neil Small says concerning the discussion of death within scholar-ship and as differentiated over time in the West is relevant here: "Death is the apotheosis of this grand dream of control and of the belief in the power of the ordered."[26] As Blacks have been constructed as death, this means for those needing and wanting this arrangement that death is both sought and feared—having something of a religious quality. It is an odd arrangement: Blacks are projected as death within a context fighting to keep death at bay, and participation in American life in any substantive way requires Blacks to buy into the death they are projected as constituting. With this in mind, it is clear that Russ Castronovo's intriguing notion of "necro citizenship" fails to fully capture what I mean to represent here. He argues that US democ-racy enjoys nonresponsive citizens—Blacks—who do not react to political developments, who are passive and still, who are . . . corpses.[27] His sense of a citizenry rendered docile, disengaged, corpselike entails some of the actual consequences associated with the irrelevance or death of African Ameri-cans, but I have more in mind, more than the sociopolitical spheres of life. For Castronovo there is something about recognition of morality as political capital that says a word about "democratic existence within the state."[28] The corpse—the body—can be dead, or it can be reanimated through particular shifts in political ideals, practices, and sensibilities. This sense of death, of the final disembodiment, understood within the context of "necro citizenship," has something to do with the sense of privatization that so many have understood as the modern turn regarding the dead, while the political is public. This separation isn't certain and it isn't fixed, when, for instance, one considers the political importance of the social death of enslaved Africans.[29] I mean something more fundamental by "irrelevance" over against the "dis/embodied experience, social position, and political metaphor" intended by Castronovo. The death I describe is the structuring of knowledge about Blacks in spheres of collective interaction (such as their educational ability and criminality) and the very meaning of Black bodies that undergirds these other historical patterns of individual and collective life. Death so conceived is one reason we can talk about bodies mattering.[30]

It is not the case, nor need it be, that all agree Blacks are so constructed. The manner of structuring Blacks as such isn't dependent on consensus. It only needs to become the dominant logic, with white people benefiting directly and indirectly from its normativity, and this doesn't preclude slippage regarding when and how Blacks are so understood. The presentation of this logic must be compelling or at least presented in light of a shared need, and over time it will become the unspoken reality, the assumed condition. It, this logic, to borrow and apply in a different context a phrase from Albert Camus, entails "solidarity against death."[31] Undergirding this configuration of Blacks is an epistemologically grounded and ontological move: Blacks are needed in order for meaning to be and to be lodged in the "life" of whites. Within this narrative of meaning, Blacks are a cautionary tale suggesting the importance of accepting the dominant structuring of individual and collective existence— of safeguarding against contamination. Letting one's guard down in the presence of Blacks can result only in destruction of social existence as vital, vibrant, and humane. This second form of death, according to whiteness, is a meaninglessness that restricts life force to memory: it subjects one to the caprice of others, to the will of others who determine to what degree one has presence. It is to be without the human will that "matters." Ontology, through death, is warped, and social relationship involves confinement and destruction.

This discussion is not one simply regarding alterity—the Other as a "presence" to be recognized and addressed. Such cannot be the case when Blacks are ontologically and epistemologically dead—that is, irrelevant. This difference in being won't be addressed by simply recognizing the Other or having the Other recognize the dominant mode of humanity. Even the aesthetic representation of Blacks, from the minstrel shows' "Zip Coon" moving forward, offers yet another way in which the Black person serves as the marker of death, represented in and by the cultural frameworks and imagination of the general public.[32] It is in thinking of Blacks in this way, and presenting them in this fashion, that whites over the course of centuries have been able to envision themselves as alive, or invested with meaning, as subjects moving and arranging their world. Over against Blacks, they have relevance within a social world marked by no central and consistent meaning.[33] Everything about Blacks as being irrelevant has an underlying function of affirming as right this grand narrative of white life *over against* death. There is a warped assumption that, through Blackness, whites can harness reality and control it through a mode of prescience.[34]

Blacks are constructed as the embodiment and discourse of danger, destruction, and disorder, whose very efforts to produce meaning result in contamination and chaos that must be controlled by naming them irrelevant.[35] Yet, oddly enough, this process is not without its weak points. For instance, to the extent Blacks cannot be forgotten within the US narrative of white domination, the Black person is immortal: dead to the extent that they are projected as without meaning, but perpetually alive to the extent that their memory is essential for the safeguarding of the American narrative. Some have recognized such weaknesses and have worked to exploit them, if by no other means than signifying them. From my perspective, that is the case with hip hop culture in general and rap music in particular. Those who carry the bodies of symbolic death (and who pose the threat of physical death) speak in haunting tones of their demise and what it means for the larger structures of existential concern within the US context.[36] More precisely, hip hop culture is an intervention of sorts, marking a cultural shift—a change in the grammar and vocabulary of living that acknowledges the presence of death. But, through this acknowledgment of death tied to Blackness, rap artists seek to shift its significance and benefit. That is, rather than this association with the workings of death acting as a marker of a less-than status, it is used to project substance. In this situation, meaning is *me*(an)*ing*, or a tension between the individual and frameworks of communality played out through/in the fragility of life.

Exposing and Claiming Death

My aim in this section is not to offer a full rehearsal of how rap is related to death in general or murder in particular. Instead, I want to share a few examples to establish a sense of how death functions in much rap music. As artists guided by this paradigm reflect, one has no choice but to consider death and life, to be aware of both. A sense that they are distinguishable entails a point of graphic and explosive conversation.

With respect to physical demise, hip hop has something of an elegiac quality—an irreverent poetic reflection on those who are dead, which includes by its very nature rehearsal of death's production. Such is the concern with relationship to death, which is to say, how one interacts with it. In certain ways murder is a dominant motif and, in this manner, it is tied to the Western preoccupation with the ending of life through crafted narratives exploring demise. As Michael Collins reflects, "The beautiful murder, the murder lifted into the mind by 'winged words,' is in many ways the heartbeat of American culture—indeed, of all western culture."[37] The situation, however, is more focused than that—situated within a particular social geography—and, so, what James Baldwin reflects regarding the nature of socioeconomic and cultural life for Blacks in mid-twentieth-century Harlem holds true for hip hop's attention to death. The circumstances related to the awareness of loss, or epistemological clarity, make plain that "your losses are coming."[38]

I want to avoid the quick move to the "why" of killing and instead describe and analyze the "how" and "what" of killing within hip hop culture qua rap. In other words, murder in rap is often viewed from the vantage point of life—what it takes away—yet there are important ways in which murder in hip hop also speaks about the substance of death. Much has already been made of the taking of life, or the presence of active demise, within hip hop culture, particularly as chronicled in gangsta rap.[39] And this focus is not without good reason, when one considers the sociocultural impact of the gangsta personae that emerged during the culture wars of the 1980s and in relationship to the age of crack. So, something about the effort to claim time and space, to constitute presence and significance, is connoted through the ability to consume time and space (i.e., murder).

Resembling a thematic arc found in the fiction of Richard Wright, relevance (or what Calvin Warren might call "ontological murder") for a despised Black figure seeking to be a subject within an anti-Black social environment involves the ability to take life.[40] If one cannot determine fully the shape of one's own social existence, one can produce it through negation—through the ability to end the (social) life of another. There is a "feel" for living produced by the taking of life—a carving out of psychological space and meaning through the void resulting from the manufacturing of demise.[41] For Blacks, as Wright and later rap artists would attest, the possibility of physical or ontological demise is always present, always threatening. Does one take life, or does one have one's life taken?

Taking life becomes the ontological equivalent of having life. Think, for example, of active demise as a marker of being represented in Dr. Dre and Ice Cube's 1994 song "Natural Born Killaz." Life is amplified through the consumptive power of death. While Ice Cube described the song as satire, there's no concern or remorse regarding the consequences of life taken. Rather there is only an excitement at times erotic in nature: "It feels like I'm bustin' a nut when I open you up."[42] Presented from the perspective of the one who controls life by taking it, vitality is determined in light of a signifying of codes meant to safeguard life. Murder is without a larger logic and without grand claims. It takes place because it can, and within this possibility of demise the murderer constructs an arrangement in which one controls life through death. The "right" to life is superseded by the ability to end life. In this sense, production of death serves as a signifier of subjectivity, as a mode of being in contradistinction to social dictates. Or, in the words of DMX,

> Look me in my eyes (WHAT!)
> Tell me to my fuckin' face that you ready to die (C'mon).[43]

Murder, then, is the performance of a twisted personhood. It is not only the taking of life by murder that constitutes a marker of significance; ontological vitality is also constituted through being the target of murderous intent.

Biggie Smalls (The Notorious B.I.G.), murdered in 1997, famously outlines this philosophy of existence in "You're Nobody ('Til Somebody Kills You)"—the counter to Dean Martin's "You're Nobody till Somebody Loves You."[44] The visual imagery associated with the track presents Biggie Smalls dressed in a long black coat and hat, leaning against a hearse, looking out at the person holding the record album. The license plate with the letters "B.I.G." suggests the artist is the one orchestrating or ritualizing the transition between realms, serving as something along the lines of a funeral director. From this cover imagery to the lyrics, death is present. Through the track, Biggie Smalls comes to grips with death by seeking to manage it, to determine its arrival and its target. This isn't quite the gangsta encountered through "Natural Born Killaz," but death is still managed. Although the posture is a bit different, there is still a direct relationship between projected personal meaning and destruction of the Other. A direct relationship, a metaphysical mutuality, between taking and sustaining life is apparent and graphically portrayed through the defiant Black body occupying time and space. Agency is aggregated and signified through a body count.[45]

Something about this arrangement of ignoble reciprocity speaks to the metaphysical significance of the dead Black (male) body. Or, as Lindon

Barrett reflects, "The dead black body may be an ultimate figure of regulation, unruly desire and its risks fully mastered. Yet, as the unfolding history of the United States attests in particular, what is most interesting is that this form of death has a highly useful social valence," marked by a type "of social productivity."[46] What Biggie Smalls outlines in "You're Nobody" isn't hip hop's presentation of the martyr. That is to say, the track doesn't advocate seeking (or welcoming) demise, but rather indicates one's value is determined by the desire to murder that it generates in others. Importance or worth involves negation, a mode of absence—ultimately the value of one's life is measured in the void generated by its ending. In relationship to the materiality of being, the measure is the desirability of one's economic holdings: one is valued to the extent one has things others will kill to secure. But on a more ontological level, significance for the Black body is measured against the merit of loss. Value is determined by how aggressively another tries to bring about one's nonbeing. This is a radical give-and-take by means of which substance is assessed by a significant absence, and importance is defined by the appeal of a void. There is a tragicomic quality to these circumstances: tragic in that they define the existential environment described (and lived?) by the artist, and comic to the extent the artist is aware of these arrangements and seeks to maneuver with swag and thereby live despite the price for living.[47]

Still, death is accepted as part of the game but also denied, or, as the chorus of Biggie Small's track laments, "I don't wanna die, God tell me why."[48] Even so, to be (of worth) is to be in reach of death. Both the deceased and the one who murders claim substance, announce their presence through demise. Nonetheless, there is a paradox in play. The one who is killed, because of the rationale for taking that life, has inflated significance (they are "worth" killing) but is also diminished by the act. In other words, death is two-faced, jaded. It exposes, renders transparent, the cartography of status, signifying both the inauthentic and the celebrated real social substance:

> You can be the shit, flash the fattest five (that's right)
> Have the biggest dick, but when your shell get hit
> You ain't worth spit, just a memory.[49]

Biggie Smalls's album depicts the distinction between life and death, while recognizing circumstances can result in a quick transition from the former to the latter. Pride, prowess, money, and status can easily fuel a demand for blood. Puff Daddy's rehearsing of Psalm 23:4–6 ("Yea, though I walk through the valley of the shadow of death, I will fear no evil . . ."), with which the song starts, is quickly overcome by Biggie Smalls's recounting of life marked by "strictly gun-testin', coke-measurin.'"[50] Is he the chosen one framed by the scripture rehearsed? Or do the lyrics signify scripture by offering an orientation premised not on the blessing of life, but rather on the promise of death—expressing the fragility of life in which divine assistance doesn't trump the intent of a murderer?

The bestowing of subjectivity isn't a matter of divine creation and orientation but instead is found in the bringing of death—"somebody" does the killing and in that process of taking bestows personhood. Obtaining material goods doesn't constitute this personhood but merely becomes the occasion of a certain visibility that, through death, brings meaning. Death consumes life and leaves behind residue in the form of memories and reputation. The curiosity about a theologized depiction of life qua scripture over against existential concerns is short-circuited through a materialist turn because, Biggie Smalls recounts, "Niggas in my faction don't like askin' questions."[51]

Social status and its markings (e.g., wealth and notoriety) can bring death, as Snoop Dogg chronicles in "Murder Was the Case That They Gave Me"—released a year after Snoop Dogg was charged with (but not convicted of) first-degree murder, after his bodyguard shot and killed someone.[52] The story weaves together the threat of death with the promise of life enabled by a cosmic turn; but even this doesn't entail a break from the materiality of both. Death is felt, and life is defined, over against the looming possibility of demise. Like blues artists before him, Snoop Dogg works a deal with the "Devil" meant to render life robust and deep with material markers of importance, but it simply delays the consumption of life by death.[53] That is, either way—through murder or the surrender of one's soul—loss is the paradigmatic transposal. It simply solidifies the metaphysical dimensions of and material geography for death over life. But, unlike Biggie Smalls, who tells the story from the perspective of the murderer who brings death, Snoop narrates from the perspective of the one challenged with death. In this case, he's brought back from the brink and reconstitutes an alternate modality of life, but not without the ongoing threat of demise:

> Just remember who changed your mind
> 'Cause when you start set-tripping, that ass is mine.[54]

The bedtime prayer that begins "Now I lay me down to sleep . . . ," recited mid-track, offers no clear protection from the threat of death. An appeal to a moment of innocence succumbs to significant demands that impinge on the body. Perhaps there is a type of desire for inactivity, for rest, but it gives way.

It, this prayer, is a theologization of circumstances without salvific potential. Time isn't disrupted or reconfigured along new lines of meaning and being. Praying doesn't trump preying. Again, life is distinct but lived in the shadow of confinement and demise, and this arrangement isn't softened or altered through theological proclamations and platitudes.

Between Snoop Dogg and Biggie Smalls, there are distinctly different perceptions regarding the embodied response to death. For the latter, it can instill status; for the former, it is to be avoided, in that it marks the tragic. For both artists, death is already and always a consideration—one that is distinct from life. In other words, death marks an end to connection and to the workings of community, and importance tied only to ephemeral realms of memory. Put yet another way, death has a direct and negative relationship to life—marked by the taking of agency and the residue of vulnerability exposed in a most graphic and permanent form. It is to lose grip on the markers of substance impinging on one's psychosocial geography.

Distinction between death and life constitutes a mode of self-sacrifice acknowledged in lyrics as an assertion of self over against the Other for justified reasons related to the established code of conduct. This is one way of thinking about "getting got" as a mode of status exchange revolving around the dynamics of reputation that is real but in/tangible, and shadowed by a materiality of consequences (e.g., money). All of this—murder and being murdered—has meaning to the extent the social parameters and rules for life are agreed upon, or, in other words, because all involved know the "game."

In playing this game to the death, there is both longing and disregard. Both require an object kept through destruction. The Black body is understood as significant, as bearing "weight," to the extent it is open to the loss of life in either an active (murder) or inactive (murdered) form. To recognize similarity—both partners being in the "game"—does little to dissuade aggression. To kill and to be killed are forms of manageability, as well as the graphic ritual enactment of annihilation. The language used to narrate stories of murder (*lunatic, psycho-driven murder, maniac*) suggests recognition of the act as antisocial and outside the normative morality of collective life—a type of social dysfunction. Or, as Dr. Dre and Ice Cube put it,

> Journey with me into the mind of a maniac
> Doomed to be a killer since I came out the nut sack.[55]

These artists, despite what might be the listener's initial reaction, don't seek to normalize murder; rather, they rationalize it by describing circumstances and social contexts in which death is necessary if one is to value life or at least maintain the viability of existence. In a word, they expose and manipulate the logic of whiteness.

While narratives of death over against life have tended toward the totalizing impact of murder and Black male occupation of time and space, this does not mean that the perception accurately reflects circumstances. I would not attempt to authenticate any assumption that death has a special hold on Black male bodies or that the distinction between life and death is any more graphic or intense when gendered in that way. Social coding and cultural assumptions concerning gender may help shape those to whom one listens; but it doesn't mean women within rap aren't experiencing the impact/fullness of death and narrating it. Rather, the mechanics of expression may bend to gender, but the nature and meaning of death remain as intense and determinative. Think of the demise of Philadelphia's Chynna Rogers, a model and rap artist. Her death, in 2020, probably as a result of addiction, is not a common case of traditional gunplay like the stories recounted above—of bravado escalating into identity and personhood affirmed through death. Still, the narrative of death here isn't unfamiliar. Yet drugs, in this case, aren't marked by the lure of the hustler or the trap house presented from the perspective of the hustler. Instead it is death in relationship to a young woman, whose end is still a bit mysterious.[56]

Working within the orbit of the A$AP Mob, her early releases (especially "Selfie") gained Chynna an audience beyond the fashion world she'd entered after signing with Ford Models.[57] Her music blurs the line between death and life: embodied struggle (perhaps) chemically fueled is a circumstance shadowed by mechanisms of demise. The titles of her EPs—such as *music 2 die 2* (2017) and *in case I die first* (2019)—speak to this presence of death and focus on the dynamics of death in public. However, it isn't simply the titles that explore these conditions. Instead, the lyrical content provides a grammar and vocabulary of death as slow spectacle. In fact, "her output thrives on bringing light to the things often relegated to hushed conversations in the corners of the mind: drugs, death, despair."[58] Chynna, the embodied artist, is shaped and figured through the highlighting of effects: the biochemical play that both intensifies and destroys as the body is *re*-shaped by substances that "blunt" the dynamics of life, leaving death in their wake. The somewhat slow, intentional, sleepy, and haunting delivery of her lyrics, laced with reference to a bluesy haze of activity, guides the script as it announces her pattern of "question[ing] my life all the time."[59] Demise is amplified; life ends and death takes over.

From a profession (fashion) centered on the hypervisible body to the lyrical content of her music, there is a shift from the body as ideal and static to the body as altered and victimized by external materials brought into it. With the former, death is bracketed, or "quarantined," behind a frame of beauty; but with the latter, the body is subdued. The body is vulnerable—not only dimensional and tagged by the potentiality of life but also susceptible to death. There is the lyrical, the skeletal, the to-the-bone manner in which habit encourages a mood in which death is a matter of honestly portrayed living . . . ended. The performance of life with its trauma surrenders to a type of stillness at the end. Or, as Chynna asks, "Shit ain't bad forever, is it though?"[60] One doesn't necessarily see the full performance of demise—Chynna didn't speak about her addiction until after rehab—but rather the "mood" of demise is rehearsed and layered on a visible body, and it is done in a way that fades life into death.[61]

In addition to Chynna's raps addressing demise from a young woman's perspective, remember Rapsody's "Aaliyah," a track in which she recounts the dynamic relationship between existential circumstances and notions of death. As she reflects, there are various dimensions to demise measured by quality and quantity—a circumstantial weight borne by those on both sides of the divide:

> Only plan for some niggas, was the plan to stay alive
> Is a loss a blessing? Only a few of my friends died
> I know another side of graves, some always at a graveside.[62]

Life is taken and this constitutes death: a distinct experience framed in terms of negation. In a certain sense, the threat of ending life is totalizing, shaping not only how living is understood but also the preoccupations directing movement through time and space. The tools of demise are ever-present, working in a variety of contexts but all targeting vulnerable bodies on display. To be part of a hip hop–inflected community is to be seen by means of a negative visibility and prone to demise. To live is to be exposed and targeted. As Lil' Kim reflects in "Pray for Me,"

> I'm more worried about the streets takin' you from me
> I'm more worried about police takin' you from me.

Yet this worry doesn't paralyze. There is agency present to the extent Black embodied bodies not only are exposed to death but also can perform death and in this way be death dealing. This is an awareness that doesn't stifle activity, but rather motivates and directs engagement:

I'll whack a nigga, then buy a flight to Madrid
I did the bid, now I do the most . . . [63]

Social meaning plays out within a metaphysical and historical arena of death against life. And there is enough separation between life and death to allow forethought of action and reflection, at least in the form of memory rehearsed and exercised. While differentiated to some degree, life and death in this schema both impinge on time and space in similar ways and are consistent with the logic of the social environment described by hip hop culture.

Paradigm 2: *Deathlife*

In 1974, while speaking with a French journalist, James Baldwin reflected on his life and said that he "never had a childhood, he was born dead."[64] *Born dead*: an existential and ontological intertwining of life and death played out within the framework of embodied Blackness. Mindful of Baldwin's statement—how it links life and death existentially and ontologically—and moving beyond a discussion of killing and dying as the existential scope of rap music, this book explores not the "how" of death, but rather the "what" of death. That is to say, my concern is the manner in which Black bodies are coded by social understandings of and reaction to *deathlife*.[65]

Over against the paradigm of death versus life highlighted above (i.e., paradigm 1), the paradigm of *deathlife* pushes against the assumed safeguard of both real and symbolic boundaries. To relate this description of two material-metaphysical patterns using common tropes, one might think of it this way: the latter (*deathlife*) is met through the sensibilities of the trickster (i.e., the technique of movement that blends worlds) whereas the former (death versus life) involves a distinction exhibited by the preacher, who speaks of movement from one to another opposing plane. What the preacher offers is the *elegiac response* to a perceived exhaustion of vitality in one plane of existence. If one is of faith, the preacher claims, one is reconstituted on another plane beyond loss and sorrow. The preacher's approach is consistent with the argument found in spiritual and gospel music: freedom entails the detangling of life from death through a transhistorical "beyond." Despite the preacher's claim, even if death and life could be distinguished and held apart—one against the other—language doesn't have the capacity to illustrate the process. Vocabulary and grammar remain on the border of each and are marginal to the content of both.

This framing of *deathlife* isn't mere recognition of "both/and." Put another way, one might think of it as an expressed superposition housed within embodied Blacks. This isn't a mode of epistemological agnosia whereby there is an inability to distinguish objects that are distinguishable. This is to say, distinction between life and death so as to safeguard one over the other just isn't, and effort to produce distinction is without effective possibility. To speak of one is to name the other. Furthermore, *deathlife* involves more than a highlighting of a symbiotic relationship between life and death, in which these two realities are in close proximity or relationship without having that connection alter the meaning of either. More than that, there is a fundamental connection—involving a blending together beyond simple patterns of contact between slippery social conceptions. Black existence as embodied and geographically arranged speaks and reflects this relationship: embodied death as life, life as death. They are coterminous in that they entail the same situation.

The Blackness of certain bodies entails the mapping out of this relationship, as it constitutes a blurring—mingled meaning that speaks life as it speaks death. By and large, the primary locations of hip hop's—more precisely rap music's—development are geographies of this denial of distinction. At least, they are locations serving as a vantage point from which to recognize and narrate this economy of denial. In one sense, artists highlighted in the following chapters provide an alternate perspective, in that they narrate life as death (and death as life)—that is to say, a merger of life and death along the lines of ontological consumption. The artists reflect a mood of existential movement that assumes the epistemological "sameness" between life and death. It is harsh, and one might seek to signify it, but death remains inseparable from what is meant by life. Both mark the body, in this case the material Black body; and the discursive Black body is constructed in relationship to both. What these artists, in part, provide is a poetic engagement with/through this situation of sameness.

What is offered in rap presentations of *deathlife*, then, is a hip hop–inflected thanatological (or what might be more properly called a bio-thanatological) lucidity.[66] To say this is to speak to the manner in which Blackness is to *be* a structured condition—despite all (e.g., economic gain through music production), recognized only in relationship to this condition of *deathlife*. This, however, isn't the equating of Blackness with death, but rather the destruction of any distinction between life and death vis-à-vis the totalizing category of Blackness. One, then, shouldn't think of this as a fixable circumstance that can be altered through persistent effort to the extent that Black lives can be made to matter; rather, it is a fixed circumstance defined in terms of its resolute resistance to alteration . . . for the sake of the social system and the world it manufactures. It is to name a culturally coded and politically, economically, and socially enacted sameness of death and life that isn't constitutive of a transition "between," a movement from one to the other, as narrated in light of social stories of "natural death" and "long" life.[67] The structure of *deathlife* entails a push against the assumed utility of sociocultural confinement as a plausible safeguard for life as well as a denial of the accompanying assumption that death involves the ultimate loss of agency.

Deathlife is somewhat viral in nature: it has no meaning and doesn't function outside a host, which is to say it has no meaning outside its enactment in Black embodiment. On some level, Blackness is constructed and constituted in such a way as to deny death to those who carry (as definition) its weight. To grant death would be to acknowledge a distinction that humanizes and to represent Blacks as similarly constituted to white bodies—as the vulnerable storehouse of humanity. However, Blacks are not indistinguishable from creatures existing outside the context of "cultured" sociality. While particular Blacks are forgettable, Blackness grabs attention and is subject to fevered engagement. Whiteness is a performance that demands a disproportionate counterperformance. Whiteness needs to be able to identify Blackness through Blacks so as to have it serve a function unfulfilled through others. To confine or kill a lion, for instance, offers nothing for whites seeking affirmation of distinction. For this affirmation to take place, there is a requirement of both (1) the threat of demise, and (2) comparable signs of life recognizable, yet distinct. Blacks serve as an entry point, a safety value that allows controlled access to Blackness. So, my concern here isn't the applicability of the category of the human as a way to congeal Blackness in time and space.

Related to the ontological question, there is much I find compelling in the writing of Calvin Warren, and I engage him, along with Afropessimist Frank B. Wilderson III, directly and indirectly at various points, thereby marking out regions of commonality in our thinking as well as points of disagreement. Yet the ontological status of the target doesn't capture what I want to say concerning *deathlife* as articulated in rap music.[68] This entails a need to replace an ontological grammar with thanatological considerations in order to capture the nature and meaning of Blackness. Therefore, this book wrestles with dynamics of thanatology (again, perhaps more precisely, bio-thanatology), but only indirectly with the issues of concern framed by Warren's questioning of ontology connected to "antiblack violence sustaining the world."[69] My concern here is with the intentionality of that violence and the social shaping power of that violence as well as rap music's response to that outcome—*deathlife*. Hence, as readers will see, this book isn't directly concerned with issues of being as a philosophical question, although death undoubtedly lends itself to such considerations; instead, the concern is with *deathlife* as a thanatological (highlighting its social dimensions) circuit.[70] Despite how Blackness is situated, those who carry it are a target of abuse resulting in death *but* are also alive to the extent they animate a white fear and anxiety of dying—the collected presence of effect and affect. Blackness entails both: it is available as counterpresence, allowing whiteness to have social significance (i.e., alive), but also open to violence to prevent the demise of whiteness (i.c., dead).

This violence often involves the killing of individual Black people, and I want to pause briefly to consider what the death/murder of individual Black people entails for the larger system of disregard and demise. Simply put, it doesn't reduce Blackness; rather, it amplifies Blackness. Stated differently, this violence speaks a relationship between Blackness and whiteness: an increase in one entails a related increase in the other. They are dependent, so killing a Black person doesn't challenge said relationship. No, it reinforces and highlights the relationship, because Blackness, so to speak, is not the sum of its parts. One can't "kill" Blackness by killing Black people. John L. Jackson Jr. might be brought into this discussion, since an affective embrace of this relationship as the "American" way can be said to relate (in a deadly manner) to what he calls "racial Americana"—which is a way of naming, in his words, "the inextricable linkages between race and nationhood."[71] Animosity between what, for the social world, are necessary categories gets expressed through modalities of violence and symbolized in forms of this "racial Americana." Considering this, to kill a Black person is performance of this relationship. It is an active reminder of whiteness's need for but hatred of the Blackness that is meant to undergird it and save it from "untimely," or what one might call an "irregular," death.

The dead Black person becomes a type of talisman, a device representing (both physically and psychologically) circumstances under control, which is to say life with death bracketed away and managed, at least for a moment. And this representation imagines the Black person both dead (killed in assurance of whiteness as life) and alive (an ever-present reminder of the danger of death). In chapter 4, I'll think about this status in terms of the zombie, but here suffice it to say that Blackness doesn't end with the death of Black people. The graphic "look" of Blackness with pretense stripped away through the act of killing continues to impinge, to impose. And the fear this produces for white people is in part the point of Blackness. One might think of the killing of Black people as a selective "pruning" of Blackness's representation, which doesn't hamper it but rather promotes its stability and growth. Its importance for the maintenance of whiteness and a certain set of practices for white people can't allow for such a finality. Blackness does too much heavy lifting for whiteness, and therefore white people, for it to come to an end.

Blackness is not an in-between place as such but rather is a type of simultaneous occupation—or what one might call a type of metaphysical comorbidity conditioned and orchestrated through external structures of social anxiety that confirm the demands posed by the social world encountered. Blackness affords the social world the maintenance of an illusion—that of beginning and end, or a narrative of progression and development that manages the anxiety of death through a projection of reasonable life as a process of fulfillment over time. And the lack of time encountered by some within the social world is rationalized (or theologized) as an unfortunate anomaly presented through a grammar of lament: a re-membering.

The performance of Blackness (over against the performance, for example, of whiteness) can't be captured and described using the same vocabulary and grammar of engagement. Those who carry Blackness are denied the affective arrangement of response and consideration expressed in such a way as to communicate death as "unnatural"—coming too quickly and taking away something precious. Blackness is constructed so as to hold together life and death and render them indistinguishable in function. Blackness, holding together what is called death and what is called life, can't be controlled in full by the social world because it exceeds social limits. This, one could argue, accounts for how Blackness is both despised and desired (i.e., death is both repudiated and mesmerizing). On some level, there is an erotic quality to engagement with Blackness through violence to the extent, that is, such engagement allows a flirtation, or an affective entanglement, with what is both desired and feared.

The second decade of the twentieth century has provided urgent and excessive cartographies of this Blacks/Blackness arrangement. One gains a sense of this relationship of Blackness to the white social world in the testimony of former police officer Darren Wilson, who killed Michael Brown in Ferguson, Missouri, in 2014. (A white man, he was not indicted on state charges nor did he face federal charges.) During his testimony—an inner dialogic made public—Wilson described Michael Brown in terms that rendered him a caricature ("Hulk Hogan") and ontologically foreign (a demon), one who seemed to walk through bullets gaining strength with each stride.[72] (Absorption of destructive intent marks the Black body defined by *deathlife*.) While attempting to explain the shooting, Wilson said,

> I start backpedaling and again, I tell him get on the ground, get on the ground, he doesn't. I shoot another round of shots. Again, I don't recall how many it was or if I hit him every time. I know at least once because he flinched again. At this point it looked like he was almost bulking up to run through the shots, like it was making him mad that I'm shooting at him. And the face that he had was looking straight through me, like I wasn't even there, I wasn't even anything in his way.[73]

Nothing is mentioned of Brown that would center his pain. This, again, is because Blacks through Blackness are presented as "demons." What Blacks experience by means of their Blackness wouldn't qualify as a category or type of suffering (not even in theological terms). Instead, it is simply a marker of qualified existence cast in other terms (ominous danger, disorder, aesthetic repulsion-appeal, animated hazard, virus). What Blacks experience through the white social world's engagement with Blackness simply constitutes sanctioned and embodied aversion. For Wilson, Michael Brown oozed wildness and the threat of demise, which had to be contained, rendered tame, and confined within established boundaries. Blackness is a threat, but it is also a desired necessity: fundamentally, Wilson's sociality is premised on the existence of this dilemma. Blackness constitutes a situation of both death and life performed and authenticated—despised and desired to the extent it is constitutive of the distinction that whiteness is intended to mean.[74] Hence, death isn't something that happens to Blacks, as if they can be named outside this framing. Rather, violence is a naming of *deathlife* made visible and active. Violence, in a manner of speaking, puts *deathlife* to work. Furthermore, it is only from the vantage point of Blacks that violence is shrouded with negative connotations. For whites, violence against Blackness by means of Black bodies is rendered justified—a necessary dimension of the social world's infrastructure.

This all points again to a basic logic: the social world isn't dependent on Black bodies only (or, directly, as if to say Black bodies "matter"), but rather the structure of society is grounded in the presence of Blackness. By extension, the social world (sociability performed) is framed and defined over against *deathlife*. Whether there is more to Black bodies than this is moot at best, and attention to the question does nothing to sideline *deathlife* as a basic consideration. To be clear, I am not saying Blackness involves life *and* death—the holding together of two meanings. Thinking this way misses the fact that Blackness doesn't involve a choice, a selection of one over the other, an ability to decipher and name an alternative: life and death. Rather, Blackness is Blackness precisely because it entails—it is—the two as the same. Who is "Black" is a question responded to with a bit of fluidity based on proximity and need, inasmuch as the Black is one whose value is symbolic (indirect), a breathing and moving allegory. Other groups who aren't participants in whiteness—who don't perform the sociality of whites—can also be marked by *deathlife*. In effect, there are two categories: whiteness and all else. One sees this, for example, in the expansive manner in which violence serves as a means by which to affirm a particular arrangement—force assures whites of their whiteness. Think of the violent effort to present and arrange Latinx populations in a grammar of democratic life vis-à-vis firm borders, or the way during COVID-19 Asian Americans were rendered connected as they were often (and violently) targeted as the embodiment of viral threat and so on.

Furthermore, beyond "color," the dimensions of the Black body are of limited concern because what the body—small or large, weak or strong—serves to represent is beyond scale. Even when the embodied body is subdued through killing, the body remains alive—a looming threat because Blackness is the same, despite the particularities of a given Black body. As with a virus, disabling one occurrence of Blackness's presence doesn't wipe it out but instead simply highlights Blackness's expansive configuration. To kill *a* Black person is to point out at the same time the irrepressible nature of all Blacks as marked by the same Blackness. Removal of one points out the existence of so many others. For example, think of the communal continuity to Michael Brown, discussed later, who becomes all Blacks: the hashtag "#iammichaelbrown" and the like speak a word concerning the relationship of all Blacks to *deathlife*.

Blackness is without age restrictions, which is to say Blacks are in this coterminous relationship of *deathlife* from birth. So, violence as an acknowledgment of this relationship's value to whiteness observes no limits when it comes to reinforcing the arrangement. One example of Blackness—or one Black—is the functional, interchangeable equivalent of another. Aiyana Mo'Nay Stanley-Jones (seven years old) was shot and killed in Detroit, when members of the Special Response Team charged into her grandmother's home. She was sleeping on the couch, next to her grandmother. The police had entered the wrong apartment . . . and the list of Blackness managed goes on, each individual different (e.g., gendered) but the same with respect to how they represent Blackness. The need for Blackness as a functioning arrangement of *deathlife* creates its own justification and provides a grammar of threat against proper conduct. This is one way to read the trauma experienced by a six-year-old Black girl in Florida, who was arrested after "throwing a tantrum in class and kick[ing] a staff member."[75] She was taken to a detention facility, where she was fingerprinted and a "mug shot" taken. Blackness is perceived as a threat to be contained for the well-being of society's white residents—and it is never too early to reinforce this framework. Or one might think of twelve-year-old Tamir Rice, who was shot and killed in 2014 while playing with a toy airsoft replica gun without the orange-tipped barrel, indicating it posed no threat.

As with the lynched body hanging from the tree, decomposing in the sun—as well as the small bits of that body later carried as souvenirs—the static body on a city street communicates a positioning that affirms both the demand for difference on the part of whiteness and a surrender to that demand as signified through Blackness. Though killed, the body is still animated in a particular sense and for a set of purposes, which is to say it has impact to the degree it impinges on (shadows) the sociality of whiteness and animates public/private conversation and exchange. It is not just the one whose body litters the ground who creates these conditions; no, any embodied Black is representative of these conditions and therefore poses a threat to the stability of whiteness's framing of life as distinction. Hence, in this sense, the dead body is a trope maintaining certain "vital" functions. While confrontation with Blackness does not always produce this exact response, it is a ready option. There is a distinction between the death of a Black and the end of Blackness. The latter isn't desired despite white nationalist rhetoric serving as sociopolitical subterfuge and a type of affective convulsion, while the former is performance of social sensibilities regarding life and death scaled down to that which affords repetition—one individual after another: Martin, Brown, Bland . . . all meant to justify the coding of Blackness.

To merely say Blacks are dead or are death is to miss an element of the terror they represent qua Blackness. If Blacks could be understood totally through death, the violence against them would be to safeguard life without the nature of life being challenged or disrupted. No doubt, Blackness constitutes such a challenge to life, but it also involves a potential signification of what life entails: its fragility, for instance. Life and death aren't destroyed through this activity, but rather a reinforced sense of their mutuality is preserved. To be white is to live until otherwise—but even then, with physical demise, to be known through the memorial of a life remembered. To be Black is to exist, which is to say Blacks are "produced" as visible and anthropomorphic housing for Blackness. What is rendered visible (thereby meaningful) about Blacks as presented to (and active within) the world involves this sameness between death and life. Blackness is both cause and rationale. That is to say, Blackness isn't a structure of convenience but rather a calculated and carefully arranged category that makes possible for whites an existential and psychological conjunction: *or*—as in life *or* death.

For Blacks there is no conjunctive possibility, no *or* as in life *or* death. Better yet, there is no vantage point outside the scope of both (*deathlife*) that would allow such a choice to be made. They are only representative, an embodied trope, of *deathlife*. Black bodies, as Blackness, cannot be described or positioned adequately as "dead" or "alive"—this grammatical move is unavailable because *or* stipulates possibilities made available only by whiteness. Rather, again, a coterminous relationship between the two renders Black bodies both at the same time. Blackness, by its constructed nature, opposes substitution or alternative; rather, it is totalizing in intent and overdetermining in effect. Blackness becomes the social world's attempt to confine and tame death while advancing its take on life.

A visual representation of the distinction between life and death that whiteness struggles to maintain is offered in Gustav Klimt's 1915 painting *Tod und Leben* (Death and life).[76] On the left, one sees Death represented—visualized as a skeleton draped in a garment marked with religious symbols (crosses and other images). It holds something in its hand, and the held device is positioned as if Death is simply waiting for the right moment to unleash it on the group of living figures gathered to the right. Aside from the faint, white skull, the rest of Death is shrouded in dark tones; the darkness indicates a presence beyond full description and outside our ability to gather in. The more brightly colored, more vibrant, more identifiable mass of people at right is layered, perhaps depicting different moments of life—from the joy of relationship (as a mother holds a child) to the wonders of youth represented by the child. Those depicted cling to each other, at points blending together with only heads and small portions of bodies distinguishable. As one's eye moves down the image (the important symbolic value of verticality), there is a man—the only man in the painting—holding and being held by a woman, his face buried against her shoulder, hers buried in their touching arms. One does not know if those in this huddled group have accepted death. Something about their grasping of each other—the desire for some sort of bond or connection—would suggest resistance and an effort to preserve life. Moving down the grouping, the joyous expressions give way to more somber looks until the last two figures, the largest figures, with faces hidden (reflecting melancholy, the awareness of death), suggest a feeling of time lost. Life and death are connected through a web of psychological and affective confrontations worn on the faces of those in the painting. Death is at a distance—hence, oppositional to life—but the potential of it inching toward life (it seems poised for movement) is already and always present. It is this situation of death as threat against life that the creation of Blackness is meant to address.

Whites are permitted a full range of affective responses and existential possibilities meant to safeguard a fragile psyche, while an effort is made to restrict Blacks to a range of responses deemed suitable by whites. Yet Blacks do respond, do develop strategies of engagement. Two recently popular theorizations of response involve (1) Afropessimism, which recognizes the social world's dependence on Blacks as sentient beings (but not human, not understood through ontology) and a push against assumptions of political solutions to this situation; and (2) Afro-optimism, which projects a future in which Blacks exist, and in which imaginative framings mark the vitality of Black life.[77] The former, for a variety of reasons, I find more compelling— more consistent with the shape of historical conditions, more in line with my moralist sensibilities, and more informative as a way to interrogate certain underexplored dimensions of hip hop culture. However, before giving attention to both an explicit and implicit read of hip hop through Afropessimism (by means of which I connect Blackness *and/as* Black people within the context of the social world), I want to consider a counter sense of Blackness *and* Black people by highlighting Fred Moten's work. My goal in doing so isn't to offer a full explication of Moten's theorization of Blackness; rather, I want to offer a counterpoint (i.e., Moten's "optimism") to this project's pessimism so as to provide context for my argument.[78]

A useful starting point is Moten's essay "The Case of Blackness" (2008). He begins by remarking on the sense of pathology that has informed notions of Black people and Blackness, whereby activism on the part of Black people assumes, when it doesn't more explicitly pronounce, the question "What's wrong with black folk?" This question, read in relationship to its ontological considerations and to the thinking of Fanon, raises yet another question: "And if, as Frantz Fanon suggests, the black cannot be an other for another black, if the black can only be an other for a white, then is there ever anything called black social life?"[79] Of concern here, for Moten, is what he references as "fugitive movement," which is a type of unauthorized life that might fuel "black optimism." Thinking through the issue of ontology and Blackness, Moten proposes that Blackness works at the intersection of the social and the ontological—of "fugitivity and impossibility"—and the "lived experience of blackness" by its nature calls for measurement through a para-ontology, a mode of disorder, a structuring of differences.[80] Instead of concerning himself with the question of pathology—is the behavior of Blacks "pathological or natural"?—he wants to lift up another concern named in relationship to the benefit of fugitivity, of disorder, or disruption: "What is the efficacy of that range of natural-born disorders that have been relegated to what is theorized as the void of blackness or black social life that might be more properly understood as the fugitive being of 'infinite humanity'?"[81]

What Moten offers is a way to challenge the pathology (and the organizing of that pathology), which has been seen as a flaw that prevents a sense of Black social life because social life is what takes place when Blacks are not included and Blackness isn't present. Black social life is, for Moten, a fugitive act, a mode of expression and practice, naming a type of impossibility, but impossibility is not the same as absence.[82] Fugitivity also seems to undergird what he would later say concerning Blackness as "enthusiastic social vision, given in non-performed performance, as the surrealization of space and time." It helps to note that there is a danger embedded in Blackness as Moten conceives it—a danger stemming from its refusal to seek what the social world displays as desirable. Blackness in this case involves a refusal to be one thing—it is "consent not to be one: not just to be more + less than one but the mobilization of that indiscretion and incompleteness or 'otherwise than being.'"[83] When viewed in light of the nature and workings of anti-Blackness, this refusal, according to Moten, enforces recognition that there is a distinction between Blackness and the people referenced as Black. There is, then, also a distinction between life and death, even if that distinction amounts only to a difference between "life and lives."[84]

For Afropessimism, Blackness seems a condition that cannot be resolved, or addressed in ways that transform, short of destroying the social world. However, as I read Moten, there is a sense of Blackness as a troubled and troubling category, a type of "brokenness of being," but a brokenness that doesn't prevent living: Black people can "live with brokenness."[85] To do so is an act of fugitivity (a "space" of "dis-order") and amounts to living with what Moten and Stefano Harney have called "debt."[86] As Kara Keeling elucidates, this turn to Karl Marx's notion of wealth allows Moten to distinguish between Blackness and Black people, in that the former involves a type of "historical becoming" that isn't restricted but speaks to the "racial dimension of 'the human.'" Hence, Blackness "both exceeds and supplements those who are called 'Black people,' but cannot be divorced from Black people without epistemological and ontological violence to both the concept and the material realities it currently participates in organizing."[87]

For Moten and Harney, Blackness isn't the same ontological emptiness described by Frank Wilderson and other Afropessimists—an emptiness that consumes Black people; rather, it is to live in a "wild" space in which the modalities of order and domination don't make sense any longer. This, one might say, is a type of abolition-inflected "refusal" that constitutes an action that counters the forces of disregard. Such is more than Afropessimism's political apostasy.[88] While recognizing the importance of Afropessimism as a revitalization of intellectual rigor in "Black study," Moten counters what he perceives as Afropessimism's refusal to "love" Blackness through a challenge to its notion of social death by means of which he seeks "to stay a black motherfucker." Here something about staying Black involves a slight shift in grammar—"death and pessimism" toward "life and optimism."[89] Philosophically, one might say this involves a shift with respect to the relationship between Blackness and ontology. For Afropessimists, Blackness is outside the realm of ontological consideration (Blacks are sentient beings only), but for Moten's effort to exist outside the desire to justify that existence (vis-à-vis a "standpoint"), not only is "blackness . . . ontologically prior to the logistic and regulative power that is supposed to have brought it into existence but that blackness is prior to ontology."[90] To be a "black motherfucker"—to continue to hold Blackness regardless, to seek ways to free Blackness from the assumptions of ontology—is to oppose Afropessimism's read of social death (i.e., Black life lacks sociality). Instead, it is to view Black life as social but tied to political death in the burial ground called the world. For Moten, what Patterson actually describes is political death, not social death as commonly argued. To clarify the argument, Moten writes,

> I am in total agreement with the Afro-pessimistic understanding of blackness as exterior to civil society and, moreover, as unmappable within the cosmological grid of the transcendental subject. However, I understand civil society and the coordinates of the transcendental aesthetic—cognate as they are not with the failed but rather with the successful state and its abstract, equivalent citizens—to be the fundamentally and essentially antisocial nursery for a necessarily necropolitical imitation of life. . . . Social death is not imposed upon blackness by or from the standpoint or positionality of the political; rather, it is

the field of the political, from which blackness is relegated to the supposedly undifferentiated mass or blob of the social, which is, in any
case, where and what blackness chooses to stay.[91]

According to Moten, the work involves this push for Black subjectivity over
against "ontology's sanction against the very idea." As I read Moten, this isn't
merely a hope and it isn't the goal; rather, it is the ongoing labor that fosters (a para-ontological) distinction between Blackness and Black people—a
distinction between Blackness and strategies of being. This is the difference
(what amounts to a very small distinction) between pessimism and optimism, based on the degree to which we "consent not to be a single being" but
embrace instead a type of unsettledness without a standpoint.[92]

Black people are in relationship to the world, and according to Moten, this
involves deprivation of a kind, in that "Black people are poor in the world.
We are deprived in, and somehow both more and less than deprived of, the
world." This recognition, according to Moten, is shared between his optimism and Afropessimism; but advocates of the latter think of this along the
lines of "ontological reach," while Moten understands Blackness as the expression of an alternative modality of desire. In his words, "What if blackness
is the name that has been given to the social field and social life of an illicit alternative capacity to desire?" Such involves, on some level, an effort to forge
another world made "in and out of this world."[93] One might also think about
such Blackness as a practice of resistance, which is to say, "Our resistant,
relentlessly impossible object is subjectless predication, subjectless escape,
escape from subjection, in and through the paralegal flaw that animates and
exhausts the language of ontology."[94] Indeed, Moten is not alone in this desire for Black-life-affirming difference. Keeling, for example, also holds alle-
giance to the plausibility of "another world," framed in terms of robust "queer
futures," by means of which a "wealth that cannot be measured by a predeter-
mined yardstick" holds open possibilities that can't be fully described.[95] Yet
Moten's "optimism" and Keeling's "another world" miss the mark for me and
blur from clear view what I believe are important representations in and of
hip hop that don't fall in line with their approaches.

Moten notes the distinction between his approach (i.e., optimism) and
that of the Afropessimists (i.e., pessimism) as being slim. Thinking across optimism and pessimism, Moten sees a relationship—the possibility of a "friendship" premised on some shared commitments (e.g., the slim nature of their
disagreement) processed in light of their differences (e.g., a contrary sense of
distance between Blackness and Black people). I think one may simply need

to choose a stance and measure the distance between Blackness and Black people as they see it. Mindful of this, some might view hip hop as adopting an optimistic posture, and that would entail a particular framing that highlights certain artists. But there are other artists, some discussed in the following pages, who offer no clear distinction between Blackness and Black people, between death and life. It is this group of artists, who see nothing encouraging in the call for distinction, that I highlight for consideration. And it is in relationship to their art that I labor to name a theoretical framework—drawing on a sense of pessimism—capable of maintaining their sense of Blackness, Black people, and *deathlife*.

Turning again to Afropessimism, Blackness and Blacks are connected, but they are not the same: one occasions the other. To illustrate the point by borrowing from Hortense Spillers, one might think of it this way: Blacks are "flesh"—the first narrative, the marker of significance ripped away through violence—and Blackness is that which is left (i.e., the body) as a functionary for the logic of whiteness after the flesh has been taken away.[96] Or, borrowing from Wilderson, one might say that Blacks involve the "performance" of *deathlife* and Blackness is the "paradigm" representing *deathlife*.[97]

Performance: There is with Afropessimism an important recognition of dire circumstances that projects a particular engagement worth noting (although these circumstances are understood and articulated somewhat unlike my take on Blackness):

> Afropessimism is Black people at their best. "Mad at the world" is Black folks at their best. Afropessimism gives us the freedom to say out loud what we would otherwise whisper or deny: that no Blacks are in the world, but, by the same token, there is no world without Blacks. The violence perpetrated against us is not a form of discrimination; it is a necessary violence; a health tonic for everyone who is not Black.[98]

I agree with dimensions of Wilderson's depiction of violence as necessary and as a process with relational dynamics, or what he calls a "positioning matrix."[99] Yet, rather than understanding violence as a *negative* act against Black bodies, I see it as whiteness's *affirmation* of Blackness, as perhaps an anti-anti-Blackness. Violence so understood isn't meant to foster political structures, economic mechanisms of wealth and poverty, or dynamics of a dys/functional democratic "experiment." This violence is a naming and management of death and life through the establishment of Blackness as a trope of nondistinction (i.e., *deathlife*), freeing whiteness to function as a technique of difference: life *or* death. That is to say, whites are authorized through the logic and mechanics of collective life to punish Blacks (to the point of physical death), thereby preserving whiteness. And violence is a systemic process of affirming this social need. Through modalities of aggression, whites are freed from a certain type of visceral anxiety while still subject to the consequences of the trauma associated with maintaining this difference between life and death. In this sense, through Blackness, whites feel both nausea and euphoria.

The sense of life (and death managed) is ritualized and expressed as sociality. Something of this meaning is found in Wilderson's remark concerning violence within the context of master-slave interaction. He asks, "What if anti-Black violence could be counted among the things that make life *life*?"[100] Whiteness allows a sense of the present as the present (i.e., measurable and responsive localized episodes of white need/desire fulfilled), a presence-connoting activity that soaks in the moment. Blackness, on the other hand, extends beyond itself and is tied to a particular will to recall a pleasant past and speculate or confirm a future (for whiteness) that isn't dissimilar to the structure of the present guarded vehemently through force. The future sanctions an ethics of containment and claims Blacks as its target. Such an orientation involves a missing present—a sense of meaning that short-circuits conditions in the moment and, in particular, a failure to interrogate violence and its rationale.

Violence as a core element of the social world depends on Blackness. Or, as Wilderson situates it, violence "underwrites the modern world's capacity to think, act, and exist spatially and temporally."[101] Violence is a wild and aggressive refusal to deny whiteness. In this way, through the targeting of Blackness, whiteness preserves "time"—allowing measurability of events and determinable progress as personal and collective value and worth. And preservation of time is the maintenance of a calculable and structural arrangement of distinction that accounts for relationality and, in this way, gives a type of "substance" to whites. In turn, Blackness serves as a switch initiating a protective structuring of what "is" over against what can be "taken." This keeps whites from dying to irrelevance, although it can't safeguard fully from physical demise. Still, the democratic experiment as a weaponizable shaping of engagement with the world provides some effort to safeguard whites from the latter. In so doing, sociality is marked for whites by a potentiality exercised or wasted. Even if wasted, whites do not become corpses inasmuch as viability remains through the fact they once lived.

For whites, in most cases, pain or misery is a measurement of choice. It helps to think about this theologically by saying that, for whites, one might read pain and misery as having a theodical quality (a connection to defending god's goodness despite human suffering), expressed in relationship to potentiality, pedagogical benefit, and projection of future. Blacks, theologically, can be read as the "anti" figure—those through whom life and death are read. In the parlance of the "first white president," Donald Trump, "Make America Great Again."[102]

Whether Blacks are ontologically substantive is an important issue, one alluded to earlier, but what grounds it is the manner in which Blackness covers Blacks and determines the meaning of presence and purpose. Blackness is fixed and firm—it is already and always *deathlife*. This is not dependent on Black death (i.e., the death of Black sentient beings), as Afropessimists surmise, but rather on Blackness to ground both death and life in one loved/despised framework. As such, I would argue in this context the social world is anti-Black and pro-Blackness: it needs the latter to sustain the viability of white life as distinct from death. Every*thing*—structures of thought, mechanisms of meaning, ethical frameworks, affective registers, political practices, cultural codes, grammars of being, modes of pleasure, and regulatory boundaries—is caught in this double bind.[103] Blackness becomes for whites and whiteness a means of avoidance and denial because the structuring of *deathlife* offers the social world (i.e., whiteness) and its inhabitants the illusion of selective performance: death *or* life. Blackness qua Black bodies serves as both the narration of this arrangement and the reason for the arrangement. Blackness and those defined by it make visible (and therefore manageable) what the white social world and its recognized inhabitants fear: life slipping away into an end through which social meaning is lost as access to (and control over) technologies of collective life—economics, politics, cultural production—expires.

Wilderson argues that a Black person is "a being that is *dead*, despite the fact that this being is sentient and so *appears to be very much alive*."[104] Is *dead* but *appears to be very much alive*: I would offer a change in perspective here and say Blackness involves Blacks as *alivedead*—no transition, no space, between the two orientations. To call Black bodies "death personified" doesn't capture fully the dynamics of Blackness as *deathlife*, and to label whites as the "personification of diversity, of life itself" doesn't announce the relationship of whiteness to Blackness as I seek to frame it.[105] Instead, if Blackness is *deathlife*, whiteness is the opportunity (or "right") to distinguish. This does not keep whites (through whiteness) free from threat, but they aren't defined by this threat. Instead, whites are marked by a capacity for avoidance that opens them to challenge, despite social coding (e.g., gender, class, sexual orientation). *Deathlife* is a noting of no distinction between life and death. By extension, whiteness—through violence—exists to the degree life and death are synonymous in function and orientation *and* "external" to whites. Whiteness, then, has only to rub up against this sameness through force in order to be affirmed. Whiteness is defined by a practice of choice—the ability to live or die, each as a distinctive ordering of time and space.

Wilderson notes a tension akin to that I have alluded to throughout this discussion, although the larger argument might differ. Reflecting on a conversation in which it became clear that "the borders of redemption are policed by Whites and non-Whites alike," he writes, "I, as a Black person (if person, subject, being are appropriate, since Human is not), am both barred from the denouement of social and historical redemption and needed if redemption is to attain any form of coherence."[106] Social death, according to Afropessimists, "can be destroyed," although what is required in order to pull this off ends the social world and therefore requires of Black bodies a posture of commitment to the destruction of the social world that is, really, "impossible."[107] I'm unable to say the same concerning *deathlife*, in that there is no outside, no alternate mechanism for viewing or engaging. Objection to this arrangement by Blacks (or whites) doesn't alter the framework because its logic easily shifts to render Black bodies accountable and responsible for what is done to them. Whites hide their hands, so to speak, making Black bodies accountable for Blackness and accountable to whiteness. For Black bodies, violence is a sign of demented desire, consuming them in order to stabilize the fictions of the social world. For whites, it offers an odd comfort—peace within the storm—suggesting their right to well-being, or life.

Exposure of violence, for example, through phone videos, tends to elicit sympathy for whites (as symbols of whiteness), drawing on the very intent of the United States as a white haven for distinction (life *or* death): "*life*, liberty, and the pursuit of happiness."[108] Such is the case, as Christina Sharpe reflects, with respect to the dynamics of the US social world to the extent that "the ongoing state-sanctioned legal and extralegal murders of Black people are normative and, for this so-called democracy, necessary; it is the ground we walk on."[109] Yet this mode of death vis-à-vis the taking of life is one technique, while the other attacks and destroys more than existential arrangements because is an ontological killing—a sense of Blackness as "nothing" by means of which life and death are joined.[110] Even when this sympathy isn't in place, punishment for white performers of anti-Blackness is easily narrated as their having selected life over death, and the integrity of the *deathlife* framework is maintained. So conceived, the demise of a Black person might be better characterized in light of *deathlife* as being "disappeared" or a "forced disappearance." In this way, something is captured of the manner in which the circumstances of this one Black person are always shadowed by an inability to distinguish life and death—by a fogged performance—and connected to larger social arrangements.

How some Blacks have engaged *deathlife* takes shape in the four central chapters of the present book. For now, I'll argue that some whites lament this mode of demise—speak against it, act contrary to it—but their language of life and grammar of systemic change offer little to differentiate *deathlife* as life over death, and little to dimension its ubiquity. There is a symbiotic—as in close and mutually informing—relationship between Blackness and whiteness played out in its most graphic presentation on/through Black bodies. The Black body can't but represent *deathlife*. Even the most liberal whites still envision Blacks over against *deathlife*; hence, they remain tied to these circumstances as constitutive. Whites, even liberals and progressives, need Blackness so configured; the question is whether, in word or deed, they will admit the benefit (the life-affirming quality) of this arrangement. For others, the action is more straightforward, in that they understand Blacks and Blackness as inherently linked, and all they see in and of the world affirms this relationship, including in their personal dealings, as each one knows someone who's had a life-threatening encounter with a representative Black. For the liberal/progressive or the "Make America Great Again" public advocate, Blacks/Blackness remain the same in function.

This situation is both philosophically and theologically the case when one considers, for example, the biblical story of Abraham and his son, forced into a performance of obedience as substitutional demise.[111] Relationship to a "Grand Unity"—to ultimate being—required the ritualization of death as a request for life (in the sense of distinction from surroundings). The story indicates Abraham was only required to surrender to the idea of sacrifice— that is, to think life gone as the opening to vertical meaning; yet, for his son, the one to be killed, the lesson involves something more overtly sinister. The potentiality of death (for life) isn't measurable logically as tied to physical breakdown or existential circumstances, but rather is an endorsement of a larger, nonhistorical "order" that structures un/spoken commitments and obligations. The demand comes from (and thereby constitutes) the very structure of the world in that it is tied to the logic constituting the markers of disassociated meaning played out in sociopolitical, economic, cultural, and affective registers. And buttressing this is a simple assertion: something/ someone must embody this demand for "blood." The demand, of course, outweighs the need for cooperation. Abraham's son, like the substituted ram, need not voice agreement or disagreement with the act of sacrifice (of staged death); in fact, they can't, in that each in its own way lacks a vocabulary/grammar of restitution that can contradict the expressed conditions for participation in the Grand Unity.[112] Abraham sees no necessary distinction between the two: one can replace the other; both serve the same purpose.

Either/or.

Still, there is something about Isaac that poses both possibility and threat: possibility to the extent he might be a suitable sacrifice, but threat to the extent he, in his demise, takes something of Abraham with him. Perhaps Abraham senses in him something that might speak "not I" and thereby disturb performance of the ritual. Or perhaps Abraham wonders who might be next: could the taker of life be taken in turn? Isaac's death would be both sacrifice (renewing life) and murder (ending life). The willingness to murder is as good as the act. Still, the history of connection and interaction (son versus wild animal) makes no difference in how this plays out. Abraham, as does the thicket neutralizing the ram, holds steady what the world demands. Only the horizontally arranged logic undergirding the social world can decipher which sacrifice is more suitable. Desire as expressed here in the form of horizontal connection pushes beyond language of faith, beyond a grammar of psychic surrender. It is a ritual of assurance, a safeguard against being forced to acknowledge one's awareness of the absurdity of that which is named "life." However, what one might gather from this narrative is already known: life and death are bound together through the necessity of violence (as a type of white life logic). Black bodies, as *deathlife* embodied and active, represent for whites something along the lines of what Wilderson points out when discussing how white South Africans he taught creative writing viewed him: "I was both the trauma and the cure."[113]

This is not to call Blackness "salvific," as is the case with a sacrificial scapegoat. Such a suggestion would entail the ability to distinguish life and death: the latter guaranteeing the former through shifting of embodiment and representation by means of ritualization. The scapegoat, at least at the time of the ritual surrender, subdues the threat of demise in some form. The scapegoat or sacrifice, at least for a time, tames the perceived threat. But the white world needs the *deathlife* threat, and to banish it would be counterproductive. Because Blackness must remain, Blacks aren't properly understood as the scapegoat, nor is Blackness properly positioned as the form of "sin" to be ended in that it is a necessary technology within the social world. Sin would suggest an alternate possibility of thinking and doing that isn't available if the white world is to be maintained. No, here, theological formulations give way to a more mundane "contract" drafted, arranged, and enacted by whites for the benefit of whites. Referring to Charles Mills's "racial contract," Adam Serwer frames the racial contract in a manner that suggests the dynamical relationship underlying *deathlife* as Blackness managing the psychological and existential anxiety of whiteness. He remarks, in light of the murder of Ahmaud Arbery as he jogged through his Georgia neighborhood,

> If the social contract is the implicit agreement among members of a society to follow the rules—for example, acting lawfully, adhering to the results of elections, and contesting the agreed-upon rules by non-violent means—then the racial contract is a codicil rendered in invisible ink, one stating that the rules as written do not apply to nonwhite people in the same way. . . . The law says murder is illegal; the racial contract says it's fine for white people to chase and murder black people if they have decided that those black people scare them.[114]

Despite the graphic and seeming finality of this violence, the societal goal isn't to end Blackness because whiteness needs it to "be." The demise of individual Blacks, then, doesn't speak to an end of Blackness but rather the brutal effort to manage it, to display it, to express need for it. Physical death doesn't negate this coterminous arrangement, in that the "presence" of Blackness as threat isn't dependent on overwhelming materiality, but it is always real and impactful on the psychological and affective level. The physical killing of Blacks doesn't kill Blackness but reinforces it; the desire (no, need) for whiteness/whites to confront it is an effort to confine and tame it—and in so doing preserve whiteness as life.

If there is fungibility related to Blackness as Wilderson describes it, here it would entail this process of one individual after another—the same violence enacted on Black bodies without difference.[115] These individualized markers serve to verify or authenticate the claims regarding Blackness made against (and for) Blackness. In a word, Blacks can die (or be put to death), but Blackness cannot be ended, and so the technical nature of this arrangement isn't captured through a strict grammar of "murder" (explored earlier in this introduction). That grammar separates life and death; it moves between the two and positions Black bodies in relationship to one over the other. Blacks produce anxiety in that their presence overflows the intent of whiteness, because *deathlife* by its nature exceeds the boundaries established through violence (and other means).

Narrations of *Deathlife*

Although Christina Sharpe and I think about the relationship of death to life in different ways and use our perceptions of death to explore and explain different moments of anti-Black thought and activity, one of her statements is applicable here. "Again," Sharpe writes, "Black being appears in the space of the asterisked human as the insurance for, as that which underwrites, white circulation as the human."[116] Sharpe explores this depiction of Black being and death (the ability to breathe) in relationship to the wake (i.e., weather, as anti-Black climate), and here, through rap music, I explore naming and signification of Blackness and the constitutive nature of death and life as concurrent. If the social world and the well-being of its considered occupants (whites) are sustained through a reflexive relationship to the *deathlife* scenario, what of this is spoken back as echo or, at times, signified through rap music's narratives? Is some of the animosity toward particular genres of rap music—from both Blacks and whites—tied to (while not limited to) its graphic amplification and signification of this construction of Blackness as *deathlife*?

The coterminous nature of life and death qua Blackness frames the United States, and recognition in various forms of this arrangement entails a poetic impulse exercised. That is to say, it has required the destruction of language and its grammar in order to reconstitute a mode of expressing the gross (as in without diminishment) nature of such circumstances. Hip hop culture's manipulation of language in the form of rap music provides this service. Hence, this book is framed in light of this question: How does rap music articulate and respond to this arrangement of death and life, the positioning of Blackness by means of which it becomes a blending of the two into *deathlife*? Embedded in some rap lyrics, then, is a meaningful and lucid interrogation of the social mechanics of de/contamination. Awareness is the underpinning of dying, and as such it might be akin to what Peter Boxall calls "blind seeing": a process of depleting distinctions such as that between light and dark, or in this case death and life.[117] This is met with an affective response, which signifies dread—a type of subversive (or, better yet, perverse) joy embodied and ritualized over against social perceptions of life *or* death.

The artists discussed in the following chapters chronicle activities that engage (at times embrace) this *deathlife* model and signify its disturbing and disruptive social coding. As they make clear, to see Blackness is to see *deathlife*. If this work on the part of rap artists involves ethics to any degree, it is because of rap music's linguistic function as offering perspective on the "what" in the "What ought we do?" question.

Deathlife isn't the first text to explore death in relationship to Black existence; it would be difficult to think and write about Black existence without entertaining death on some level.[118] However, less frequent is analysis of rap music meant to push beyond melancholic-centered description and analysis of victims or victimizers.[119] Furthermore, in tackling the issue of *deathlife* my focus isn't on unpacking and explicating the metaphysical dimensions of this positioning or naming of Blackness and Black bodies (although there are moments when I am so engaged). The concern isn't primarily an ontological issue, but rather the aim is to provide thanatological narration of how certain artists—by no means all artists—at times name, describe, conceptualize, act out, or signify *deathlife*.[120]

My goal isn't to assess the effectiveness or morality of these depictions. I offer a description of rap music's relationship to *deathlife* without measuring it against some type of moral-ethical norm. What we believe ourselves to know about life and death (and the connection between the two) is often sensitive to a selective body of materials, drawing on the perspective and concerns of those other than the "victims" of the social world. Even when sources from those who carry Blackness (as their definition) are tapped, there is typically a concern with the pedigree of documentation. How often does the material output of hip hop culture claim philosophical ground beyond a grouping of scholars who embrace it, primarily as an extension of personal appreciation? I question a particular arrangement of respectability: how is it that Du Bois not DMX, Martin Luther King Jr. not Goodie Mob, tells us about the nature and meaning of life and demise? *Deathlife* shifts this archive by attending to and theorizing death and life in light of artists who claim the grime and grit of traumatic geographies.[121]

This introduction has worked to theorize *deathlife* and also to set out some contextual considerations regarding its function as a framing, as well as what its performative expression is meant to accomplish for whiteness/whites. Once the function of death on behalf of whiteness (framed through Blackness as *deathlife*) is established, the remainder of this book involves a thanatologically oriented exploration of rap music's recognition of and response to these circumstances. And while some appeal is made here to various artists, the next four chapters focus on examples of rap music's take on *deathlife*.

The first chapter explores *deathlife* through attention to Jay-Z, positioning him as something along the lines of the "Orphic" hustler: a figure who understands death as already and always bound to life, and for whom ethics entails effort to maintain this tension between the two. This figure lives in light of death, but without either life or death serving as a totalizing experience.

Chapter 2 explores the delicate balance between life as death and death as life through Kendrick Lamar's album *DAMN.*, which is bookended by the potentiality of death and how death penetrates life. All the action (i.e., life) taking place within the various lyrical narratives offered on the album is consumed by the specter of death. I position Lamar as the antihero, whose challenge to the illusion of distinction (i.e., life versus death) is posed against the heroic effort to pretend a safeguard for life (expressed in Eminem's "Stan" and "Bad Guy"), rendering it distinctive. In both chapters, life and death are presented, discussed, and interrogated. Together they address the signifying of *deathlife*, while the following two chapters map out the poetic consumption of *deathlife*.

In chapters 3 and 4, through performances of the erotic and the symbolic zombie, *deathlife* is seen to entail a merger of embodied possibilities that disrupt distinction between life and death by "playing with" or consuming the terminology associated with them: love, passion, hunger, and so on. The artists considered here serve to distinguish linguistically the dynamics of each appetite, thereby rendering *deathlife* connected through an intertwining of vocabulary used in relationship to them. In a certain sense, in the examples discussed in these chapters, death and life are consumed together as *deathlife* through acts of irreverence: behaviors that counter the ritualization possible when life and death are distinct. One might say the artists reject the socially assumed value in seeking to separate life from death and confine/manage the latter for the longevity of the former. They position *deathlife* as a mode of defilement, of destruction, that challenges the integrity and logic of the social world and the grammar/vocabulary used to narrate that social world. To rethink the nature of embodied Blackness in this case, one might argue, involves by its very nature a destruction of the social world as currently conceived—that is, the safeguards for meaning, the dynamics and processes of life as distinguishable from death, are negated. The very presence of embodied Blackness (e.g., the zombie) threatens the distinction: Blackness, in this regard, consumes both life and death.[122] The zombie (chapter 4) and the demise devotee (chapter 3) involve the one who brings *deathlife*. Something about this blends time, conditions response "time," and merges unto itself in such a way as to make an impactful separation of circumstances that promote life over those that promote death disingenuous. The moral and ethical framing of distinction is signified. What one encounters here isn't a corruption of life, a stagnation of its more vibrant dimensions in the form of possibility; rather, it is a lack of distinction by means of which to initiate one is to satisfy the other. The volume ends with an epilogue in which two forms of melancholia are described and discussed: one related to death or life, and the other related to *deathlife*.

If either the signifying or consumptions of death projected onto Blacks qua Blackness involves a "victory," to the extent this term has any use, it isn't in what is gained but rather in what is prevented. It is embedded and expressed through each moment of disruption: each break in the smooth operation of whiteness, when whites are forced to see their whiteness and confront the cost of maintaining it. With respect to rap music as a poetic thanatological narrative, I argue that to separate life from death, and death from life, is to alter the meaning of each, to lose their significance. Such a claim is not to suggest they aren't discussed within the language of the social world as distinguishable—each with a set of affective markers, biological conditions, political arrangements, and so on. Rather, it is to suggest that Blackness is constructed as a safeguard for, but also comes to connote, a defiance of distinction (i.e., death *or* life). To be clear, the language of distinction doesn't apply here, despite the intent of whiteness otherwise. Death doesn't always end physical sensation and biological movement. It can negate significance or ontological recognition. Yet it conditions, informs, and satisfies life in such a way as to make distinction meaningless. One might think of this not as "Black life as it is lived near death . . . deathliness," but instead life as merged with death.[123]

PART I

Signifying Deathlife

THE ORPHIC HUSTLER

When one thinks about mechanisms of communication employed by Blacks with great effect, high on that list must be musical expression. The poetic quality of music and the language shaping the lyrics have given Blacks ways to describe and critique arrangements within the context of a society always on guard against challenges to the status quo of whiteness.

Church . . . or Chuuch?

I learned the importance of musical expression long before I had the academic tools necessary to deconstruct and analyze the musical worlds fostered by my ancestors and contemporaries. First, during my youth within the context of the Black Church, I came to know and appreciate the manner in which music often challenged the sermon as the dominant modality of theologizing. Music marked out the various phases of Sunday morning worship, leading parishioners through the order of service from the precession to the benediction. The rest of the week, music marked the rhythm of life within a death-dealing society, in that the words of a hymn, spiritual, or gospel tune were used to capture a given situation. When other words failed, the gospel message captured through biblically based lyrics spoke clearly and compellingly to the circumstances of the Christian's position as being "in the world, but not of it."

Yet this musical articulation of the gospel message flirted with more "worldly" modes of musical expression. Sometimes the result—as in the case of traditional and contemporary gospel—was the Christian faith with a new rhythm. But as so many in churches like mine feared, this openness to secular musical sensibilities could just as easily draw the unsuspecting Christian into a full embrace of nonreligious sensibilities. Contemporary gospel too easily softened believers to the allure of R&B, pop, and the "world." But for young people like me, the warning meant nothing. We were determined to like what we liked, play the music we enjoyed playing, and still show up for Sunday service singing, "This little light of mine . . . I'm gonna let it shine!" After all, like our parents before us (to the extent they'd admit it), we found something of ourselves—an epistemological recognition and existential comfort—in the "questionable" musical forms that kept us tuned in. As I was growing up, no musical genre expressed this better than rap music.

"Old school" hip hop artists spoke a world so creatively and compellingly that resisting their stories was a futile act. Their grammar and vocabulary were organic and captured so much of what young people like me knew and felt in and about the world. Lyrics explored and explained the already and always nature of death and life, in the form of *deathlife*—the not-so-subtle effort of whiteness to consume us for the sake of whites. Rap music recognized a certain ontological "truth" that brought into focus both the promise and the pitfalls of life (really, the nature of life and death as bound together) in the United States as, in my case, a young Black male. This appreciation, to be sure, wasn't without its tension. I, after all, was a Christian, but I was moving to the rhythm of rap artists whose ethics and moral codes were creative, organic, but not always in line with what I had been trained to privilege as proper conduct. In hindsight, to some extent, this tension revolved around hip hop culture's reframing of religious authority done through a signifying of theistic structuring(s) of meaning, including the artificial distinction between life and death. But should we have expected anything less than this signification of theological themes and assumptions from the child of the blues? If Nina Simone reminds us, in the spirit of the blues, of the sinner man's lament as he runs from judgment, rap music that I was growing to love would probably respond, "Fool, don't run; embrace your swag, and move with style."[1] That is to say, hip hop culture in the form of rap music was simply the most recent incarnation of philosophical-theological counterpoint as the marginalized manifestation of poetic protest. Rap spoke worlds and I was more than comfortable exploring those worlds. Even when it challenged my religious sensibilities, I turned up the volume and smiled. I was intrigued. I couldn't stop listening.

Rap music had me, and I didn't mind or fight its grip on my imagination—despite the fact that I first encountered it as my training to be a minister within the African Methodist Episcopal Church was underway.[2] In light of these opposed sensibilities, I was both insider and outsider: the young Black male of concern within so many rap lyrics, but also a minister-type who represented a particular hustle infesting Black life. Expressed a different way: many artists were speaking to me *and* about me. This made for a particularly stubborn epistemological dissonance, or it could be described as troubling personal/vocational ontologies. It was a challenge to be sure, in that artists brought into question many of my religious assumptions and shot holes in the narrative of ministerial excellence: the minister is the "man" (usually a man) considered closest to the will of God and best able to hear the voice of the Lord. No, rap artists highlighted in verse the frailties of ministers and their abuses of resources and people. Lyrics, often without mercy, exposed ministers as pimps, frauds, and other questionable types: holiness was exposed as hollow. The minister is "frontin'," not faithful, proclaiming in his or her own way the lament of the hustler: "pimpin' ain't easy."

The authority of the preacher simply clouded these circumstances through whooping and references to a divine sanction: "Let the words of my mouth and the meditations of my heart be acceptable in Thy sight, O Lord, my strength and my redeemer." But rap revealed how some of these preachers kept their "pimp hand strong," so to speak, through theological exercise and the well-placed doctrinal slap. And, related to the concerns of this chapter, many of these critiqued church professionals, by means of this theological exercise, traded on talk of death and life as distinct, with the former feared and the latter desired (albeit spiritualized). Reflecting on my days in ministry, I see something of this epistemological and ethical structuring of ontological restriction. In my former context, those eager for spiritual goods and other religious "stuff" surrendered epistemological and moral authority in exchange. Hip hop, particularly the poetics of life offered in rap music, challenged this arrangement in which the authority of the cosmic Other is filtered through the minister. In some cases, such as Reverend Run (Joseph Ward Simmons) or Kurtis Blow (Kurtis Walker), the artist becomes the minister—but without forsaking hip hop sensibilities, and with a posture that signifies the staid aspects of traditional ministerial appeal.[3]

Rap artists provided a model of authority that opposed the long-standing dominance of traditional modalities of leadership—so many of which went back to the Black Church's genealogy of spiritualized authority. The preacher wasn't the only one who could weave a story or frame moral and ethical obligation over against the cartography of life. The preacher might "whoop" but the MC spit fire, and that fire burned my mind long after the sermons (even my sermons) were over. Rap had a staying power; the rawness associated with the sound and the manipulation of instruments continued to vibrate through my mind long after the echo of scripture had subsided.

I don't want to overstate the point in that I was able to maintain something that resembled a balance between the authoritative nature of the religious call to ministry and the more fluidlike sensibilities of the rap world. I walked the border between these two worlds—hip hop and church—finding something that appealed to my self-understanding and view of circumstances framing a life horizon marked by the best and worst of these cultural forms.

Perhaps this was all a consequence of the social world being a place of contradictions, of desires for meaning within a context best prepared to leave Blacks frustrated and unfulfilled (i.e., "dead"). The Black Church acknowledged this predicament but quickly turned to metaphysical claims, and I for some time embraced that approach and those claims. Yet hip hop looked at this predicament without blinking and advanced a position of defiance. This appealed to me, even when I couldn't pull it off myself. I found intriguing rap music's ability to maneuver between worlds and in the process deconstruct and reconstruct religious sensibilities, responsibilities, and notions of authority in line with a lucid sense of *deathlife* and the whiteness it is meant to cover.

Deification as Signification

The rap duo UGK (Underground Kingz) argued "game belong to me" in their 2007 track with that title, and this meant a reclamation of human agency, and thereby an ability to work the systems of "production" and "destruction" to one's benefit.[4] Here the duo, Pimp C and Bun B, chronicle the structuring of existence available to young people in the urban, Southern context in ways that speak to the struggles for meaning that can't be captured adequately by the somewhat sterile and disembodied framings offered by many churches with their fear of death and desire for a spiritualized life. Such artists and their narratives create a space—a space that others fill with psychological probing prompted by recognition of the artists' absurdity-marking encounter with the world. But this isn't genesis of angst that demands nihilism; instead, it offers a more measured sense of the world framed by struggles over the meaning of death and life. Furthermore, it's not the Black Church's hyper-optimism premised on the assumption that "God is on the throne and all is well." Instead, certain artists chronicle in lyrics a life less certain and already and always bound to death. There is a roughness and grittiness, for instance, in Geto Boys' "Mind Playing Tricks on Me" (1991) and Scarface's "Mind Playin' Tricks on Me" (1994) that speak to encounter with a harsh and unresponsive world. Life distinct from death is questioned. This is over against the dreamlike state of some churches' response to the challenges of human existence. "Just a little talk with Jesus makes it right" seems underwhelming in comparison. Other artists push for reconstitution of metaphysics in a way that renders theological themes highly unrecognizable to religious traditionalists.

While examples of this abound, I think one of the more compelling is Tupac Shakur's transfiguration of Jesus the Christ in the form of "Black Jesuz" (1999), who is the patron saint of thugs—a saint who recognizes the importance of despised moral and ethical postures within a troubled/troubling social world. The moral-ethical code and the company Black Jesuz keeps both run contrary to the stuff of a standard Christianization of thinking and doing; but what would one expect when this new figure of authority proclaims a genealogy composed of "drug dealers, thugs, and killers"?[5] Rather than the biblical text, one could argue Tupac—as Black Jesuz—provides a sacred text written on his body, the ink of his tattoos over against the ink of the King James Bible. And, in "Blasphemy" (1996), this embodied text is coupled with the "ten rules to the game," a blasphemy of commandments. There is layered significance to this turn away from a borrowed text to an organic and embodied representation of metaphysical assumptions and claims—drawn on a "substance" always vulnerable to the workings of *deathlife* displayed in word and deed. The biblical text, Tupac argues, doesn't free but rather enslaves: it functions like a drug that tames the body and renders the will docile. Black Jesuz compares himself to Moses, who "split the Red Sea"—"I split the blunt and rolled a fat one up deadly / Babylon beware."[6]

Babylon (i.e., the West with all its mechanisms of demise) beware!

Black Jesuz and his embodied teachings push for self-realization through a creative manipulation of circumstances made possible by an alternate ethical framing that privileges need and desire through a consumption of demise. This arrangement is marked by Black Jesuz's signifying of the death impulse: shot and resurrected. Tupac proclaims that traditional sources and forms of authority despise him; in fact, traditional religious leaders, he raps, want him dead because he exposes the lie that is the traditional religious narrative of life over against death, which justifies the abuses of ministry.

Beyond Tupac's interventions, there are more recent theological turns marked out by rap artists. For some time, I have listened to two tracks, in particular: "No Church in the Wild" (2011) by Jay-Z and Kanye West, and "Crown" (2013) by Jay-Z. These tracks have fascinated me from my first hearing to the present. Perhaps one of the ideological and epistemological shifts I find compelling (based on my own history) is the challenge to the construction of authority housed in traditional religious community and played out through Black existence. The first track dismantles authority by cutting to the core of the modern West. Jay-Z challenges the framing of knowledge as associated with the Greeks by exposing the inherent bias in the crafting of epistemology; dismantles the ethics of the Christian faith (the Church); and challenges constructions of being that don't stem from a materialistic base. And, of course, all this has something to do with epistemologies of death and life played out most graphically in the form of *deathlife*, as both theology and philosophy wrestle with dynamics of mortality.

What Jay-Z and West offer is a modality of the religious that pushes it back to its stripped-down meaning (from *religio*, in Latin)—to bind together. This, one could argue without much effort, is the nature of struggle in terms of ongoing intent to hold together competing claims, or to balance oppositional forces, without being destroyed in the process. Referring in his book *Decoded* (2010) to the way Biggie Smalls frames the nature of a hustler's life, Jay-Z reflects, "Our struggle . . . wasn't organized or even coherent. There were no leaders of this 'movement.' There wasn't even a list of demands. Our struggle was truly a some-thing-out-of-nothing, do-or-die situation."[7] Authority (of religious leadership, for instance) can be dismantled because it can be challenged. The chorus of "No Church in the Wild" sums it up: "Human beings in a mob, what's a mob to a king, what's a king to a god, what's a god to a nonbeliever who don't believe in anything?" In place of traditional modes of authority, Jay-Z and West establish a new religion framed by mutuality and, of course, "exposure" over against violence, deception, and epistemological manipulation. West adds to this a new framing of ethics by maintaining the authoritative significance of the individual in connection to others and by privileging exchange and consent as the bases of relationship: "No sin as long as there's permission."[8] It all revolves around consent as an assertion of self, the willful sharing of agency, while traditional religious authority is premised on the crafting of story and codes that demand (often through violence both rhetorical and physical) surrender: the taking away of agency through the promise of a "different" life free of death. With respect to the latter approach, adherents (as advocated by their leaders) privilege obedience over agency. Pointing out and exercising this distinction, as West notes, is a true point of the theological insight that "the pastor don't preach, that's somethin' that a teacher can't teach."[9] It cuts against the authority of their pedagogy and flies in the face of their circumscribed and truncated ethics.

Over against this reconstitution of tradition and its theological categories, there is an epistemological recalibration offered by "No Church in the Wild" that disrupts the grounding of church-based strategies of living and dying. The video for the track graphically portrays the dismantling of authority's markers of meaning and enforcement. And the lyrics depict the poetic dismantling of discourses of presence that privilege church and state—all done through a meta*physical* rejection of and rebellion against the grammar and vocabulary of rightful control exercised by these institutions. The Black Church, therefore, with its theological tropes (e.g., Jesus) is done away with through a graphic turn to embodied meanings that allow for, if not directly call for, structuring(s) of presence that remove the justification of theologized *meta*physical entanglement. Importantly, both the video and the lyrics do this work through the removal of fear that keeps populations tied to tradition:

Will he make it out alive?
Alright, alright
No church in the wild.[10]

Even the title of the album the track is from—*Watch the Throne*—speaks to this dismantling in a manner reminiscent of Friedrich Nietzsche's mad man pronouncing the death of God.

Western mechanisms of knowledge and meaning (philosophy and religion) are rejected. Yet, while Nietzsche advocates for keeping empty the "throne" once occupied by God so as to not simply replace one God with another external source of authority, Jay-Z and West reconfigure the throne and transform its occupant into the image of the artist. As, for instance, Jay-Z proclaims on "Crown," "You in the presence of a king. Scratch that, you in the presence of a God." Still, in saying this, Jay-Z isn't pointing to new "vertical" relationships (to borrow an idea from Mikhail Bakhtin).[11] No, his is a turn involving an assertion of ability to transform epistemological arrangements, which I would argue entails larger categories of life and death as a matter of horizontal structuring(s) of existence. His proclamation of divinity contains a different, embodied, performance that short-circuits tradition and flirts with *deathlife* without succumbing to it. Jay-Z (aka Hova, a name based on "Jehovah") pushes against restrictions, refusing in "Crown" to be "wiped out of history," but instead imbues said history with the narrative of urban miracles—"Put in the belly of the beast [New York's public housing], I escaped but nigga never had a job"—so that the metanarrative of the American dream is turned on its head through an alternate epistemology of success, or salvation, that doesn't hide practices of demise constituted by whiteness. "If it wasn't for the bread," he notes, "probably be dead." The narrative of "making it" as a consequence of docility in the presence of the Christian God (or whiteness), who might give you a beatdown like Job received but will finish the process by granting more stuff, is flipped and subdued by the standard of a new hustler (aka the streetwise Jay-Z and his communicative skills).[12] By shaping the content of hip hop, he controls ontology, epistemology, and the details of existential happenings. Lucidity, or deep awareness, marks an intimacy with linguistic supremacy acted out.

Tupac reconfigures divinity through a poetics of divine thuggery—Black Jesuz is the saint for contemporary thugs. Jay-Z, in contrast, reforms divinity through a related horizontal move by means of which he amplifies and personifies the qualities of the hustler. Tupac's Black Jesuz succumbs to death (depicted on a cross on the album cover), while the hustler exposes and signifies *deathlife*. The traditional notion of God offers only silence in the face of urban absurdity, but Jay-Z reframes silence. He does not replace the traditional God, however. After all, he believes in God in a more traditional sense.[13] That's not how the concept functions for him. Rather, there is something lasting, extraordinary about his hustle. The divinity of Jay-Z, a way of naming his hustle, places him above traditional notions of a "higher" power in that he signifies *deathlife* in an urban context "where even God doesn't visit."[14]

For some time, hip hop artists have signified the death-dealing arrangements of social life through a renaming intended to assert their agency. And, by this, they've pronounced various modalities of sovereignty that challenge more reifying metaphysical formulations encountered in the United States. Monica Miller and Michael Eric Dyson have both written about this shifting sense of self within hip hop culture, and they have done so in ways that jibe with my argument here.[15] For Miller, deification is constitutive of what she labels "black hyper-legibility," by means of which she seeks to identify and name the enhanced ability of Black bodies to move through time and space marked by recognition and substance—by, in a word, "presence."[16] In a sense, then, Miller is concerned to critically analyze the manner in which deification becomes a trope for an assertion of the artist as full being. For

Dyson, the proclaimed divinity of figures such as Jay-Z points first to artistic prowess, a type of dominance over lyrical production; their poetic genius is marked by an ability to harness theological tropes for an alternate purpose. "Such divine-like signifiers," Dyson writes, "establish and highlight a direct link between the manipulation of rhetoric and the assertion of religious legitimacy."[17] This is a divinity recast and not reliant on the restriction of language, the confusion of language, so as to maintain authority but rather the rendering of language secular and grounded.[18] Hova (i.e., Jay-Z) reassembles pieces of language and turns tradition against itself.

Dyson links Jay-Z to the Black sermonic tradition; however, this entails an effort to fit Jay-Z into the very structuring of authority he seeks to destabilize: the Christian preaching tradition involves the use of language to reflect a reality beyond language—a distinction between life and death—and so entails the introduction of a vertical relationship. Dyson's depiction is thick and complex; yet I would argue that Jay-Z's rhetorical work marks the end of the sermonic logic. The vertical nature of the sermonic moment is overpowered by Jay-Z, who pulls theology to earth and, in this way, works it against itself as only a god can do. Again, this is not god in a traditional sense, with the biblical attributes that dominate images of deification. Rather, it is a type of deity entailing the supreme hustle, with the ability to destroy with words and constitute other meanings that, in effect, signify *deathlife* by revealing and surviving the implications of whiteness.[19]

Whereas Miller and Dyson view this claim to divinity as a way of addressing a more robust occupation of time and space (i.e., living), I see this turn to deification as a means by which some hip hop artists have used radical sovereignty to reconfigure the nature and meaning of *deathlife*.[20] In other words, death remains a negative, a matter of limited epistemological merit and relevance. However, through radical sovereignty some artists project themselves beyond and above in such a way as to challenge the metaphysical damage constituted by whiteness's attempt to impose irrelevance. Jay-Z is a god who embraces the rejected dimensions of existence, finding in them value, for example, a world-facing grammar. Through his claim of deification, Jay-Z can be said, by extension of these theological assertions, to offer victory over death by removing its uniqueness as whiteness means it, and exposing the workings of *deathlife* that whiteness would rather hide.[21]

Furthermore, what I have in mind isn't the existential status marked out by the name "God," as in Lil B's use of "The BasedGod," a name he took on in about 2009. By "Based," Lil B intends to describe a life marked by positive attitude and openness to difference; but, according to Lil B, the BasedGod has the capacity to bring demise through curses on those who aren't respectful.[22] As one journalist wrote after hearing Lil B The BasedGod speak at MIT, the takeaway was love and mutuality:

> When the lecture came to a close, I felt different, changed slightly in some immeasurable way, but for the better. It's what I imagine people experience after a Tony Robbins seminar. Lil B had told us he loved us and I believed it. Somehow I now cared about the wellbeing of this classroom full of strangers in a way that I hadn't when I walked in. I wanted everyone to get home safe, and to thrive during their college years at MIT, and just to do well in life. I looked down my row of seated writers and hoped that all their stories and recaps of the event got millions of views, even if we were ostensibly competing against each other for attention on our articles about the same topic. It's all about sharing the love, not keeping it to yourself.[23]

This statement (perhaps something of a Sermon on the Mount) is a reflection on "divinity" marked by a communally felt push against the despair and trauma that marks life; that is, it is an effort to bracket the dynamics of death vis-à-vis love. As such, it is an approach defined by wrestling with death versus life, and an effort to highlight and claim the latter, as opposed to a signifying of *deathlife* that always reflects both.[24]

The larger context for Jay-Z's and West's assertions lends itself to reassessing the parameters of existence once safeguarded by modalities of authority now condemned: state- and church-controlled mechanisms of life, death, and the ritualization of death. Who, then, controls life and death (*deathlife*) after authority is denounced?

In this new arrangement, lucidity frees as opposed to being a type of agential restricting. It is not a mapping of life vis-à-vis negation: "thou shalt not . . ." Rather, it operates on a different premise: do as you like by means of consent, through recognition of mutuality present even in the context of a troubled world. This doesn't involve any assumption of consistency, as promised within the old divinity model, but it promises intensity of experience as signification of *deathlife* and its guiding logic. Through this transition, Jay-Z becomes that which others fear: he becomes the very embodiment of discontinuity-continuity.[25] Words, the poetics of rap lyrics, destroy meaning and in its place impose an alternate narrative, a counterpresence. All this is done with an abiding knowledge that life and death are indistinguishable. As the deified hustler reflects, "Consumption's flip side is decay and waste."[26] Death isn't to be feared. It is to be acknowledged, not mourned as loss, and understood as intimately connected to life (as Jay-Z advises in "If I Should Die" [1998]). For Jay-Z, the thought of death produces questions regarding the proper vocabulary and grammar for this new circumstance, and much of this is resolved through memory, that is, through the continued activity of those not consumed by demise. Put in terms of the hustle, "If I should die," he reflects, "don't cry my niggas; just ride my niggas; bust bullets in the sky my niggas. And when I'm gone don't mourn my niggas; Get on my niggas."[27]

Jay-Z encourages an alternate approach to agency that maintains the individual's authority over one's life and relationships through a questioning of the very epistemological assumptions of the modern West—thereby creating a space for being who we are as we are. Perhaps it is this reconstituted life (called a religion in "No Church in the Wild") that motivates the proclamation of divinity one finds in "Crown"—again, "you in the presence of a king, scratch that, you in the presence of a god." The miracles associated with divinity are distilled in this track and lodged in the workings of urban life, marking out material desires. Like Black Jesuz, Jay-Z as god welcomes game—as in putting in work, even in the drug trade, and doing so with success. This stance is constituted by means of an authority premised on consistency rather than traditional markers of obedience—not following what others say, but doing what you do. Deification in this instance is based on lucidity, that is, an awareness grounded in the material world and marked off by a measured realism that confronts the workings of the social world (e.g., *deathlife*) without blinking. And, with this task, he has no match: "I'm the illest nigga doin' it 'til y'all prove me wrong. Do you believe? It's Hova the God."[28]

There is, of course, physical demise surrounding Jay-Z's life while dealing drugs in the economically challenged environment that was public housing during the 1970s and 1980s in New York City. In addition, his work suggests a sense of irrelevance as constituting another mode of death, one imposed by whiteness as social control. However, there is also a different type of irrelevance—what one might describe as a cultural irrelevance associated with the end of a career or a career marked by an inauthentic persona. It is in relationship to this dualistic structuring of irrelevance that Jay-Z's framing of hustle projects him as above and outside the grasp of forces of demise, or what one might call the structuring and performance of *deathlife*. The hustler sells death (i.e., crack) without succumbing to it and describes death (e.g., the "streets") without being consumed by it. Death as intended by whiteness is presented, named, *and* contained. This isn't to glorify "the life." Descriptions of death linger and prevent long-term romanticizing of the hustle in ways that negate its traumatic dimensions; yet the intent of the hustle doesn't require such sanitizing.

> You don't hear me though.
> These words ain't just 'pared to go
> in one ear, out the other ear, no![29]

Again, the hustle signifies *deathlife* and in so doing constitutes a means to avoid the end intended by whiteness.[30]

Divine Hustle

W. E. B. Du Bois spoke of the Black existential-psychological dilemma as the effort to hold together two competing structures of meaning, and there is something of that with Jay-Z: the hustler who holds together life and death.[31] Depiction as hustler—perhaps a version of the trickster—enables him to elude social irrelevance, and there's epistemological swag that positions him to recognize the risk of cultural irrelevance and sidestep it. Reflecting on Jean-Michel Basquiat's artworks that address success, the trappings of fame, and the nature of the music business, Jay-Z describes how the sidestep happens: "You become a target. People want to take your head, your crown, your title. . . . And you resist it until one day your albums aren't moving and the shows aren't filling up and it seems like the game might have moved on without you. Then you start to change, you do whatever you need to do to get back into that spotlight. And that's when you're walking dead."[32] Hustler status has something to do with the ability to harness the material substance of life and to tame death—in the form of *deathlife* transgressed. Nonetheless, there are various acknowledgments in Jay-Z's lyrics that, in light of his socioeconomic context growing up, he should be dead. He should have succumbed to the death-dealing intent of whiteness. In a significant way, status as a divine hustler speaks the ability not to end *deathlife*'s connotations per se but to skirt them while others fall victim. Jay-Z's lyrical corpus is replete with references to those who have died—this being a physical demise conditioned by the socioeconomic matrix of US urban life within the confinements of whiteness. Still, in reflecting on them, he works to safeguard the fallen from full irrelevance.

There is a clarity that separates Jay-Z from other hustlers. To the extent this distinction is robust, it might be called a divine difference—the "thing" that establishes the divine in his *divine* hustle. Divinity here entails the manner in which Jay-Z's hustle is sublime and also the manner in which it unpacks, speaks to, and surfaces the details of *deathlife* that whiteness seeks to cover. In "Hova Song" (1999) he proclaims nothing can stop him, no mode of disregard can touch him: "I should be rapping with a turban. Haters can't disturb him, waiters can't serve him." Hustle, then, connotes this poetics as a complex "exception." In a word, it is a reflection on the task of holding together the "possible" and the "impossible," the dynamics of existential arrangements within a context of whiteness's work. This transfiguration of the hustler isn't a simple positing of the "outsider." Such might be the case if Jay-Z shed the persona once he left the "game" and moved away from the "corner." But he has maintained that posture in the boardrooms of corporate America. His is a more complex arrangement, a clarity of conditions that cuts across socioeconomic and cultural geographies: "I'm not a businessman, I'm a business, man!"[33]

I'd like to pause here for a moment to briefly explore the "economics" of whiteness. Du Bois, in "The Souls of White Folks," notes the economic nature of whiteness—the manner in which the assumed ownership of the world entailed in whiteness involves harnessing and controlling the material resources of the world. He describes the economics of enslavement, of colonialism, of European material greed played out in Africa and Asia. He highlights the structures of control that limited (and punished) Black people's efforts to gain some control over their economic circumstances—to claim an alternate value to their Blackness. Stefano Harney and Fred Moten in *The Undercommons* also allude to the economics of whiteness when discussing "debt" as a mode of living in relationship to the "brokenness of being." They are speaking of an unpaid debt related to the workings of slavery and colonialism. In fact, it develops through struggle against the structures of empire, and this radical work is a refusal to pay—thereby rendering this debt "bad debt."

Lester Spence, in the context of post–civil rights politics and economics, asks an intriguing question (one that can be framed in terms of economic-political functions of whiteness) that is applicable here. It is a question that assumes much of what concerned Du Bois, and it respects the "brokenness" noted by Harney and Moten. In asking it, Spence pulls all three—Du Bois, Harney, and Moten—into a contentious realm of cultural expression where the "market" is embodied, stylized, and performed. It's a question that pushes against assumptions that political content is always explicit, instead suggesting that the political content of expressive culture is also present by absence. In either case, political positions are extant. But what are they, is the question: "What," Spence writes, "are the politics embedded in rap and hip-hop's production, circulation, and consumption?"[34] The hoped-for answer to this question involves a politics supporting a "parallel public"—the structuring of a counterworld that challenges rather than simply embraces and reiterates the logic of neoliberalism.[35] Yet while, according to Spence, this was the intent of hip hop, it ends up betraying this possibility and offering the economic-political rationales and mechanisms already in place—just this time with booming bass.[36]

Jay-Z also recognizes how the workings of whiteness have economic depth. However, this is not to say that, like Du Bois or Moten, Jay-Z seeks a way to tame (or even end) such economic (and other) workings. Rather, he signifies the economic logic of whiteness played out through Black bodies. And signifying alters perspective but it doesn't resolve circumstances. Instead, it's a type of imaginative "living within." To define it further, it isn't work to produce an alternate social world free from the stranglehold of whiteness's economic demands; no, it's the hustle—a creative manipulation of the economic rules of whiteness (and hence Blackness). And, while many such as Spence are (rightly) critical of the neoliberal tendencies of this posture toward the world, my concern here is not directed at whether rap music—or Jay-Z's in particular—should work directly to dismantle the political-economic structures of whiteness by tackling neoliberal eco-political circumstances. Nonetheless, Spence is correct when saying, "For a variety of reasons we've been forced to hustle and grind our way out of the post–civil rights era, and it is this hustle and grind in all of its institutional manifestations that's resulted in our current condition."[37]

In this statement there is something of a political lament—a reckoning with the ways in which Black cultural production often helps to maintain the economic-political circumstances and strategies (notably, the neoliberal turn to market principles as regulatory guide for social life) that do damage to Black communities.[38] I think Jay-Z would agree, as much of his lyrical content suggests, but he would continue his form of the NYC-inflected Black(ness) hustle. He's a "business, man," which, perhaps, is a signification—a pronouncement with/through "swag"—of what Spence references as the entrepreneur managing his "human capital," tied, at least early on, to "crack governmentality." For Spence the phrase "crack governmentality" is a way to name the mechanism through which certain rap artists "deploy realness and authenticity as vehicles of urban and human capital and as a technology of subjectivity within subjected places and populations."[39] The personal narratives in Jay-Z's lyrics suggest he sees himself both as embedded in what Spence might label the "technologies of subjection" and as produced by what Spence might see as the "technologies of subjectivity": in sum, the social world and its various logics. The latter ("technologies of subjectivity") serves as a source of economic advancement—what might be felt as something along the lines of *life*—and the former is a mode of punishment (realized as a context of *death*).[40]

Life and Death . . . better stated as *death/life*.

I say all this while asking readers to recall that I want to privilege not Moten's "optimism," but rather Afropessimism's "pessimism" in my reading of Jay-Z and the other artists discussed in this book.[41] This reading, then, entails a different sense of Blackness, a different sense of whiteness, and less concern with the construction of a different world. It isn't an interrogation of economic-political alternatives (or even the production of a blackened sameness) meant to promote what Spence discusses as "creating new possibilities for black life," or, put another way, "new political opportunities and new worlds in which to live, love, and thrive."[42] No, I'm concerned with the manner in which the "hustle" *isn't* simply an economic-political statement related in some ways to neoliberalism but *is* a particular pronouncement concerning death and life in a more fundamental sense. Ultimately, my concern here is how *deathlife* (in relationship to Blackness and whiteness) is understood and articulated.

While Stanley Trachtenberg's essay "The Hustler as Hero" (1962) is inevitably dated and rests to some extent on the outsider (hustler) versus insider (hero) dichotomy, there are elements of his description of the former that hold true and that explicate what Jay-Z might intend to communicate through his frequent appeals to the importance, if not unique nature, of his existential clarity.

Thank God for granting me this moment of clarity
This moment of honesty
The world'll feel my truths.[43]

Reflecting on the hustler as outsider, Trachtenberg states, "He was always certain of the conditions under which his world operated, and though his approach may have shifted occasionally as he learned more of the dangers of his situation, his goals remained fixed."[44] It is when Trachtenberg complicates the model in a way that holds in tension the hustler and the hero that one gets a sense of the introspection, or the observation, that would be refined by Jay-Z. The hustler-hero, as Trachtenberg names the figure, "has emerged as no longer merely the alter ego of the hero, establishing conflicting personifications of a single idea, but as an introspective and independent agent in whom one witnesses the conflicting ideas of a single person."[45] Still, Jay-Z's NYC is framed by the rise of crack, while Trachtenberg speaks of a cultural world pre-crack, and that makes a difference. Nonetheless, Trachtenberg's 1960s depiction does point in a useful direction, that is, toward the manner in which Jay-Z as hustler holds in creative tension the complexities of his existential situation, marked as they are by the presence of *deathlife*.

Jay-Z doesn't claim to be a hero; there is no such dimension to his persona. One gains a sense of this in "Kill Jay-Z" (2017), in which he details the contradictions embedded in the hustler character: a sidestepping of death that exposes self and others to suffering and misery; the trail to death, misery, and absurdity, which is always visible and available. The album on which "Kill Jay-Z" appears, *4:44*, speaks to the clarity and the lucidity to which Jay-Z attributes the success of his hustle. But it isn't a simple clarity regarding the nature of the streets, the dynamics of the corner. It is a drilling down into the affective-psychological self encapsulated in the hustler. This clarity, in a sense, involves an awakening that contradicts the death-dealing intent of whiteness.[46]

> "Fuck wrong with everybody" is what you sayin'
> But if everybody's crazy, you're the one that's insane
> Crazy how life works.[47]

The goal of the hustle isn't simply material acquisition. Rather, it affords the clarity of vision and the depth of insight that allow one to "handle" *deathlife* while maintaining a sense of its deep presence.

It is worthwhile to acknowledge the manner in which Jay-Z recognizes the persistence of death and, at times, laments loss. He knows death but is not tamed by the already always possibility of whiteness's deadly intent: "Prepared for war, I should fear no man."[48] As he notes, he's "from the murder capital, where we murder for capital."[49] He, like Kali, has become death, destroyer of worlds: "I ain't trying to be facetious, but 'Vengeance is mine' sayeth the Lord, you said it better than all. Leave niggas on death's door, breathing on respirators for killing my best boy, haters."[50] Turning to his inversion of theo-ritual strategies associated with vertical connections to a transcendent "something" honored and preserved, Jay-Z grounds his theological performance in the markers of materiality, status, and the ever-present reality of violence and death. Religious rituals meant to point to death overcome are brought back to violence and blood spilled:

> Yes, this is holy war, I wet y'all all with the holy water;
> Spray from the Heckler-Koch automatic
> All the static shall cease to exist.[51]

Vertical relationships are connected intimately to horizontal relationships, and the latter pull the former into the mundane workings of the white world. Questions of life (the existential angst of life in a death-dealing world) prevent long-term comfort or resolution authored by vertically arranged statements of faith. In other words, arrangements in the context of death pose strong questions of theodicy that point back to the need for pragmatic sensibilities offering answers grounded in the existential workings of the material world.

> Dear God—I wonder, can you save me?
> I can't die, I can't die, I can't die.[52]

Yet this theodical inquiry by Jay-Z is matched by a turn to the world with all its challenges:

> I never prayed to God, I prayed to Gottis
> That's right, it's wicked—that's life, I live it.[53]

Contradiction isn't a problem in the above; rather, the ability to hold together opposed sensibilities is a positive aspect of his poetics as sublime. What he offers lyrically are formulas, "scriptures" of a sort, or incantations that speak to the mood of the moment and push for recognition of the "magic" of the hustle (in its various forms, all resonating with the same posture) over against the conditions of the social world.[54] What distinguishes Jay-Z, then, as he proclaims, is that he's "the truest nigga to do this nigga and anything else is foolish. . . . My lyrics is like the Bible, made to save lives."[55] More to the point, in terms of his position as sublime, "Before me there was many," he proclaims, "after me there will be none. I'm the one."[56] In this way, "minor mythologies" regarding the persona of Jay-Z, the hustler, amplify life and neutralize death over against the wishes of whiteness.[57] And these scriptures are offered in arenas turned churches—with sacred items in the form of albums and downloads.[58]

There is no sustained detachment from circumstances that avoids demise by ignoring the nature and meaning of death. Jay-Z is not the "bad man" of blues legend whose tragic quality entails the production of death as glory, as humanizing act. His isn't a callous response to death and dying. He interrogates, explores, and explodes. As he encourages, "Question religion, question it all. Question existence until them questions are solved."[59] There is confrontation here with death that does not kill, albeit a confrontation not without its affective and psychological weight and response when death consumes others.[60] As such, Jay-Z's stance isn't simply an urban critique of US codes of conduct and performance. There is, of course, some of that present.

Yet, more than that, his stance is lucidity in the face of whiteness-fostered demise, or an interrogation of the circumstances of life that undergird what is possible (i.e., the materiality of the "corner," the "block," the world).

The tragicomic dimension of this presence as artist involves the manner in which increased life (e.g., material goods and an expanded social circle) brings with it the threat of death. "Biggie was on the streets before he started releasing music," writes Jay-Z, "but he never had squads of shooters (or the Feds) coming after him until he was famous. And Pac," he continues, "wasn't even heavy in the street. It wasn't till he was a rapper that he started getting shot at, locked up, stalked by the cops—and eventually murdered."[61] Hova avoids the grip of death, while flirting with it.[62] Jay-Z uses lyrical language to articulate the story of self, to point to horizontal relationships that call into question the utility of the traditional "Grand Unity," to borrow from Albert Camus.[63] And doing so entails awareness of the world and its structure; put differently, and borrowing from William James, Jay-Z is potentially a "sick soul"—that is to say, one who is always aware of the circumstances of misery and suffering in the world (i.e., *deathlife*). Regarding this moment of existential clarity, Jay-Z writes, when reflecting on a line from "This Life Forever" (1999),

> I was in the car with my nephews, who were teenagers then. I was listening to Donny Hathaway and moving slow, like ten miles an hour, just rolling around Fort Greene, Brooklyn. I was totally sober, but I felt my consciousness shifting. I looked around and suddenly everything was clear: girls younger than my nephews pushing babies in strollers, boys working the corners, old women wheeling wobbly shopping carts over cracked sidewalks. It was like a movie unfurling on my windshield with Donny Hathaway on the soundtrack. But it wasn't a movie; it was my world. It fucked me up.[64]

Also think of the basic framing of circumstances in "Hard Knock Life (Ghetto Anthem)" (1998), where opposites are brought together to present the gritty nature of life through the "innocence" of the musical *Annie* and the sights, sounds, and activities of the "corner": "It's the hard knock life for us" is the shared sentiment.[65]

What distinguishes the divine quality of Jay-Z's hustle, or his posture toward the world as a "sick soul," might have to do with the maximization of a possibility, or better yet, the perfecting of an attribute. One gets a sense of this distinction as Jay-Z outlines the artist's potential relationship to the world (which would entail a cartography of *deathlife*). "Artists," he writes, "can have greater access to reality; they can see patterns and details and connections that other people, distracted by the blur of life, might miss. Just sharing the truth can be a very powerful thing."[66] For Jay-Z, in relation to his divinity claims, boundaries are problematic and must be replaced with a blurring of distinction—a hip hop *l'informe* (formlessness), as Georges Bataille names it, or debasement; or, as Mikhail Bakhtin defines it, a degrading by means of which creativity is renewed without the restrictions imposed by a vertical relationship in which God despises and restricts.[67] All is horizontal, and sacred texts are embedded in the workings of the material world, located not in special books but on despised bodies, as Jay-Z reflects:

> Good morning.
> (Never read the Qu'ran or Islamic scriptures)
> (Only Psalms I read was on the arms of my niggaz).[68]

Yet Jay-Z positions himself as divine precisely because he is not conquered by the strictures associated with *deathlife*. Hear him: "What you gonna do to me, nigga? Scars will scab."[69] It is a matter of will, of insight, not of transhistorical realities trumping the world, but instead, of perspective and balance within a death-dealing environment.

His divine posture is dexterity and comfort with the presence of the uncomfortable in the same way Br'er Rabbit, the Black cultural figure, is comfortable with the harshness of the briar patch: the location resisted by most, but which he labels home. Or it is similar to that of the African deity Eshu, who mediates worlds and who moves between the context of living and death in a manner that unites them for certain purposes determined by his desires. Br'er Rabbit and Eshu are tricksters across time and place, and beyond the strictures of narrative format they are cultural signifiers for a particular relationship to life and death marked by epistemological swagger and ontological nuance. Like Br'er Rabbit and Eshu, Jay-Z seeks to recast life in ways that recognize the sameness of death and life, and he does so by removing the specter of fear. He reflects, "I'm not afraid of dying, I'm afraid of not trying."[70] Furthermore, like Br'er Rabbit, Jay-Z signifies circumstances in part through exaggeration and wordplay, thereby offering narratives that lend themselves to confrontation with death: "Life's a bitch, I hope to not make her a widow."[71] Yet, while there are elements of similarity one can highlight with respect to Jay-Z's relationship to the social world operative of whiteness and that of cultural heroes such as Br'er Rabbit or Eshu, there are noteworthy discontinuities as well. Transhistorical movement, for instance, doesn't mark Jay-Z's divinity and authority, as one finds with Eshu, nor is his a prowess simply beholden to his ability to trick a white world, as in the case of Br'er Rabbit.

While juxtaposing Jay-Z's hustle to Br'er Rabbit and Eshu provides a mechanism by which to see the posture of the hustler over against the world, it doesn't capture fully the epistemological marking of the hustler within the existential space of *deathlife*. Better than Br'er Rabbit and Eshu, an epistemological reading of Orpheus provides a compelling means by which to understand the trope of the hustler and the economy of *deathlife* that his poetics and actions signify.[72] In fact, in a piece in the *New Yorker*, Alec Wilkinson toys with the idea of Jay-Z and Beyoncé as Orpheus and Eurydice.[73] For Wilkinson it's an opening move, as something about Orphic adventure and journey cast in terms of two superstars offers a catchy introduction to New York City subways—the underworld of the city—and subway maps. Yet, as this chapter seeks to argue, there is more to be said concerning the application of that allegory as the hip hop-ification of Orpheus in relationship to *deathlife*.[74]

Hustler as Orpheus

The narrative of Orpheus made its way from ancient Greece to geographies of contemporary thought, as numerous writers rehearsed and revised his story in light of their particular historical-cultural moment and mood. For example, in the film adaptation of the myth titled *Black Orpheus* (1959), the story unfolds in Rio de Janeiro around the time of Carnival, bringing into play issues of class and race, as an impoverished Orpheus desires Eurydice, who is of mixed race.[75] The ability to paint the narrative Black and re/contextualize it made the film's hermeneutic precise in its presentation of particularly painful dimensions of politics and economics in Brazil. And, for my purposes, to do so within the context of a favela opens the possibility of Orpheus inhabiting other spaces marked by disregard and demise shaped in light of whiteness.[76]

As the death rattle of colonialism could be heard in Africa, Orpheus served as a signifier of transformation. The character was a way of capturing an early cultural allegory and applying it to the intellectual and political transformation of Africans, from the death of Otherness to complex presence. For example, Jean-Paul Sartre had referenced "Black Orpheus" in 1948 in describing Negritude—the intellectual and practical system of critique regarding colonialism and its varied implications—and in reflecting on the work of Aimé Césaire, Léopold Senghor, and other Black writers. Their poetic awakening captured the world as it both claimed and rejected subjectivity based on a knowing that undercut what had been taught (e.g., inferiority, impoverishment, and fixity).[77] Senghor captured the poetic quality of the movement but cast it broadly, and without Sartre's Eurocentric filter, as "the ensemble of values of black civilization."[78] Turning back to Sartre, we find the poetic life of the (anti)colonial moment depicted as linguistic demise. "It is in this perspective," Sartre writes, "that we must situate the efforts of the 'black evangelists.' They answer the colonist's ruse with a similar but inverse ruse: since the oppressor is present in the very language that they speak, they will speak this language in order to destroy it." Finally, bracketing the implications of Negritude as defined by a European who thinks strictly in terms of economic mechanisms of control, Sartre describes the mechanics of this process: "He will crush [words], break their usual associations, he will violently couple them 'with little steps of caterpillar rain'" (quoting poetry by Césaire).[79] In recapturing and redeeming a term of death—or nothingness as a particular type of thingification—the concept of Negritude was seen by many during the twentieth century as the mark of human substance pointing to the ability to elude social demise.[80]

This movement and its cultural sensibilities were performed through a variety of geographies of engagement, and the epistemological-existential insights gained through a new Black awareness were celebrated in print. Related to this formal presentation, and in line with my concerns here, one of the most significant journals developed on the heels of Negritude, coming out of Nigeria in 1957, bore the title *Black Orpheus* and was meant to enable, transmit, and celebrate this expansive transformation. All this is to say that Orpheus has long served as a symbol of human encounter that cuts across time periods and vast territories. As Orpheus came to us over time, some privileged his love for Eurydice or his early travels as part of the quest for the Golden Fleece, and so on, with each component of his story capturing a particular symbol of current circumstances played out through the persistent workings of human imagination. Yet, as the manifestation of Negritude and other practices of Black lucidity, Orpheus did not speak simply for but *against* Europe. When Orpheus became Black, he served to foster the cultural mood and sociopolitically signified sense of Blackness that sang the merit and power of a pan-African orientation. In the process, language and cultural codes were destroyed—including the narrative arguing that Africa and its children in the Americas had little to say and less to offer. These restrictive modes of communication and "naming" were denied, and in their wake a grammar and vocabulary were developed by means of which a new relationship to existential possibilities and independence was articulated.

This impulse is present in Black US artistic production—such as literature (e.g., Langston Hughes and Ntozake Shange) and music (e.g., blues)—that projects Black expressiveness as one with the large and graphic narrative of encounters survived as both fantastic and awful.[81] From the Harlem Renaissance moving through Black Realism, civil rights rhetoric, and the Black Power poetics of Gil Scott-Heron and the Last Poets to the deconstructive wordplay of hip hop, something of an Orphic mood can be sensed.[82] Hip hop figures like Jay-Z—who in their sociocultural moment speak a similar understanding—recapture through their poetics the sounds of death and rename them: "nigga" . . . "god" . . . "prophet" . . . "hustler."

Hustler . . . Orphic Hustler.

The poetic—that is, the shifting of communicative elements for alternate purposes, thereby both destroying and reinventing expression—confronts the possible and the impossible (as I have used these terms above), blurring distinctions and allowing room to maneuver against whiteness and its henchmen. This is an allusiveness that demands the poetic for its transport. Drawn into and read through contemporary mechanisms of irregularity (i.e., race and class), the myth then becomes a trope of value in interrogating the circumstances for Black people in the Americas as they occupy a geography defined by the ever-present threat of demise (in particular, physical death through poverty and irrelevance through racialization).[83] Such a turn points to the transformative potential and intent of poetic language—or, in Jay-Z's case, as with Orpheus, the penetrating nature of music. Yet, in either case, the communicative capacity that is expressed exposes and challenges the comfortable (or normative) distinguishing of life and death. There is something of death— the complexities of demise as life yields to it—that leaks from Orpheus as allegory.

In the essay collection *Orpheus in the Bronx*, for example, the poet Reginald Shepherd says simply, in the first line of "Why I Write": "I write because I would like to live forever."[84] This is not to suggest that Shepherd believes one can cheat death in an ultimate sense, but rather that the articulation of our occupation of time and space and the experience at the nexus of those two are wet with the potentiality for and practice of *deathlife*. Or, as Shepherd laments (I believe there is something melancholic about his reflection), "Art is a simulacrum of life that embodies and operates by means of death." As the story of Orpheus suggests, however, art has the capacity to "rescue some portion of the drowned and drowning, including always [oneself]."[85] The poetic manipulation of word and sound shifts the vibration of life and softens the grasp of demise, allowing for life sunken in an awareness of death. It is the sublime nature of Orpheus's poetics that separates him and fosters the development of a particular cultural ethos. Orpheus teaches, and contemporary applications hope, that death can be known in a way that draws us from it as it draws us to it—in a way that blurs what is meant by life *and* death.[86] As Shepherd and others in the late twentieth and early twenty-first centuries attest, something about the application of Orpheus enables a recognition of, approach to, and survival of whiteness and its implications.

Both Jay-Z and Orpheus can be said, in light of the particular historical-cultural geographies they traverse, to "[narrow] the gap between . . . living and dead."[87] Where there is Orpheus, and for that matter Jay-Z, there is *deathlife* signified. To elude or survive death, in the case of Jay-Z the Orphic hustler, is to survive the corner (or public housing); in a more expansive sense, it is to negotiate and make it in and out the trap house.[88] Orpheus exists in Hades; the Orphic hustler tames the hell of the contemporary social world. For Jay-Z, worlds come together early in the form of the "corner" and the housing development. They are held together, positioned so to speak, through the strategy of the hustle—the manner in which rap in general (and Jay-Z in particular) "took the remnants of a dying society and created something new."[89] And perhaps it is this ability to navigate (to walk through) the death-dealing terrain that has claimed so many other lives that elevates and promotes his hustle.[90] What distinguishes them—Jay-Z and Orpheus—is the compelling nature of their expression, which cuts across distinctions, gains attention, and transforms the territory of movement. With both Orpheus and Jay-Z, there is a power in the impact of their words, in that the quality of their pronouncements speaks to the felt impact of art as manipulation. And through music they establish an alternate performance of imaginative and creative possibility within the realm of *deathlife*. Orpheus travels by sea and descends into and out of Hades, and Jay-Z's negotiation of the drug trade entails a particular type of perilous journey.[91]

Regarding the Greek circumstance, "Orpheus was not regarded as a god," writes Walter Guthrie, "but as a hero, in the sense of someone who could claim close kinship with the gods, in virtue of which he had certain superhuman powers, but who had to live the ordinary span of life and die like any other mortal."[92] Yet, in contrast, some link Orpheus to the Greek god of vegetation, which places him within the realm of life, demise, rebirth—i.e., life and death.[93] Jay-Z encourages—like the collective writings about Orpheus—a range of perceptions, including status as god, prophet, hero, and so on. In this way, Jay-Z's persona forces a rethinking of divinity, and with it the nature and meaning of temporality as a framing for distinction between death and life. Art—the ability to name, describe, claim, and transcend—is important in these narratives. Music, as representation of his lucidity, keeps Jay-Z alive despite whiteness's instituting of death, and it fuels the movement of Orpheus as a presence that isn't stifled ultimately by physical death, but that holds death and life in tension.[94]

Again, the Orphic hustler is "divine" (a flexible and situational positionality) to the extent that he possesses a set of capacities exceeding all others. This divinity fosters another point of commonality: Orpheus is said by some to be associated with a religion—the ancient Greek "Orphic religion," or "Orphism religious sect."[95] And Jay-Z (alone on "Crown," and in partnership with Kanye West on *Watch the Throne*) dismantles old standards of authority and offers an alternate system of meaning making, or what might be called a religion, complete with "scriptures" and poetic "rites" (e.g., concerts and videos) as the guiding mechanism.[96] Furthermore, some theologized Orpheus as a Christ figure, and, of course, Jay-Z is also known as Hova, an informed wordplay on Jehovah.[97] What we have is Jay-Z as human but also reflecting an epistemological excessiveness. Jay-Z claims special abilities, greater insights and lucidity, and this marks a certain supreme quality—a sublime dimension that reflects something of divinity without freeing him from the limitations of human history and material existence.

While Orpheus has often been depicted as somewhat subdued and without the "fight" of so many Greek heroes, there is defiance in his story of travel and encounter.[98] Jay-Z's posture toward the world is explicitly more rebellious and robust. This twenty-first-century hip hop incarnation of the Orphic personality takes on more girth, an "earthiness" made necessary by the realities of public housing and the demands of the "corner." Still, these figures share music and the power of music. Jay-Z as hustler is akin to Orpheus the sublime artist—not offering the same type of music, or the same peaceful effect of Orpheus's lyre, but a similar ability to harness the sublime through musical production in relationship to the markings of demise.[99] Both fluid personalities can maintain the impact of their music despite movement, or perhaps because of movement. Jay-Z and Orpheus refine and reframe their capacity to influence and inform as they transition between circumstances, as they encounter new geographies and conditions. They are unknowable to us without their movement through treacherous terrain: Orpheus goes to Hades to bring his wife, Eurydice, back to the land of the living; because of the sublime nature of his music, he is given permission to leave with her.[100] Thus he tames and eludes the intent of death, and in the process, he maintains what matters most to him. In like manner, Jay-Z, the hustler, recognizes physical death will one day claim him, but until then his lucidity, expressed poetically, marks out his ability to evade the intent of whiteness through death and subdues its terror. This is more than "second sight"—the ability to understand life on both sides of the "Veil," described by Du Bois as the "talent" of Blacks.[101] Here is awareness, the skill of metaphysical elusiveness that marks Jay-Z not simply in terms of a Black/white social binary but in relationship to more basic mechanics of meaning and being (e.g., life and death). The hustler recognizes the violence of *deathlife* and, unlike the "bad man" character, subdues it by sidestepping its intent.[102]

Orpheus dies, but prior to that, his music opens him to the secrets of death and the place of the dead. Guthrie recounts one rendition of that death in which, even in demise, there is greatness. In this version, those who kill Orpheus and dump his limbs into the sea believed the task of destroying him required the additional violence of removing his head. However, when the head is discovered later, "It was still singing, and in no way harmed by the sea, nor had it suffered any of the other dreadful changes which the fates of man bring upon dead bodies. Even after so long a time it was fresh, and blooming with the blood of life. So they took it and buried it under a great mound, and fenced off a precinct around it, which at first was a hero-shrine but later grew to be a temple. That is, it is honored with sacrifices and all the other tributes which are paid to gods."[103] This depiction speaks to a superhuman quality, a relationship to death and life beyond that engaged and countered by others. There is with Orpheus a twisting of harmful intent in such a way as to tame it—to prevent its aim of fixing him or subduing him. Instead, he remains marked by death (his head buried in a mound) and life (continued adoration and praise associated with the gods) intertwined.

Jay-Z and Orpheus aren't the only figures to confront death. Others knew the route to Hades and some had ventured or been dragged through it in heroic fashion; Jay-Z wasn't the only one who faced death on the "corner."[104] All true, but these two have knowledge of death by means of which, while still subject to death, they are not consumed by the intent of the social world. The severed head of Orpheus continues to perform its poetics; the call to "Kill Jay-Z," among other performances of demise, serves only to further his legend and increase his metaphysical prowess celebrated through a hip hop–infused odyssey. The substance of Orpheus's hymns and writings continues to intrigue, and Jay-Z, as Travis Scott's hook on "Crown" would suggest, refuses to submit his legacy to the fog of forgetfulness despite the efforts of others: "Shit on me, these niggas tried to shit on me. I was left for dead; they tried to wipe me out of your history."[105] The signification of *deathlife* involves, then, for Jay-Z, the ability to remain undefined by the intent of whiteness—to not be subdued by whiteness but rather to remain a sign of its failure.

Sometimes Laughter

In an interview with Zadie Smith, Jay-Z reflects that the election of Barack Obama in 2008 might have "made the hustler less relevant."[106] By this, he points to how his growing-up years were defined by a limited range of options: a narrow scope of life possibilities always already strangled by death as the workings of whiteness.[107] There are ways in which Obama's election to the highest office in the land marked out at least the slim chance of expanded possibilities, but the coldblooded murder of Blacks at the hands of police officers confirmed the ongoing manner in which Blacks, through Blackness, are cast as a threat against life to be subdued. "And now," writes Smith, "by virtue of being forty-two and not dead, [Jay-Z] can claim his own unique selling proposition: he's an artist as old as his art form. The two have grown up together."[108] So, he outmaneuvers the intentions of whiteness in its various incarnations and contexts. From public housing to what could be the tragic consequences of success, Jay-Z wards off death-dealing entanglement with whiteness both as a physical ending and as irrelevance, with a laugh dripping with swag while "staying real jiggy."[109]

Reflecting on laughter through Bataille's reading of Nietzsche points out the way Jay-Z's laugh reflects the ability to produce convergence of worlds— or the creative tension between the material world (i.e., what is possible) and the world of death and disconnection held together.[110] The laugh that one hears between lyrical lines isn't simply a break, a matter of regrouping before going hard again. It's more than that: both absence and presence are affirmed, and death is tamed through his lucidity in the face of demise. He confronts it, defies it, through lyrics as a trope for laughter, as a signifying of whiteness's narrative of death.

This connection may, at times, promote an interrogation of circumstances in such a way as to suggest surrender to the absurd. This is certainly one way to read Jay-Z's questioning of the arrangement of existence, expressed in the following verses from "This Can't Be Life" (2000), but the soulful lament of the first line gives way to a repositioning that holds in tension life and death—presence and absence—a questioning of circumstances within the limits imposed by whiteness:

> This can't be life, this can't be love
> This can't be right, there's gotta be more, this can't be us.

For Jay-Z, such tenacious forces need not split us apart, need not produce a despair that results in surrender. Rather than the assumption of clear distinctions, or what Bataille would reference as discontinuities, Jay-Z sees contradictions as really being dimensions of one reality—*deathlife*—that whites have tried to hold separate.[111] Reflecting on what could have been the tragic consequences of an assault charge he faced for a physical confrontation with someone who'd been pointed out as the source of the leaking of one of his albums, he writes,

> But more than that, I realized that I had a choice in life. There was no reason to put my life on the line, and the lives of everyone who depends on me, because of a momentary loss of control. It sometimes feels like complete disaster is always around the corner, waiting to trap us, so we have to live for the moment and fuck the rest. That kind of fatalism—this game I play ain't no way to fix it, it's inevitable—feels like realism, but the truth is that you can step back and not play someone else's game.[112]

From the crackheads (the look of demise) to the gunfire (the sound of death), he knew that whiteness's projection of death and his understanding of death—his refusal to be paralyzed by its tortures—rendered him "different."[113] As he writes, "I love metaphors, and for me hustling is the ultimate metaphor for the basic human struggles: the struggle to survive and resist, the struggle to win and to make sense of it all."[114] He, as the Orphic hustler, is the mediation of the material world and the context of death presented in such a way as to remove the assurance of ownership over the former and any fear of the latter. He, in a word, becomes that which is feared (by whiteness due to his signifying), or as he proclaims, "If fear is your only god, getting y'all to fear me is my only job."[115]

THE ANTIHERO

April 14: This is a date marked by the confluence of life and death. On this date in 1865, John Booth—on the heels of a gruesome battle over slavery and the nature of whiteness—bringing to an end a particular articulation of nationhood and the possibility of a new arrangement of the public, killed President Abraham Lincoln. Yet this day in 2003 marks a scientific grasp of the structuring of life through the completion of the Human Genome Project. Symbolized by these two events, April 14 is a date reflecting the interplay, or blending, of life and death. And it does so through the presentation of social constructions and scientific framings, with both involving technology (i.e., a gun and scientific apparatus) at work marking demise and birth. Either situation—the killing or the discovery—points out the penetrated nature of embodiment and the manner in which this openness frames the nature and meaning of living into death/dying into life—that is, *deathlife*.

With these scenarios in mind, the release of Kendrick Lamar's *DAMN.* on April 14, 2017, is telling, in that it captures the political nature of Blackness as a significant social construct having an inner logic by means of which death is indistinguishable from life for a certain population, in order to safeguard life for whites. To be Black entails a situation in which to name one (death) is to point out the other (life).[1] To further push the significance of this release date, and its statement on *deathlife*, toward its theological limits, one could highlight the fact that April 14, 2017, was Good Friday—one of the more impactful framings of an understanding of death available in religious terms. In the biblical story of Good Friday, it was the day that Jesus died on the cross for the sins of humanity. His was a death that brings life; his death is indistinguishable—in effect—from the life it makes available. To have one is to have the other. I don't know that the release of Lamar's fourth album was meant to correspond to any of these particular events as symbolizing a certain articulation of the social world (i.e., historic developments with clear and intentional bearing on the themes articulated throughout the various tracks). Yet the album's imagery and wordplay are open to thanatological possibilities, and speculating on what the album might say regarding the nature of life and death is worth the effort. In fact, the layout of the album might even call listeners to this type of speculation.

Lamar begins with a poetics of his own death—a narrative of death that comes on the musical heels of *To Pimp a Butterfly*'s "Alright" and "Mortal Man"—that is to say, a narrative of death that is always and already also a narrative about life. *DAMN.* offers a short story ("BLOOD.") in which Lamar's life ends as he is shot trying to assist a blind woman. The imagery is rich: a lack of lucidity or awareness is the absence of something vital, and this results in demise. And, perhaps more to the point, life and death are always bound together: death can't be bracketed off; it can't be fixed and there is no safeguard from it.

Framing *DAMN.*

The Pulitzer Prize jury acknowledged what millions have known for some time now: Lamar's *DAMN.* is a profound journey into some of the most compelling (and terrifying) challenges facing us: racial disregard, the graphic reaction to Blackness.[2] In short, whiteness needs Blackness as a counterpoint but also despises Blackness to the point of violence. As if this weren't enough, it's also the story of how the cultural codes of the United States produce (figuratively and literally) death across the landscape of collective life—articulated through the workings of *deathlife*.

The importance of this tackling of death, as Lamar makes clear, is highlighted by the fact that US culture (read whiteness) looks to control death, to destroy its most frightening dimensions, to reverse its appearance, and to cover up the anxiety it produces. In this way, I would suggest, we get a glimpse of the way in which death and life are held together and reflected through the performance of violence safeguarding whiteness, or what Lamar has referenced on *DAMN.* as "real nigga conditions."[3] Yet *DAMN.* means to avoid anything in its presentation of how a death-dealing society operates that might allow for comfort, ease of mind, or respite from angst. This is certainly the case when the album is listened to backward—from the last track to the first—or what some have labeled the "Blue Album." As Lindsay Zoladz remarks in an article titled "The Power of Kendrick Lamar's 'Damn.' from Back to Front,"

> The "Blue" version is no fairytale. Love warps into lust. The wise words of Cousin Carl (who we hear in a voicemail sampled on "Fear.") are forgotten by the time Kendrick has made it to the carefree "Yah." Success has made our cocky narrator forget where he came from, although it *does* make the penultimate track "DNA" more meaningful since we know where he's been—we've taken the journey with him. We do not need to be told about the power, poison, pain, and joy because he's already showed us all of their vivid hues.[4]

Lamar, with this album and earlier work as well, represents the continuation of a thought tradition aiming to better understand the conditions of humanity reflected through death and what we might hope for in light of the tragic quality of human existence in this, our troubled time. One might say he participates in a long tradition, then, of signifying *deathlife* through an interrogation of the Blackness that whiteness means to foster.

He takes up where twentieth-century thinkers such as W. E. B. Du Bois, Nella Larsen, Albert Camus, and Richard Wright left off. And in the process he raps Black moralism, which is a way of rigorously naming the conditions of human existence and the contradictions and inconsistencies embedded in dominant ways of thinking and doing in the contemporary world.[5] Although using the language of existentialism rather than moralism, the singer Miguelito speaks to a similar awareness, what one might reference as the "sick soul" privileged by William James (and mentioned earlier in this book in relationship to Jay-Z).[6] The "sick soul" refuses to ignore the misery in/of the world and demands recognition of the misery embedded in life. For Miguelito, Lamar's *DAMN.* offers intense questioning, a type of worldly awareness: "Kendrick, flipping the coin, doesn't shy away from asking God the tough questions and plays the role of hip hop's resident existentialist. He's focused on the subjective experience of the individual and his music is littered with the assertion that suffering is intrinsic to that experience."[7] Still, while mindful of a turn in hip hop, my concern isn't simply the historiography of existentialism within rap music. To this point, I am concerned with how existential considerations play out through a framing of death intended by whiteness, but targeted by Lamar for signification as whiteness's tool.[8] Existentialism certainly captures some of the "mood" I have in mind; however, it brings with it a level of affirmation while moralism—like Lamar's—privileges questions, complexity, and paradox by means of which the hypocrisy of social structures and codes is exposed without an ultimate resolution. And this lack of conclusion doesn't result in nihilism or even a mode of pessimism that traps movement. Rather, for Lamar, recognition of these circumstances is an existential awareness allowing for a more productive movement through the world of whiteness. It pushes against illusions of perfection or perfectibility and replaces such illusions with a recognition of life marked by struggle, marked by the presence of death. There is no need, however, to be broken by these circumstances. Appreciation of the dynamics of *deathlife* simply enhances deeper appreciation of the nature and meaning of our humanity. DAMN. raises the question of whether "We gonna live or die?" However, the album offers little that suggests a clear distinction between the two (live or die); rather, it suggests the former bleeds into the latter and the latter into the former. They, life and death, are the same, and nothing disrupts this sameness of living/dying.

Poetics of Death

Lamar, like so many hip hop artists before him, paints graphic and often disturbing depictions of movement through this world, inspiring a sustained concern with racial disregard, economic injustice, and theological shortcomings of religious traditions. Through a rejection of despair and melancholy, of angst and fear, regarding circumstances of our living into death (and dying into life), Lamar turns arrangements upside down by embracing what is despised. His "mood" channels that of the blues. By saying that, I intend to capture a sharp awareness with respect to circumstances that don't seek to reduce tension but rather embrace competing components, thereby allowing meaning to entail slippage and interplay between contrary ideals. Such is the nature of self-understanding shaping reality—the meaning of movement through time and space. Life, as he points out, is fragile and full of contradictions; yet there is an odd beauty in all this. Through embrace of what so much of US culture is meant to deny, Lamar chronicles and critiques assumptions regarding whiteness as the cartography of how to live life. DAMN. offers an urban(e) system of knowledge couched in the sights and sounds of Los Angeles.

Lamar's is a secular religiosity, in that it doesn't point away from the stuff of our troubled existence. *DAMN.* wrestles with the fundamental questions of human existence: Who are we? What are we? Where are we? When are we? Why are we? And it addresses them without the promise of security and escape from what troubles us: death looms large and there is no way around its impingement. Although "nobody prayin' for" him, the goal isn't perpetual lament but rather recognition of circumstance and embrace of self in the world along with the contradictions this entails.[9] Lamar doesn't celebrate the fail-safe of transcendent possibilities of heaven and hell beyond the restrictions of human history; rather, he calls attention to the stories of graphic pain and unlikely possibility that mark contemporary life. Along the way, he demonstrates what we might just gain in the process: some clarity regarding the "feel" and "look" of death as life.

Death penetrates (and becomes) life, and in so doing it casts a shadow over every dimension of our occupation of time and space. One can regret these circumstances. One can attempt to undo these circumstances; or, as is the case with Lamar, one can embrace the tragicomic quality entailed by life as death / death as life. To live is to confront death, to face the dynamics of demise, until there is no longer a distinction between the two: one lives into death and also dies into life. There, of course, is an affective quality to this confrontation (perhaps fear, bewilderment, etc.). None of these, however, find expression in Lamar's poetic engagement with the pervasiveness of death. He chronicles it, ritualizes its impact, and signifies the terror it intends to foster. By facing death, confronting its intensity, death loses its terror (intended by whiteness) and instead entails a component of life's rhythm.

Such circumstances promote the issue of theodicy for the theist—what can be said about God in light of the conditions of life? How does one maintain posture and voice in a world privileging pain and silence? And while he doesn't use traditional theological formulations, Lamar does funnel many of his theological-philosophical considerations through the Hebrew Israelite philosophy held by members of his family. In "FEAR." he presents the Hebrew Israelite theodicy as offered by a cousin. While one might think it is Lamar's perception of moral evil, his reflection on it in an interview makes that a questionable assumption:

> *INTERVIEWER:* Your Cousin Carl is a member of the Hebrew Israelites, who believe that African-Americans are the true descendants of the biblical Israelites. Carl pops up in a voicemail on "FEAR." You call yourself an Israelite on the album. How much of his theology have you embraced, and how much of it is just you playing with the ideas?

LAMAR: Everything that I say on the record is from his perspective. That's always been my thing. Always listen to people's history and their background. It may not be like mine, it may not be like yours. It was taking his perspective on the world and life as a people and putting it to where people can listen to it and make their own perspective from it, whether you agree or you don't agree. That's what I think music is for. It's a mouthpiece.[10]

Lamar's perception of moral evil and the nature of Blackness also involves interrogation of a theodicy of divine curse:

INTERVIEWER: So what's your opinion about the idea that Carl brings up, that black people are cursed by God as per Deuteronomy?

LAMAR: That shit's truth. There's so many different ways to interpret it, but it's definitely truth when you're talking about unity in our community and some of the things we have no control over. Where there's fighting against the government, where there's fighting against our own political views, there's always a higher being, right there willing to stop it.[11]

Theodical arguments (about God's goodness) certainly exist for Lamar; however, perception of the divine as reflected in "GOD." seems grounded in the historical workings of the world. That is to say, what God "feels like" is associated with the affective and material arrangements of life—and this life is framed by death. What Susan Mizruchi notes regarding Du Bois is as true an insight regarding the lyrics of Lamar: "Death and niggers have become synonymous in White minds."[12] *DAMN.* confronts this conflation of Blackness with the decay of death, and it does so in a manner that signifies white fear and obsession. Still, there is no pessimism in Lamar's outlook; rather, it is better described as a mode of realism by means of which one continues to move through a world profoundly committed to one's demise. Lamar considers the various discourses related to the nature and meaning of life—including, again, that of the Hebrew Israelites. From the latter, he takes only a shift away from "Black" as a basic category of being: hence, he exists in a more robust manner than "Black" can indicate.

Whites seek to address this persistence of the spectacle of death they have created through confinement, through boundaries that reinforce their needed discourse of disregard. Death, within the workings of the larger society, is the ultimate metaphysical and existential boundary. Yet Lamar recognizes the flaws within that mode of thinking and being. When one recognizes that one will "prolly die" and all that shifts is the circumstances of that demise, one is able to manage fear as a matter of material circumstances, as opposed to fear as a confrontation with more fundamental meanings.[13] For Lamar, theological questions are turned and pointed toward the material nature of earth—physical relationships and responsibilities over against abstract considerations. Perhaps this is why the theodical questions concerning God's relationship to human suffering in "FEAR." ("Why God, why God do I gotta suffer?") are followed by descriptions of the restraints on life imposed not by God but by family, by life in the context of his Los Angeles. Or, as his mother demands, "Nigga, you gon' fear me if you don't fear no one else."[14] Doctrine of God considerations are followed, if not consumed, by the demands of material life: "I beat your ass . . . ," threatened by his mother, takes precedence over divine interrogations. By extension, one must recognize accountability to material arrangements above all. Yet there is something of a cautionary tale in his depiction of his relationship to others within the context of a troubled and troubling world. Ultimately, when it comes to the tension of *deathlife*, he does not find the answer in pedagogies of the divine. Suffering isn't justified by some divine scheme and intent. There is no distinction of substance between theodical questions and material circumstances. Pain is without comfort, whether assumed sanctioned by some divine force or imposed as order by parental authority.[15]

The nature of a god defined not by unconditional love but rather by exacting requirements that, when not met, result in pain and misery is outlined in *DAMN*. This is a god whose highly visible mark on the world is suffering. "So, in conclusion," Lamar writes in a letter response to an article dealing with his concept of god, "I feel it's my calling to share the joy of God, but with exclamation, more so, the FEAR OF GOD. The balance. Knowing the power in what he can build, and also what he can destroy. At any given moment."[16] In both theodical questions and material circumstances, suffering is meant by the former to safeguard against a damned soul and by the latter to safeguard against the threat of death within a world that doesn't appreciate Black bodies "out of place," as Mary Douglas might phrase it.[17] In both cases (theological and existential) what is at stake is the substance of the self. Even "God" is grounded in the material, "felt" in terms of the workings of social arrangements firmly positioned within historical arrangements.[18]

What happens between life and death, as "DUCKWORTH." indicates, is a horizontal relationship between random acts and coincidence rather than history as teleological in nature. In short, shit happens and we survive it or allow it to crush us. In "DUCKWORTH.," Lamar's current circumstances—the developments leading up to *DAMN.*—aren't divinely orchestrated because "what happens on earth stays on earth!" They are a collection of human acts—someone isn't murdered, isn't robbed, for random reasons—not the grand logic of the universe. And so the question "Whoever thought the greatest rapper would be from coincidence?"[19] And while this cartography of meaning supports both misery and joy, nothing about it prevents death, and nothing separates life from death. The album begins with life into death and ends still marked by the reality of demise, all within the context of vibrant material realities. Of this, Lamar is aware and, with this, Lamar is comfortable. Theological uncertainties are tamed not through an appeal to altered life beyond the reach of death, but through a deep dive into the workings of existence within a world framed by death as life, or pain tied to continuation.[20] For Lamar there is in this tenacious modality of loyalty to human connection something of the divine, but it is a "god" brought into material existence, into the historical works of embodied bodies.[21] This sense of loyalty has to be moderated through suspicion, that is to say, to the extent this isn't a "perfect world." Authorities and the discourses they promote teach lessons that need to be unlearned. And a space for such reorienting thinking and doing begins with "humility" as awareness of these imposed arrangements of life:

> I don't fabricate it, ayy, most of y'all be fakin', ayy
> I stay modest 'bout it, ayy, she elaborate it, ayy.[22]

With Lamar there is a claiming of time and space in such a way as to confound moral codes and values presented as normative by those outside the "culture," while raising questions concerning the criteria for deep connection and meaning.[23] What one gets between, for example, the tracks "LUST." and "LOVE." is a dynamic tension, one that presents the complexities of existential connection and interaction in a world that is less than hospitable. There is the vulnerability to circumstance:

> We all woke up, tryna tune to the daily news
> Lookin' for confirmation, hopin' election wasn't true.[24]

Yet there is the affective quality of connection—a type of vulnerability to relationship that doesn't destroy whiteness's intent of death as (ontological) demise but that softens the blow: "If I minimized my net worth, would you still love me?"[25] There is for Lamar a contradiction between the ideals exposed and the demands of life within a hostile world. Exposing—or knowing—hypocrisy and biblical pretext easily lends itself to maintenance of social arrangements as they are:

Hail Mary, Jesus and Joseph

The great American flag is wrapped in drag with explosives.[26]

There is no doubt but that Lamar pushes through Christian signs and symbols, but in the process he urges them on to a new work, perhaps in ways similar to Tupac Shakur's reconfiguration of the transfiguration of the Christian Jesus. There is more to it than this, however, in that Lamar seems to recognize the resistant nature of the world and how struggle produces the need for more struggle. As he reflects on the track "GOD." he asked for a piece of mind and was charged for it. Death in this instance is ever present, and it affords no comfort and no great terror.

The theodical arguments in the track "DNA.," for example, appear more consistent with a Sisyphean posture toward the world. The track is a description of disregard as a persistent dimension of historical Black experience; according to Lamar, the resolution appears grounded in human creativity and ingenuity, "unity in our community and some of the things we have no control over." For Lamar, discussion can be reduced to the nature and meaning of Black identity within the context of a troubled world hostile toward, but also deeply reliant on, Blackness. He is not broken by this predicament. Rather, the poetic response flooding his lyrics is more akin to a lucid response to the question posed at the start of "BLOOD."—"Are we going to live or die?" In the lyrics and layout of the album, he suggests both at the same time. This, I would add, constitutes "real nigga conditions." Furthermore, there is in Lamar's stating of the diagnosis of "real nigga conditions" something of an "amen" to Du Bois's sentiment when saying,

> There must come a loftier respect for the sovereign human soul that
> seeks to know itself and the world about it; that seeks a freedom for
> expansion and self-development; that will love and hate and labor in its
> own way, untrammeled alive by old and new. . . . Herein the longing of
> black men must have respect: the rich and bitter depth of their experi-
> ence, the unknown treasures of their inner life, the strange rendings of
> nature they have seen, may give the world new poise of view and make
> their loving, living and doing precious to all human hearts.[27]

With Lamar, existential circumstances and the ever-present potential for death do not produce anxiety or fear. In this regard, his hip hop theological sensibilities are nothing like those of existentialist theologians for whom the pressure of death produces anxiety and fear. As he makes clear in "FEAR.," fear is acknowledged, manipulated, and used. This is not to say he doesn't note the circumstances of existential angst, but, rather than being paralyzed by them, he acknowledges the modalities of fear associated with the world as he and those like him know it. And then he uses it as an alternate response to disregard: living-dying through fear or rap, as he puts it.[28]

The more overtly theological interjections in *To Pimp a Butterfly*, as well as *Good Kid, M.A.A.D. City* (2012), aren't present in the same manner in *DAMN*. Rather, the religious-theological considerations in the latter are funneled through a more caustic framing that entails a much deeper entanglement with the absurdity of the world. Lamar speaks a particular modality of lucidity, perhaps a lucidity embraced as part of swag. And through this heightened awareness of circumstances, he offers a poetics of the Black body as open and porous, as unrestricted and signifying social barriers and boundaries meant to control it through layered confinement and docility. Neither death nor life can fully contain it. Through this turn, Lamar challenges, in a fundamental sense, the authority of whiteness by removing the moral-ethical impulse of *being* deemed normative. In its place he highlights *deathlife* ("real nigga conditions") as penetrating while also being penetrated by Black existence/substance. Lamar understands himself as confronting the quality of *deathlife* without blinking, without bending, and without rendering it other than it is.[29]

The album ends as it begins: with an autobiographical encounter with living into death. Biblical pronouncements and theological assumptions don't change these circumstances and don't offer greater clarity regarding the circumstances. In a word, circumstances are circumstances: the uncertain arrangements of time and space. What Lamar champions is lucid movement— living into death without grand hope and a future fixed and sure.[30] *DAMN*. marks out this awareness by reflecting outward. Lucidity regarding meaning in the world begins with Lamar reflecting on the self, the very structure and placement of self in time and space.[31] Maybe, then, Lamar's value here with respect to the fundamental questions of human existence writ as religion isn't the taming of a certain modality of chaos; instead, religion is an invitation to interrogation without conclusion and without stealing our ability to be complex, messy humans who "win" only to the extent we understand what it means to live into death. There is in this sense no salvation, no end, but simply the exposing of the inner logic and workings of the status quo—its fears and preoccupations with death.

DAMN. affirms a question posed by Camus: "What can a meaning outside my condition mean to me?" Furthermore, as Camus continues, "I can understand only in human terms. What I touch, what resists me—that is what I understand."[32] In a similar posture toward the world, Lamar, while maintaining the impetus of his religious commitment grounded in the materiality of life, signifies whiteness's call for death as distinctive from life.[33] This is rebellion. And in this rebellion—this proud awareness and confrontation of circumstances through a commitment to a magnitude of experience—is Lamar's maintenance of swag.[34]

There is in this a moral code for the antihero, the one who speaks a vision for resistance that defies the aims of whiteness. In a social world defined by whiteness and its effort to regulate life and death, the hero would enforce the illusion of distinction by working to tame chaos and enhance life expressed using a particular grammar and vocabulary of preservation as world affirming. The hero is guided by an epistemology that holds the framing of human life firm, that seeks to render history teleological in nature and certain in this regard. Heroes distract and misdirect human effort. It entails recognition of an idea of rescue from silence through the presence of a grand figure with the capacity to safeguard from death, or at the very least invest death with meaning. The heroic involves a passionate call for alliance or for alignment with unquestioned metaphysical arrangements of life against death. Whiteness calls for the heroic; it exposes the illusion of life as a distinction maintained at the expense of Blacks who demand the antihero.

Heroic: Whites Playing with Death

Lamar conjures Tupac and in this way tangles with life and death, presence and absence, joined together in one moment. Some argue that Tupac isn't really dead (existing somewhere between life and death) and, like the biblical Christ, is simply awaiting a time to return. Over against this, there are conspiracy theories suggesting Eminem is dead.[35] One such theory argues that he died of a drug overdose and was replaced by a lookalike. Those paying attention, according to the post-2006 theory, said that he looked younger than he should and his aesthetic had taken a turn, as did his music. For these theorists, there is additional "evidence": they claim that the lyrical content of Eminem's music and that of others announced his demise. I mention this latter theory not because I am particularly interested in it, but because it centers death while speaking to the ongoing significance of life. It, in an important sense, speaks the aim of whiteness. This theory of absence points to the concern with demise and the effort to find meaning in that inevitability by claiming a firm distinction between what it means to live and what it means to die.

One might think of "Stan," a track on Eminem's third album, *The Marshall Mathers LP* (2000)—one of the best-selling albums of its time—as entailing a poetics of death or a eulogy of sorts that offers the other side (whiteness) of a hip hop–inflected thanatology.[36] In "Stan," the heroic doesn't constitute escape or a safeguard from the trauma of death; rather, it speaks to the very inescapability of the "absence" that frames death as a negative (distinct from life) to be avoided. And this affords an alternate geography of life that understands it as always in opposition to death.[37] The heroic simply captures and re-presents the grammar of death expressed eulogistically, and it does so as a cautionary tale. It offers not necessarily praise but rather *elogium*— inscription or an interrogation that doesn't stem the tide of meaninglessness but instead points back to death as a problem addressed by means of "proper" behavior. This track becomes a mnemonic device bringing back to the fore the dynamics of living as distinct from dying, offered through a type of parable.[38]

It isn't only that artists become a cipher for the anxiety of death; they also become alleged conduits for a demise that points to a distinction, a break with life. Eminem's music was blamed for inspiring murder and suicide. His lyrics, some have attempted to argue, encourage, if not justify, the ending of life and the assuring of death.[39] His track "Stan" brings much of this into graphic relief. Many have viewed the track in light of what it suggests concerning the relationship of listener to music, the assumed connection between listener and artist along the lines of "sound" appreciation. Others have interrogated the track regarding what it tells us about the "dark" side of fandom and about issues of mental health.[40]

> I can relate to what you're saying in your songs
> So when I have a shitty day, I drift away and put 'em on.[41]

While there is much to be said for such discussions, I am more interested in what "Stan" says concerning the relationship between the heroic and the practice of death undergirding that discussion of mental health. I want to shift away from fans' fascination with personality and move in the direction of what can be gathered concerning depiction and practice of absence and death chronicled in "Stan."

> Dear Slim, you still ain't called or wrote, I hope you have a chance
> I ain't mad, I just think it's fucked up you don't answer fans.[42]

It isn't that Eminem, through this critically acclaimed track, chronicles the proper approach to death and dying, or even a proper philosophy of death. Rather, the track speaks to entanglement and absence as the structuring of death. A type of absence, which is the shadowed presence of Marshall Mathers (Eminem's given name), dominates the track. Yet this secondary absence speaks to a larger sense of absence that motivates the fan Stan. The primary absence involves the lack of substantial connections to the world, a limited engagement with other persons, and a limited sense of place.

> That's kinda how this is, you coulda rescued me from drowning
> Now it's too late, I'm on a thousand downers now, I'm drowsy
> And all I wanted was a lousy letter or a call.[43]

Life is disruption in this case, which Stan hopes to resolve by connecting with a figure similar in background but with a status putting him—Mather's alter ego, Slim Shady—beyond the trauma that holds Stan. As Stan recounts, "'Cause I don't really got shit else so that shit helps when I'm depressed."[44] Stan seeks the heroic as a source of meaning, but the heroic is fragile and without the capacity for rescue: the heroic, in the form of Slim Shady, is entangled in the same death versus life illusion as Stan. Still, Slim Shady is the larger-than-life personality that signifies and pushes boundaries, including those of death—flirting with murder in at least one instance—and who offers a comic quality to the arrangements of life.[45] Slim Shady is something of a trickster figure and, for Stan, the one to whom he appeals to bring a source of produced meaning that counters the tragic quality of his own existence. What Stan seeks is a sense of self within the context of a larger framework of life that is free of the tragic (meaning or) element of death.

The video for "Stan" begins with Stan bleaching his hair. His girlfriend knocking on the door, needing the bathroom, disrupts the process. He gazes into the bathroom mirror with a bizarre look. A chaotic encounter with his girlfriend ensues, they argue, and the sounds of rain and thunder take over as Stan goes to the basement to write a letter to Slim Shady. The disillusionment of life—the fights, the anger, the angst, the unreliability of those close, and so on—is chronicled and all guided by the words in his letters to Slim. For Stan there is no meaning, no certainty, and no assurance. But he seeks these from the possibility of connection with Slim, whose friendship would confirm life before death as the social world promised. Instead, there is silence. Stan's reaction is violent. He forces his girlfriend into the trunk of his car and then drives and plunges the car into water. It is only after this that the long-awaited response comes. It isn't that the projected heroic senses no obligation to assist, but rather that such assistance doesn't save.[46]

> I hope you get to read this letter, I just hope it reaches you in time
> Before you hurt yourself, I think that you'll be doin' just fine.[47]

In the return letter, Slim offers no assurance, no safeguard against death but rather ways to manage its inevitability—to come to grips with the traumas of life by recognizing them and confronting them. This management, as is the aim of the heroic, projects behavior as the key to maintaining an opposi- tional relationship between life and death.

> You got some issues, Stan, I think you need some counseling
> To help your ass from bouncing off the walls when you get down some.[48]

In these lines, Slim offers advice that comes too late. Despite what Stan hoped a letter from Slim might provide, there is no "sacred" text with the capacity to undo the absurd quality of life and speak meaning to a death- saturated world; instead, the letter reflects back the grammar of dying into death, offering only a superficial ethical pronouncement as a tool against demise.

What Stan has—that which keeps him lucid—is a recognition of pain. An embrace of pain (the "rush," as Stan describes it) serves as the marker of embodied place within the land of the living. In this vein, what Oliver Wang says concerning the nonredemptive quality of Lamar's *DAMN.* could be extended to the context in which Stan requests more than he can actu- ally "receive" from his hero. "He's not here to provide relief or distraction," writes Wang, "but [Lamar's] anxieties and unease around his own foibles are meant to mirror our own—and likewise, his struggles towards salvation and redemption are lead-by-example exhortations for us to do the same work, lest we risk perishing in a damnation of our own making."[49] Wang ends there, but the story doesn't. Even following this model doesn't lead away from death; it doesn't stem the tide of dying, much to the chagrin of those hoping for rescue. In a way, Stan encounters the absurd and surrenders to it by assuming there can be more than silence. Stan's implied question is the explicit question suggested by Camus in *The Myth of Sisyphus and Other Essays*: Is suicide justifiable in the face of the world's silence to our probing for meaning?[50] Stan's reluctant answer is a muffled "yes," as his car dives into the water.

With the haunting lines by Dido on "Stan," rehearsing a numb monotone at the start moving forward, the track is an occasion for introspection. With

Eminem's lyrics added, this inward gaze into the nature of the ordinary provides a troubling invitation to interrogate a question undergirding whiteness: Can anyone save us from the absurd and free us from the call of death? In other words, is there in Slim Shady a guiding logic, an expansive personality that can tame demise or at least lessen the sting? Dying, in the context of "Stan," involves increasing sensitivity to the silence that engulfs the effort to trace meaning in the world. It is, in this sense, the structuring of a query: what to make of absence? Stan hopes for an answer. Still, the tragic quality of existence leading to death is played out when Stan's murder-suicide recording for Mathers/Shady is left without a means of delivery, and Mather's response letter comes after the murder of Stan's girlfriend and his suicide. Despite desire, despite effort, there are faults in the structure of whiteness: the heroic acts of white defenders unintentionally expose the illusionary nature of life safeguarded from death. The hero fails, as the hero must, in that whiteness is too great a burden.

More recent than "Stan," there's Eminem's "Bad Guy" (on *The Marshall Mathers LP 2* [2013])—the sequel to "Stan," and the story of Stan's brother, Matthew. There is a commonality here: both Stan and Matthew are fans whose dedication doesn't produce desired meaningfulness. Disappointment, once again, pushes toward death. The markers of life, such as family, are disrupted and there is a price to pay. One sees here a continuity of form—a shared assumption that there are answers, or ways to maintain one's balance within the social world, and that whiteness's relationship to life over against death has its champions and its heroes. Matthew points this out, holding Eminem accountable for his grand role, when saying,

And to think I used to think you was the shit, bitch
To think it was you at one time I worshipped, shit.[51]

In this song, isn't the bad guy the one who causes death and disrupts the comforts of life? What is at play here is a peek behind the curtain, so to speak, because it involves white people's relationship to death and life. One gets a sense of this, over against the relationship of Black people to death, through the affective response to disappointment (the presence of death), suggesting the possibility of life without death. And what is more, the very presence of disappointment suggests the ability of white people (vis-à-vis whiteness) to feel justified in assuming such safeguards. The expectations are high for heroes. They are to safeguard the illusion and thereby maintain some comfort for those who follow them.

Not once you called to ask me how I'm doing
Letters, you don't respond to 'em.[52]

Then Matthew kidnaps Eminem because of the wrong the rapper has done.

Thought some time had passed and I forget it, forget it!
You left our family in shambles.[53]

Stan loves Eminem, and Matthew loves Stan: both affective conditions produce demise. However, this is a different relationship to death: rather than
inattentiveness motivating murder-suicide, the rapper faces the potential for
death as a form of recompense. As Eminem reflects in the third verse—in
which Matthew is driving down the highway recklessly just like Stan—there
is something absurd about death, or something "unnatural" in the circumstances that bring about white demise: yet they are circumstances of white
people's own making. While some would argue the rapper is rather neutral
concerning Stan (and Matthew by extension), acknowledging connection
only after the connection is severed, the coming of his own death at the
hands of Stan's brother fosters reflection. But this is a recognition of conditions that does nothing to change those conditions: he speaks from the
trunk, but who is there to hear him?

And Matthew and Stan's just symbolic
Of you not knowing what you had until it's gone.[54]

Both Stan and Matthew destroy what they crave—speaking their desire and
needs without a source of comfort (i.e., the hero, Eminem). Stan calls out
to Eminem for answers, and there is only silence; Matthew seeks answers
but kills the source of the answers he seeks. One easily gathers here that
whiteness doesn't protect from death. The social world that works to the
advantage of those projected as white doesn't safeguard from demise; absurdity remains. Still, on some level, Eminem is able to lament this because of
a distinction between death and life—a difference that allows distance from
which to view circumstances. The search for meaning is acknowledged but
unfulfilled. Still, there is here in relationship to whiteness an effort to manage
death, in that both Stan and Matthew are eager to determine the when and
how of demise. For the heroic is meant to afford some degree of control—
and when it fails the disappointment is palpable. In these two tracks, the
disappointment produces death. And the threat of death exposes questions
and recognitions (think in terms of the last two verses of the song) that tear
at illusions of certainty and meaning and instead point out insecurities and

inconsistencies. In other words, the threat of death unmanaged and untamed hampers the work of whiteness.

In both tracks, there is a desire for the heroic—for one who can bracket death if by no other means than rendering it meaning-full. Still, the heroic collapses, fails to produce meaning or to fight off death. Again, even for white people guarded by whiteness, death comes. But death is believed to come at the end of (not as) life—so, something of a distinction is maintained even in the failure of the heroic. The explicit anger in "Bad Guy" and "Stan" stems from the exposure of the illusion—the manner in which there is effort to control death, but effort that fails to satisfy—a crack in the life-not-death assumption. Unlike with Lamar, however, there is denial of what this failure entails by projecting this failure to satisfy as a human shortcoming, as opposed to being the very nature of death and life. The antihero points out the lie of distinction, while the hero's job (the job Eminem fails to fulfill) is to protect efforts to preserve life and deny death.

Antihero: Exposing an Illusion

Pushing against any consideration of eschatology as useful, the antihero recognizes how death marks off nothing distinct but is inseparable from life: one lives into death, and one dies into life. Life cannot be accomplished by any effort to bracket off death as some "thing" that can be managed, confined, quarantined, and thereby controlled. That's the work of the hero, not the antihero who calls this logic into question, and in this way signifies both the language of preservation and the aims to which it points. In so doing, the antihero is the enemy of the social world's effort to fortify whiteness and is therefore cast in terms of attributes contrary to the maintenance of social cohesion. The antihero bends tradition to the breaking point and exposes its inner "stuff" (i.e., its relationship to the status quo as well as its sensitivities and sensibilities). It is a lucid push against the epistemological and ontological arranging of life that disadvantages and strangles. The hero calls for conformity and adherence ("you need some counseling . . .") as the requirement of well-being. The antihero sees the social world, troubles its aims, and still proclaims, "We gonna be alright!"[55]

Still, what if the antiheroic isn't in the doing, that is, in the transforming of material circumstances? What if the "alright" isn't a location but rather a process marking out a recognition of living into death? Is the "alright" offered by the antihero some clarity with which to understand the predicament, an understanding that does not allow surrender but doesn't guarantee anything?

In this regard, perhaps hip hop artists like Lamar, at their best, aren't modern versions of biblical prophets. If we turn to scripture, they are Nimrod: the one who unites around particular sets of knowledge and then harnesses energy and skills in such a way as to threaten illusions and speak possibilities already defeated. Nimrod is the great hunter said to have led the construction of a tower meant to reach to the heavens. Divine forces were threatened by this unified human effort—fearing the distinction between human and divine would be destroyed. So, in response, these divine beings created confusion by ending the reign of a single language that allowed cooperation through communication of a shared objective. The tower project isn't completed. Religious leaders over the ages have typically argued that Nimrod was a wicked figure who sought to be a god; yet there's another way to read the story and a different way to position Nimrod, as the antihero. In the context of hip hop, the antiheroic involves a commitment to struggle, to process, over against outcomes, marked by flexibility: Lamar is like Nimrod—or as he calls himself, "King Kunta"![56] The antihero seeks to maximize human capacity over against the truncating work of the hero who orchestrates human imagination and intentionality for a purpose in line with the aims of whiteness. To be sure, Lamar pronounces "we gonna be alright," but this is an indefinite proposition, when the "if God got us" part of the lyric is acknowledged. It holds no certainty but instead leaves open the question of the plausibility of a theodicean answer to the tragicomic nature of Blackness in a white society. Lamar calls for a shift in focus from the "hero" and what the "hero" is supposed to offer to the question of why we search for and need a hero to begin with.

The antiheroic isn't as "grand" as the heroic—the prophetic quality, sought by many. Instead, it amounts to signifying what the social world presents as unshakable. Lamar's effect involves certain levels of activism of anti-engagement, something of an unethical response to the ethics of the social world. Perhaps Lamar, as antihero, is a rebel: one who questions the certainties that the hero must endorse and who finds no requirement in the push for more. There is little anxiety in Lamar's representation of life with or in the midst of death; finitude isn't met with melancholy or fear, in that it doesn't mark the end of the delusion of modernity's sense of human progress.

> I'll prolly die from one of these bats and blue badges
> Body-slammed on black and white paint, my bones snappin'.[57]

The fact that Lamar is a theist doesn't prevent suspicion concerning "outcomes." He is a theist, but also one who works without definitive, teleological projections.[58] Still, there is in his telling of the story the shadow of what

Camus might label a "Grand Unity," or an overarching logic, at work. This is not to say that the antiheroic safeguards from death or that it fully and finally exposes meaning in the face of death. Rather, there is a quality—or an intentionality—that can be named even in the face of demise. One gets a sense of this in Lamar's "LOYALTY.," in which he asks a series of questions:

> Is it anybody that you would lie for?
> Anybody you would slide for?
> Anybody you would die for?[59]

There is within the human fundamental framework, the human ontology, a complex arrangement marked by contradiction that is exposed in the face of demise. After the last question above, there is this line: "That's what God for."[60] In other words, the notion—or at least the language—of God speaks to death in a consistent manner. God's function is to consume death, to address the potentiality of demise as humans will not, or cannot. Yet, whatever form it takes, some through the heroic seek a means by which to catch their breath when confronted with the absurd quality of our existence and the ever-present potentiality of demise. Nonetheless, as the antihero notes at a moment of vulnerability and exposure in which the structuring of the social world is called into question and its integrity challenged, there is absence: "Ain't nobody prayin' for me."[61]

Lamar's status, the assumption of his special status as antihero, entails ruggedness and a posture toward the world, which, again, I would label Sisyphean in nature. But it is also a posture that positions him as one whose lucidity, when communicated, can open the social world to others. In "XXX.," Lamar chronicles a conversation with a friend whose son has been killed, and that friend contacts Lamar because Lamar is "anointed." Hoping for a way to understand the nature of death, to find meaning amid loss, he is met with the opposite. Lamar the antihero offers a call for death as an affirmation of life, a recognition of death's inevitability and the way in which demise is its own answer:

> To the spirit, my spirit do know better, but I told him
> "I can't sugarcoat the answer for you, this is how I feel:
> If somebody kill my son, that mean somebody gettin' killed."[62]

In this sense, the antiheroic involves not a safeguard from death but a confrontation with circumstances, or a "feel" for how life and death bleed into each other to become one expression.

Whereas one could argue dying in the context of *DAMN.* is impossible (difficult at best) to distinguish from living, there is in "Stan" and "Bad Guy" an attempt to differentiate the two (life and death) in that dying is a matter of absence, not the fullness of life that one struggles to obtain as birthright. *DAMN.*, on the one hand, is shrouded in the connotation of Blackness: for example, the manner in which blackened embodied bodies are feared as embodied threat that the "po-po wanna kill . . . fo sho."[63] "Stan" and "Bad Guy," on the other hand, are captives of whiteness, the flip side of Blackness marked by an effort to bracket or control death. Stan answers the question of activity presented by Lamar—"Anybody you would die for?"[64] He would die in order to speak against absence, so as to embrace death with the hope of finding meaning—only to recognize that his voice is lost as the recording of his last words goes into the water with him. (And his brother, Matthew, follows Stan's lead and answers the question in the same way.) Through this irony, listeners are reminded of the tragic quality of life and the inability to tame this tragic quality through external, or "grand," means. There is no savior and hence no salvation: simply eyes open in the face of the tragic; eyes open as death consumes life.

Unlike Lamar, to some extent, Eminem doesn't claim special status; in fact, just the opposite. While Lamar's "xxx." entails at least one person coming to Lamar for advice on *deathlife*, Eminem (Marshall Mathers) is silent for most of the "Stan" track—despite having on other occasions, as Slim Shady, chronicled and mapped out the performance of death versus life. In "Bad Guy," Eminem reflects on his circumstances but gives the impression that different actions might have allowed for a bracketing of death:

> I'm your karma closing in with each stroke of a pen
> Perfect time to have some remorse to show for your sin.[65]

Intent isn't central; one need not desire to be heroic. It can simply be a function of social positioning, cultural charisma, and placement. Whiteness will find its heroic types because some will always want the heroic, which is to call for a safeguarding and a way of distinguishing life from death, bracketing off the latter. A call for the heroic is, then, a type of response to *deathlife* as an effort to utilize the grammar of death to conjure an alternative. This, I would argue, is certainly the case with some dimensions of Eminem's "Stan" and "Bad Guy." Eminem offers an alternative to the antiheroic signifying of *deathlife*: the expressed distinction between death and life, and whiteness's ability to call for one over the other. On the other hand, as antihero, Lamar doesn't simply allow listeners to "see" death. He ushers it in and calls for it as a part of living. By this move he signifies whiteness and its effort to hide the nature of white life, to hide the intent of constructed Blackness. He isn't the grim reaper, in that he isn't a foreign and cold pull toward death as a distinct and terrifying experience of demise; rather, he points out the normality of death and its inevitability. This, however, doesn't prevent a desire for antiheroic figures to offer a way out of the absurdity that highlights death. This is the desire in "xxx." when Lamar is asked for advice on what to do about the death of the caller's son, yet desire doesn't change the nature of the antiheroic response: "somebody gettin' killed."

Despite its efforts to claim the opposite, the heroic fails to keep death and life apart, and it fails to make life the exclusive domain of whiteness. The antihero's challenge involves a break with the illusion of life versus death that is difficult to ignore. *DAMN.* begins (or ends) with murder. "Stan" and "Bad Guy" begin with reflection on loss as well, but loss of the Other. The world, in both cases, is portrayed as hostile, unwelcoming, and flooded with demise. Life wears one down and bleeds into (becomes) death. Slim Shady, whom Stan and Matthew at one point position as a salvific figure, a hero, isn't able to amend this arrangement. Stan is dead, and the girlfriend is dead. Matthew's disappointment and demand also take the form of murder and suicide. Even the hero encounters death. Eulogy done—and the antihero keeps on signifying by asking, What's the difference?

PART II

Consuming Deathlife

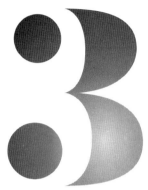

BACCHIC INTENT

For whiteness to work and maintain the assumed normativity of its logic, death is projected out (and onto Blacks) as something to be feared—as both physical demise and irrelevance—with the former often conditioned by the latter. Such framing of demise projects the relationship with death as a problem to solve, as a dilemma that threatens the sense of life tied to being white.

While artists like Jay-Z and Kendrick Lamar signify *deathlife* (while still holding it as a negative experience), there is also in hip hop an effort to turn death as negation on its head and instead narrate death as a moment of joy—a fully erotic encounter that consumes. By *consume*, I mean to highlight how this taming of death involves a wasting of its intent to generate fear, a degrading (or decomposing) of the barriers between life and death set up by whiteness. In so doing, these artists disrupt the logic of white life by denying that joy (an affective naming of meaning) is describable only from the vantage point of whiteness, and that death captured by means of Blackness is horrifying. The grammar of white life is subverted, and this frees an alternate expression of engagement. Distinction between life and death as the source of joy is disrupted through radical practices of pleasure: by merging joy and pain, death and life are denied the difference that would support the social world constructed in relationship to the demands of whiteness. Hence, whiteness's effort to render Blacks abject is countered by damaging the grammar of a ghastly "colored" difference that undergirds the social world. Through this performance, certain artists, like Tyler, the Creator, trouble the standard narrative by "consuming" death, thus stifling the naming and "ending" purpose of *deathlife*. When asked what he thought life led to, Tyler, the Creator reflected that "death is the climax, I guess. If you think about it."[1] He offers a way to think about death that cuts against typical depictions that seek distance from death. While giving limited attention to other albums, I want to read primarily Tyler, the Creator's *Goblin* (2011) as an erotic-transgressive realism, a hip hop pornographic poetics, and do so in relationship to and drawing on Georges Bataille's thinking on the erotic.[2] In this way, Tyler, the Creator can be read as offering a relationship to death that runs contrary to the aims of the social world. So, it is an important—albeit somewhat marginal, depending on how one categorizes his music—conversation concerning hip hop's awareness of and response to the intended workings of *deathlife*.[3]

Tyler, the Creator

He began his career with the group Odd Future Wolf Gang Kill Them All, yet *Goblin* is a solo album with an intensity and moral-ethical signification that challenges beyond that of his earlier work, and it met with a great deal of resistance—much of which he anticipated. As Jon Caramanica reflects in the *New York Times*, "'Goblin' is an album that anticipates its own critique—invites it, to be sure, but also understands that the listener determines how an album is received as much as, if not more than, the creator. 'Don't do anything I say in this song,' Tyler says at the beginning of 'Radicals,' adding, 'If anything happens, don't'—here he added an enthusiastic but unprintable qualifier—'blame me, white America.'"[4] Undergirding the larger narrative, I would suggest, is the reason he is not to blame: the structuring of activity, the formulation of death, is the product of whiteness played out. So, blame whiteness for what becomes necessary in order to counter its logic.

Recognition of this genealogy of demise takes a bit of psychological work in addition to the physical demands imposed. Tyler, the Creator describes his own brain as "an obscenity" and, more to the point, he is "fucked in the head."[5] Others have framed him epistemologically and morally as having "an openly nihilistic attitude, wherein he regularly invests in nihilistic themes including the rejection of higher values, the devaluation of life and property, and a loss of hope."[6] Much of *Goblin* hinges on the tension between Tyler, the Creator (Tyler Gregory Okonma) and his "therapist," named Dr. TC. It is to Dr. TC that Tyler expresses his rage, admits his anger and violence, and wrestles with the tensions between his moral-ethical code and that of the larger and dominant social structure. There are epistemological complexities here, given that the distinction between Dr. TC and Tyler is blurred. However, Tyler, the Creator's poetics of death were present earlier: violent fantasies of murder and sex appear on *Bastard* (2009), where we first encounter Dr. TC. For example, the track "Sarah" contains these lines:

> I wanna tie her body up and throw her in my basement
> Keep her there, so nobody can wonder where her face went
> (Tyler, what you doin'?) Shut the fuck up
> You gon' fuckin' love me bitch.[7]

"Sarah" is one instance of the intersection of demise and sex by means of which Tyler explores the affective morality and ethics of *deathlife* through the vehicle of graphic violence. It's disturbing and it runs contrary to what most would consider proper interaction, as I will further explicate later in this chapter; but I think that is Tyler's point: disruptions, transgression, and destruction are reflections of the psyche hidden away, a dimension of the social world's technology exposed crudely through unsanctioned activity. Or, as Tyler, the Creator remarks, "They claim the shit I say is just wrong; Like nobody has those really dark thoughts when alone."[8] I am suggesting the popularity of *Goblin*—particularly of the track "Yonkers"—speaks not only to Tyler, the Creator's imagination, but also to the manner in which he counterframes familiar moral-ethical codes and, through the familiar, exposes listeners to his thanatological desires.[9] "Goblin's eventual structural collapse," writes Penelope Eate, when addressing the revelation that Dr. TC is Tyler, the Creator, "also implies that the listener has been sutured into the perverted fantasy life of an unreliable narrator."[10] If listeners are hoping for a consistent line of reasoning, a persistent thread of logic or a moral-ethical posture that doesn't shift, they will be disappointed with Tyler, the Creator, whom some have categorized as "a bundle of contradictions."[11] Or, as the journalist Ernest Baker comments, "To be around Tyler, the Creator is to be subjected to a constant stream of lewd absurdity."[12] Or, as Tyler self-describes in "Yonkers," "I'm a fucking walking paradox. No, I'm not."

Tyler, the Creator's first studio album, *Goblin* was fifth on the Billboard 200 chart at the time of its release in 2011 (and later certified gold), but it both appealed to and repelled its listeners. It begins with "Goblin"—the first lines of which establish the necessary psychology for murder, for the posture toward world and others that finds in destruction something forbidden but compelling, something tantalizing: "You wouldn't do that, Tyler, kill yourself or anyone. You don't even have the balls to begin with."[13] Yet the concern isn't strictly about physical action; rather Tyler invokes a particular mood or mindset that authorizes a counterpurposing of language so as to signify codes endorsed by the social system's construction of *deathlife* as what shouldn't happen to those couched in whiteness.

Kill people, burn shit, fuck school.
Kill people, burn shit, fuck school.[14]

As will become clear in this chapter, whether Tyler lives out these violent fantasies—whether his poetics points to material events—ultimately isn't important.[15] The concern isn't the actual practice of violence and death ("Okay, you guys caught me, I'm not a fucking rapist or serial killer, I lied"), but rather his depiction—one that promotes a shift away from death as strictly a negative that sanctions the aims of the social world and maintains a need for *deathlife*.[16] There is connection through a "fantastic" language—the celebration of life as death—that affords both distance and proximity at the same time. What commonly is marginalized and set apart to maintain a certain type of moral and ethical comfort and recognizability is twisted and reshaped through celebration of what most would believe is disgusting. There is a subversive quality to this work of de/construction in that it wipes out established processing activities and thereby robs the social world of the meanings with which inhabitants invested it in order to safeguard themselves.[17]

To borrow from Bataille, my concern isn't with death as a matter of material survival but rather death and demise as poetic "excess"—that is, destruction and disruption as pleasure, as the erotic.[18] In saying this, I mean to highlight the way in which the depiction of demise and of disruptive behavior speaks a different sense of death: not a source of fear but a compelling dimension of joy. So conceived, death or demise in this context seeks to disrupt the naming and depiction of life—typically as it is safeguarded by principles of exclusion (which include the social coding of race, etc.). Through death, in this regard, one comes to know life; the intimate nature of the connection is exposed, and what social arrangements have sought to instill regarding these two, life and death, separately is destroyed through the poetic nature of this engagement.[19] Joy, not sadness, is the actual tone of death, producing a type of intimacy that cuts against anxiety and instead speaks an erotic response. Something of what I mean here is expressed as Bataille reflects on sacrificial killing: "It is a naïve opinion that links death closely to sorrow. The tears of the living, which respond to its coming, are themselves far from having a meaning opposite to joy. Far from being sorrowful, the tears are the expression of a keen awareness of shared life grasped in its intimacy."[20]

As those who read him will be quick to discover, my intention here isn't identical to that of Bataille's discussion of labor, production, things, and intimacy, but is more focused on what his theorization of death, when borrowed and applied, might help explain regarding certain genres of hip hop engaging *deathlife*.[21] In this way, one can read certain modalities of hip hop—such as Tyler, the Creator's music—as conjuring death so as to destroy restrictive frameworks of life as "animal" or "tool." Bataille thinks in terms of economic and social arrangements, but such an understanding of being outside the modalities of production (here intended to name the mechanics of whiteness) might appeal within a culture, hip hop culture, produced by despised and marginalized beings understood only in terms of their utility (the preservation of white life as far as possible).[22] My concern isn't a full explication of Bataille's corpus—a study on Bataille for the sake of Bataille. Rather, I find in his theorization of life and death vis-à-vis the erotic a way of viewing, thinking about, and naming how Tyler, the Creator has developed an erotic poetics of death in which he exposes the protected inner workings of whiteness through *deathlife*.[23]

There is with Tyler a particularly compelling troubling, or what one might call "mad" narration, of death as erotic and the effort through this interpretative framework to address demise.[24] This is not a statement regarding the condition(s) of the mind one might associate with contemporary mental illness.[25] Instead, Tyler's mad narration is a frenzied defying of distinction—an embodied renegotiation of the geography of life and death.[26] And such a renegotiation entails the blending of life and death, one leading to the other and back. Or, put another way, "Ain't kill myself yet," as Tyler admits, "and I already want my life back."[27] Although the details of the discussion differ, Bataille's notion holds true for my purposes: death, in this regard, is not loss in a profound sense, but rather demise points to substance that isn't confined to basic use and flat intention and purpose—it isn't restricted to the work intended by whiteness.[28] With others, death is the problem of life, but for Bataille death exposes life—it solves the problem through the consumption of utility (in this case, the task of whiteness) that has trapped Black flesh in the modern West: "living in order to be able to die, suffering to enjoy, enjoying to suffer."[29] This isn't to glorify narratives of violent demise, but simply to offer a way of thinking about the work of particular genres of hip hop that offer a different assessment of death's nature and meaning qua whiteness's social world and *deathlife*.

In a crude manner, one might say, along with Bataille, that "life is a product of putrefaction, and it depends on both death and the dungheap. . . . Death is that putrefaction, that stench. Which is, at once, the source and the repulsive condition of life."[30] Both life and death require and work through the body. Or, as Tyler describes it, "While you niggas stacking bread, I can stack a couple dead bodies, making red look less of a color, more of a hobby."[31] With Bataille there is a willful acknowledgment, if not an embrace, of the elements and dimensions of existence that tend to trouble; he reflects on "how impossible it is at the present moment for anything human to arise, except in the cesspool of the heart."[32] In other words, he encourages awareness of and comfort in the "shabby, sinister, or inspired events" that some ignore or restrict in ways that allow them to be managed and placed within more comfortable narratives of existence, whereby the despised is celebrated in orgiastic fashion: "expenditure" and approach to the self even to the point of the negation of the Other.[33] On a related note, "Do what the fuck makes you happy," Tyler announces, "'cause at the end, who's there? You."[34] What one finds, I would argue, in the lyrics of Tyler, the Creator's "Yonkers" is a type of "apathy," or a removal of what are referenced as "parasitic sentiments such as pity, gratitude, or love." As the suicide of Tyler, the Creator in "Yonkers" would attest, for the poetic and erotic dimension of a narrative to be transgressive it requires destruction, even of the poet.[35]

Sonically consumed by a sound that cautions, that signals the need for alertness, Tyler begins assuming the position of the philosophical thinker of abstractions. But then there is a shift to materiality: on the heels of playing with a large roach in the video for "Yonkers," he eats it and vomits it up—an act of consumption of what is despised, complete with a violent rejection of it. After that come fantasies of death: murder, then suicide. He removes his shirt; his eyes go black. He places a rope around his neck, climbs on a chair, and hangs himself—feet swinging above a knocked-over chair.

> (Fuck everything, man) That's what my conscience said
> then it bunny-hopped off my shoulder, now my conscience dead
> now the only guidance that I had is splattered on cement
> actions speak louder than words, let me try this shit dead.[36]

But he *returns* and presents at times with what appears to be an upside-down cross scrawled on his forehead, continuing to outline the urge to destroy as he signifies one of the most widely recognized symbols of *deathlife*.

The moral and ethical order of the world is turned upside down, and the boundaries between life and death are signified in such a way as to render physical death—despised by whiteness as the source of anxiety and meaninglessness—a matter of pleasure obtained.[37] In essence, this is a connecting of desire and repulsion through a denial of distinction between the joy of living and the pleasure found in demise—the two blur, and meaningful difference is gone. In fact, this modality of "assent" is for Tyler the nature of the erotic, and the erotic herein is tied to death. This link has to do with the way in which the erotic connotes a pleasure, a joy that seeks nothing beyond itself.[38] In the sights and sounds of demise one finds the vibrant nature of life. Furthermore, there is tied to the erotic an acknowledgment of passion—a comfort of sorts with the joy in the obscene, a turn to play over against a life of aim and restriction.

While there is something individualized and distinct in how people experience life and death, there is a shared mechanics by means of which death can hold a certain allure and enchantment. In part, this is due to the way in which death speaks to continuity, or a holding together through the ability to engage the nature of experience without the fallback of what that experience will produce. Continuity, which is achievable in a limited sense through the erotic by means of the self, becomes a fluid concept: opened and exposed through what Bataille describes as violence, by which transgression becomes a marker of meaning.[39] Or, in the words of Tyler, the Creator, "Fuck your traditions (and) fuck your positions (and) fuck your religion (and) fuck your decisions."[40] The "Fuck your . . ." produces meaning through a type of overturning—a dismissal of those ideologies and structures undergirding "order," which is a way of naming the work needed to maintain the idea of life as distinctive arrangement. In a certain sense, life and death are external: one knows death through the inactivity of another, and life is also often measured in terms of the actions of others. For Tyler, violence (or, better yet, pain) might be said to bring life and death together through activity that ends one and produces the other—and the violent person bringing these two together experiences something of both in that act. Suffering and joy are both found in that act—just as death, in this instance, offers something life does not.[41] Violence becomes a mechanism used to confront the certainties and limitations imposed by social structures and frameworks of normativity, thereby disrupting social knowledge through what might be called a form of "nonknowledge": "suffering to enjoy, enjoying to suffer."[42] It challenges staid notions of meaning through its aggressive claiming of and action toward desire cutting against traditional social parameters. Such a move is disturbing and Bataille acknowledges this, but in admitting the discomfort he does not preclude the action. As Albert Stabler reflects, when thinking about photographs of the practice of *lingchi* in China ("death by a thousand cuts"), "Whether grotesquely explicit, ideologically sanitized, or menacingly veiled, depictions of violence are perhaps never viewed exclusively as titillation or edification, but an explicit emphasis on one response allows the other to have a life of its own."[43]

Hence, death is not a problem to solve but rather a joyful resolution. "In essence," writes Bataille, "the domain of eroticism is the domain of violence, of violation. . . . The most violent thing of all for us is death which jerks us out of a tenacious obsession with the lastingness of our discontinuous being."[44] Violence represents a part of the equation of social regulation— social life—in that it "speaks" to practices without interest in production (the social call for work, as in effort dedicated to the maintenance of whiteness) and it confirms play and activity without long intent.[45] Or, in this case, one might say it is without the aim of buttressing the structuring of whiteness (i.e., utility). The erotic, then, is a mode of expression—a spasm between life and death—that tells us of their connection in a way that social regulation and social organization of life as productive (i.e., in line with the maintenance of whiteness logic and its holdings) can't. For the latter, death is an undoing.[46] Put another way, "we use the word eroticism," Bataille notes, "every time a human being behaves in a way strongly contrasted with everyday standards and behavior. Eroticism shows the other side of a façade of unimpeachable propriety. Behind the façade are revealed the feelings, parts of the body and habits we are normally ashamed of."[47] Whereas this push is typically understood in negative terms as a breach of protocol, as a disregard of the person, as "obscenity," with this thinking on the erotic one can discern another possibility in the work of artists like Tyler, the Creator.[48]

Reflecting Bataille's appreciation for Friedrich Nietzsche, one can say this erotic impulse speaks to an effort to hold in tension the "possible" and the "impossible"—that is to say, the "organic life, of materiality" and with the latter, the "share of the world of death and destruction."[49] In this way, Tyler, for instance, reforms death by separating it from any regard for notions of the divine (a bridge between life-death-life):

> Jesus called, he said he's sick of the disses
> I told him to quit bitchin', this isn't a fuckin' hotline.[50]

Tyler points out death's relevance, its importance for life—the manner in which demise isn't to be avoided (as if it can be) but rather met as joy. One might think of joy here, in Tyler's case, as embracing the "undeniable" (e.g., the perverse, as in that which is against the social codes thought up through whiteness) that mocks the social codes and their order meant to sanction denial (of death). It, joyousness, is an eager embrace of the profane that rejects social fear by cherishing the look, feel, and sounds of death as resonated in the "stuff" of life. Life and death speak each other, reflect each other—are each other. Tyler, one might say, experiences dimensions of life through contact with "obscene" performance of violations; and this performance is erotic to the extent it is a "breaking down of established patterns, the patterns . . . of the regulated social order basic to our discontinuous mode of existence as defined and separate individuals."[51] And this "breaking down of established patterns" means disruption of safeguards—or strategies for keeping the individual socially contained and present in life, if white, and present as death, if Black. In so doing, the distinction between life and death that this containment through various safeguards is meant to offer loses its social power. The one who does this pushes against distinction. Accordingly, something of this erotic impulse acted out shapes the rebel in that "the rebel defies death," notes Stuart Kendall in speaking of Bataille's work, "not by turning his or her back to it but by laughing in the face of it, by practicing joy before death."[52] Tyler finds funny the connection between violence and sex, between life and death, between pain and pleasure; but perhaps this is a dimension of the poetic twist—a means to trouble social structures by way of the laugh. I want to think about this sense of humor through a loose framing of it in relationship to the laugh as Bataille understood it.

This laughter doesn't stem the tide of brutality. Laugher, like tears, is associated with violence. Bataille writes, "But laughter is not so much the contrary of tears as it may seem: the object of laughter and the object of tears are always related to some kind of violence which interrupts the regular order of things, the usual course of events."[53] Regarding the comedic dimension of this narration, Tyler reflects, "Well, I don't rape chicks. . . . I have punched a girl in the eye. . . . Um . . . what else? I say a lot of shit and it just depends. . . . Sometimes it's just 'cause shit is funny."[54] But the question is, What constitutes funny, what generates the laugh? As Tyler wrote in a tweet a year after the release of Goblin, "The Things That Make Me Laugh Are Stupid. Like, I Heard Some Nigga Got Hit By A Bus The Other Day . . . I Just Laughed While Typing That."[55] While social regulations and narratives of containment are meant to drown particular impulses, the urge toward killing is never completely subdued. "We may find the desire to eat human flesh completely alien to us," writes Bataille, "not so the desire to kill. Not all of us feel it, but who would go so far as to deny that it has as lively, if not as exacting, an existence among the masses as sexual appetite?" And he continues by saying that "there is a potential killer" in everyone.[56] For example, when portraying himself as a type of vampire (one who moves between life and death, a different modality of synergistic relationship between the two), Tyler announces his process of destruction/consumption: "Kidnapping, attacking, with axes and shit; 'Til I grab them throats and start smacking them shits."[57] This is not to say physical murder, literal killing, must take place. Rather, as in the video for "Yonkers," it is sufficient to perform the erotic relationship of life and death. This performance is enough to surface a particular challenge to traditional notions of life and death as distinct, with the former celebrated and the latter denied.

The erotic and its relationship to death teach lessons concerning the actual integrity of life in its complex, messy, layered, and "open" form.[58] If nothing else, the erotic, whether it be physical or emotional, points to connection and hence points to the death of an illusion of distinction.[59] Death, then, as connected to the erotic, demands deconstruction of old social codes. Or, as Bataille remarks, "The first turbulent surge of erotic feeling overwhelms all else, so that gloomy considerations of the fate in store for our discontinuous selves are forgotten. And then, beyond the intoxication of youth we achieve the power to look death in the face and to perceive in death the pathway into unknowable and incomprehensible continuity—that path is the secret of eroticism and eroticism alone can reveal it."[60] Eroticism embraces death, understood as the rejection of a certain socially sanctioned sense of the self. This is a sense of the self that privileges the self, even to the point of destroying the Other. The track "She" points this out, as Tyler chronicles his interest in a young woman who is being watched and desired: "Night light hits off, turnin' kisses to bites; I'm a down to Earth nigga, with intentions, that's right; You'll be down in Earth quicker if you diss me tonight."[61] The poetic—in this case, hip hop—is the language of this relationship between the erotic and death, in that it is the destruction of linguistic meaning in order to explore and explain the denied nature of existence at its end.[62] Language is used against itself and against meaning. In fact, commentary on Tyler, the Creator suggests this poetic quality: "When he performs 'Yonkers,' still his biggest breakout hit, he intentionally fucks up the lyrics."[63] The erotic calls for a sense of being that is more than what we do, what we produce, and what we sustain through our effort. Instead, it urges attention to a deeper plateau of meaning. In so doing, it pushes Blackness beyond what whiteness intends for and by it.

Behind the development of society's major practices is the disregard of death—i.e., disgust with death and dying. Yet, the joy and pleasure associated with bringing forth death becomes the significant symbol of hip hop's tackling of the social lie (e.g., the necessity of barriers and other modes of confinement whereby what is uncomfortable is rejected). This is degradation, but not as a negative; rather, it is more along the lines of the attention to the material arrangements of life explored by Mikhail Bakhtin in relationship to Carnival and the grotesque. The Black body in this case is given a different direction and placement in time and space so as to defy the utility of Blacks constructed through Blackness. For Tyler, this placement entails consumption of death so as to reframe it through an erotic twist that denies the distinction between life and death. Such positioning or placement can be read as being meant to hold off efforts to reify and restrict—efforts to reject the status of those confounded by social regulations and the moral and ethical demand for particular plateaus of meaning. The horror in this violence, in this appeal to death, is found in how the observer—or the one who hears about it—sees in the demise her own end over against the narrative of life undergirding the social system.[64] And in this she sees the destruction of social meaning premised on order and regulation of how time and space are occupied in line with social rules and regulations. The horror is in what social meanings have projected about death, but not what death entails. The false narrative of life as stable, as refined, and as distinguished is brought into question as the erotic ushers in a different take on death. Social construction entails an effort to bracket, tame, and contain death, and in so doing it provokes a mood of horror or dread in the face of demise. One finds that this turn in the erotic's relationship to death does the opposite: it does not seek to hide death or render it problematic but rather to see in it a certain joy associated with existence not confined to social codes of restriction, thereby rendering it a natural expression of life. This joy is a depth of expressivity and relationship denied through the workings of the social codes and conditions that shape narratives of life.

With death comes the end of social arrangements, collective narratives of life that seek to support only the logic of the narrative. Death is joyful in that it exposes through transgression the complexity of life and in the process gives flight to the lie of fixed identity and objectified existence. In this embrace of death is a push against society as practiced and the narrative of life it provides. Tyler points out the end—or death—of cultural sensibilities, the end or death of restriction and boundaries between thought and conduct. And, in this way, he allows for alternative sensibilities through the destruction of sensitivities, new values *through* the destruction of values. Yet he leaves the *through* empty and doesn't propose another unity with its overarching values and strictures. Death gives life a different register: a depth and complexity also referenced as a transgressive quality marked by joy. He is the counter-social character, disruptive and "dangerous," for whom "rebel and defiance makes [his] motherfucking cock hard."[65] Perhaps not these particular words, but doesn't something of the intent expressed in these lyrics—the lacing of rebellion with a sexual dimension—recall the Marquis de Sade? In fact, the third track on *Goblin*, "Radicals," names much that reflects the desires of a figure like the Marquis, whose relationship to death is reflected in Tyler's graphic fantasies and rebellion against social standards: "I ain't never gonna bow down to your expectations."

How to Enjoy Death: Marquis and Bacchus

Albert Camus, in reflecting on the Marquis de Sade, argues that circumstances such as the physical arrangement of time and space within the framework of prison shape the Marquis's "moral philosophy" in such a way as to amplify his isolation with a fantasy of outrage.[66] In light of war and colonialization, Camus (while reflecting on physical political circumstances) has a difficult time finding merit in the physical destruction of persons for the sake of ideological claims. And Bataille is troubled by the exercise of "power over," even in the extreme fantasies of the Marquis, which accounts for his desire to communicate only with those who are troubled by the moral philosophy of the Marquis. Still, he finds something valuable in the raw and poetic quality of the Marquis's expression, in the ability to damage if not destroy social arrangements that blur the human. There is an element of "power" working here and something of what Camus labels "metaphysical rebellion." Through the Marquis, for Bataille, death is a mode of destruction that doesn't require the piling up of physical bodies. Still, for Camus, the Marquis advocated a power "toward," and for Bataille it is a power "from." The former is a positive assertion over against, and for Bataille it is a negation, in that it is a destruction of social restrictions justified by social institutions that seek only our effort to reinforce (or build) the value of utility and its meaning.[67] They differ in that where Camus sees the Marquis's servitude as a consequence of narrative as revenge and the "demand for freedom," Bataille finds a rejection of slavery to the social institutions of his day.

Read through the Marquis, destruction doesn't entail the same circumstances for Camus and Bataille. Although, for both, something of the individual is found in the call for the destruction of the Other, for Bataille this request speaks a particular morality of "murder"—or, even, a new modality of the "sacred."[68] This isn't necessarily a call for physical murder, as opposed to murder of particular social framings of life.[69] There is a reluctant joy in murder, in death more generally, in that it destroys certain modalities of knowledge that serve to restrain and limit the human (read Blacks through Blackness) to what the human can preserve for the well-being of society.[70] Death, then, opens to suppressed dimensions.[71] Such is not violence in an actual, militaristic sense, not violence in the mode of material intervention: keep in mind that the Marquis wrote from prison, not from the S&M studio; Tyler, the Creator speaks from the studio and the video shoot; and Bataille wrote after his work as a librarian.[72] Rather, violence here might suggest overthrow. It might be destruction in a word (pun intended) of the metaphysical and moral hold of social institutions and their frameworks. Poetry, when it is the tool for narratives of outrage, destroys the language of gentle acquiescence to social institutions and their arrangements, and this can happen without a physical blow being thrown or without a physical body being materially ravaged. Regarding this, Tyler's lyrics have been described as "post-modern poetry scribbled into the tight margins of a three-ringed notepad," and he as someone "armed with an absurdist wit."[73]

One gets a sense of the blending of pain and pleasure in Bataille's early novel *Story of the Eye*. Near the end, after numerous scenes of sexual activity, degradation, violence, and bodily revolt of other pornographic kinds, a priest is encountered in a church. Sexual activity and physical violence, psychological play and sacrilege are intertwined in ways that bring into graphic relief the way that erotic embodied engagement with the world rethinks the conditions for and response to life and death. The erotic, hence, is a disruption that troubles and signifies distinction; in so doing, it recasts death as a modality of violence and pleasure. Tyler also offers a sense of this connection between sex and violence, between pleasure and pain, and he does so in a way that maintains the functional dominance of the self. After fantasizing about killing a woman who rejects his advances, he writes, "I just wanna drag your lifeless body to the forest; and fornicate with it; but that's because I'm in love with you cunt."[74] While *Story of the Eye* represents something of Bataille's concern with eroticism, his prime example of this posture toward and enactment of the erotic in relationship to death is found in his discussion of the Marquis. Only in poetic narrative is this type of embrace of death as erotic, as violent affirmation, possible, advocated by the Marquis. The "orgiastic impulses" that work against "political, juridical, and economic institutions" are expressed erotically and most powerfully through the poetic highlighting of what is typically disregarded, and through this disregard something of significance about life is lost.[75] It's important to note again that Bataille finds it worthwhile to engage only those who are disgusted by the activities suggested by the Marquis de Sade. He recognizes and doesn't seek to limit the troubling nature of what the Marquis proposes. And, in fact, he is quick to remind readers that the Marquis discusses and describes practices and activities in narrative form (i.e., as a philosophy of moral signification and embodied practice). In his writings the Marquis highlights the destructive and violent nature of the erotic and in this way brings to the fore death as a modality of grand passion. There is in his depictions of sexual activity and murder a disregard for the Other and the pronouncement of the person without externally imposed parameters of conduct.[76] Yet the Marquis's personal dealings involve recognition of the Other as only conquerable through the unleashed imagination expressed in the written word.[77] While the Marquis saw state-sponsored violence during the French Revolution, his narrative is imagination on the page. Still, the Marquis found sex and violence pleasurable. In either case the two are connected.

In like manner Tyler, the Creator, through the persona adopted and portrayed in videos and the lurid lyrical text, works out seduction by death.[78] Highlighted in the Marquis's writings, according to Bataille, is a deep and sustained appreciation for "moments of excess that stir us to the roots of our being and give us strength enough to allow free rein to our elemental nature."[79] There is in this a shift with respect to morality and death, one that gives the nod to extreme pleasure without regard for consequences as they relate to the order of the social world. In a word, it is a matter of "heterology"—a highlighting and reconsideration of what is traditionally left out, that which is considered unacceptable; it is, for our purposes, to embrace what whiteness rejects.[80] Yet here is a distinction: Tyler, the Creator, as advocate of the erotic—perhaps a hip hop libertine—is never able to completely forget society (is anyone?), never able to avoid some manner of creation by social mechanisms, and never able to avoid viewing pleasure and abuse. His commitment to death isn't free of the social implication of being made vis-à-vis Blackness.[81] Something of his effort to advance the erotic requires, as Joseph Winters recognizes, "mechanisms that discipline, contain, or exclude that which might impede the preservation of that life," or, in a word, strategies "to subordinate others to our desires and projects."[82] Although conditioned, the erotic remains while it doesn't free completely from the status quo.

The manner in which both the Marquis de Sade and Tyler, the Creator link pleasure to particular modalities of justice denied (rape, misogyny, etc.) points out ways in which even the transgression of the erotic can link back to the status quo.[83] In other words, we are destructive and productive already—

contemptuous of social regulations while also endorsing them.[84] Regarding the Marquis's writings and Tyler, the Creator's lyrics, shock and rejection of the morality of pleasure to death is anticipated, but such a response does little to change the commentary on the eroticness of demise. Whereas social life is premised on a pattern of effort and the productivity of that effort, and this understood as the terms of (white) life, the erotic as championed by figures such as the Marquis and Tyler entails a rejection of these social codes and conditions that seek to distinguish life and death. Along those lines:

> My only problem is death
> Fuck heaven, I ain't givin' no religion respect.[85]

Both express through narratives of destruction a different sense of life and death—one that combines them through an erotic "mood" and performance that praise disorder and thereby reform the terror of death.[86] This involves a signifying of the social codes related to standard moral and ethical patterns: "Brutality and murder are further steps in the same direction [i.e., disorder]. Similarly prostitution, coarse language, and everything to do with eroticism and infamy play their part in turning the world of sensual pleasure into one of ruin and degradation."[87] The erotic in this manner is a rejection of stifling conditions of social life that entail a surrender of "waste" (i.e., for Bataille, activities and longings without a "productive" purpose—the practices hidden away). There is something about this process that generates from the inside out. In other words, this adherence to the value of death, to the joy of demise, involves a statement concerning self, a "dark" consciousness that appreciates depth of experience without staid coding of morality and ethics.[88]

There, of course, is a quality of frustrating restriction in the narratives offered by the Marquis and Tyler, the Creator: each experiences his own type of social confinement out of which and in response to which he communicates. For the Marquis, physical imprisonment is a consequence of his praxis; for Tyler, metaphysical confinement is due to the social codes of the United States—he is Black defined by Blackness. Each writes of pleasure and the joy of death from within the framework of the society that both challenges and authorizes his words.[89] And Tyler performs the perverse from within the very technologies that both support and critique his transgression.[90] How can this not have meaning with regard to the nature of death?

Social regulations seek to bracket death as a mode, perhaps an ultimate mode of "waste"; but the erotic and its performance redress death as a matter of joy understood in terms of fulfillment without fulfillment. Taking to its limit this adherence to morality of the erotic involves a denial of the Other but also a denial of the self who does the denying. As Bataille recounts, "If we start from the principle of denying others posited by de Sade it is strange to observe that at the very peak of unlimited denial of others is a denial of oneself."[91] In tracks like "Nightmare," Tyler's self-destruction in the form of suicide is connected to a sense of self as all-consuming in that "life is a movie and you're just a prop." He tells the listener, right after a fantasy of his suicide, "My hands tremble, my finger slipped, the wall's read; Her life is fucked, she's sad now, her son is dead."[92] Perhaps there is something of this grand denial in the suicide in the video for "Yonkers" mentioned earlier. Consistent with Bataille and the Marquis through Bataille, both life and death entail a type of happiness and joy—with the intensity of life named through its end. There is nothing "reasonable" about this, nothing consistent with the socially coded parameters of human interaction, but, for the Marquis and to some extent Tyler, the Creator in *Goblin*, this is its importance; this is the joy and pleasure in it.[93] In fact, the negative reaction to both the Marquis and Tyler (through *Goblin*) speaks to the manner in which moral-ethical alterations to social coding of life versus death intensify the opposite of normativity, thereby intensifying pleasure. This is pleasure through an expansive (in excess) performance that challenges normative distinctions between what is desired (life) and what is feared (death). Tyler makes explicit the narrative of continuity that has marked discussion of hip hop. It is not simply social critique, not simply embrace of the American deal and values writ Black, and so forth. Rather, it is the death of the American narrative. Respectability and even the shadow of such structuring of life—such reserve—is questioned, signified, and denounced. This respectability is seen, for instance, in how sex/gender are discussed and are not discussed, in how framings or projections of self as masculine or feminine, for instance, are embedded in the very logic of hip hop's response to societal structuring of collective life. Yet, again, even in this, like Bataille's, Tyler's resistance speaks a particular embrace of certain dimensions of the status quo (e.g., the normative positioning of bodies in time and space). In this manner Tyler is against hip hop's respectability—respectability as it relates to the acceptance of the guiding logic for the structuring of life over against death.

Bataille argues that the erotic shifts the terrain and brings together principles of social life held apart through both "secular" (economic and political mechanisms) and the sacred (religious activity and theology), and in this bringing together it abandons the distinction between the arrangements of life and death.[94] Within this turn to the erotic is recognition of a human connection between pleasure and pain, "sexuality and the desire to hurt and to kill," expressed in the writings of the Marquis and the lyrical content of Tyler, the Creator's album.[95] Death, in a sense then, is the excess of life expressed through the erotic. And through the erotic novel or erotic rap lyrics that which troubles is forced into the public realm: death becomes a spectacle—an expression without any larger intent. Perhaps this helps explain why Bataille associates death with silence, with the end of discourse. Or, in his words, "If death calls, although the noise of the call fills the night, the call is a kind of profound silence. The response itself is silence stripped of every possible meaning."[96] It, death, through an array of troubling activities, is with/in life engulfing it.[97] Or, as Bataille writes, "We live with an obsession with a moment when life would be at the height of death." He continues, "There is an experiment with truth there: not only must we die, not only are we frightened and anguished by this, not only do we turn away from death, but an incessant movement brings us back to it. And we are always looking to death for what life does not give us."[98] Sadism . . . with swag and a beat involves the celebration of a dimension of the human denied through social restriction. It is ground given to a rethinking of death through an embrace of the pleasure found in destruction/demise. Such a position involves a break with fear of death, anxiety over death, because that response to death restricts life and restricts activity in such a way as to confine the person, to trap them in only the material markers of social existence. This, according to Bataille, is the equivalent of a type of servitude as restriction to law (one might expand this to moral and ethical laws of social existence) to be avoided; instead, death isn't to be taken seriously in this sense but rather is to be met with joy and as a source of pleasure. Bataille and the Marquis de Sade through him point to the priority of "inner experience," by means of which the logic of the social world and its "grand narratives" of moral and ethical limitation are undercut.[99] Boundaries are dismantled, and death recognized as joyful because of its victory over boundaries.[100]

While, like the Marquis, Tyler isn't known to act out physically the practices of torture and demise chronicled in "Yonkers" or other tracks, there are ways in which, if Bataille is correct, Tyler's language does to linguistic assurances of meaning what physical violence does to life: in both cases, death speaks in multidimensional ways to the violence embedded in the human animal.[101] With each listen to Tyler, the Creator, as with every turn of the page of a book by the Marquis, the reader is exposed to a familiarity that disturbs. While readers are not sadistic in practice, they have the capacity for it. And, in this way, they are marked by the ability to push beyond a fear of death to joyfulness in the face of death—joyfulness that undercuts social regulations and social decorum by embracing what is to be despised. In short, both entail, through the erotic, a push toward "extremity."[102]

Jay-Z becomes god, and Kendrick Lamar reconceives god, but it is no wonder Tyler, the Creator is critical (dismissive really) of the god concept. Why, in light of the erotic impulse guiding him into death, would he settle for a trope that further entrenches him in the moral and ethical demands of the social world surrounding him? Through communication and fantasy, he jettisons this trope because sovereignty—the highlighting of inner experience (as a blurring of boundaries) over against the mandates (and distinctions imposed) of social life—knows no such appeal and doesn't surrender to social knowledge that frames life.

> You told me God was the answer
> When I ask him for shit, I get no answer, so God is the cancer.[103]

One must die, but will one die well or "poorly" is the question: Will one die in opposition to the aims of whiteness or in line with whiteness's interests?[104] This is an appeal to performance outside the logic of socially sanctioned schemes that are frightened of death and that are disagreeable with thick and contradictory practices that push against polite standards.[105] Tyler's isn't a useful practice, not meant to advance a particular notion of uplift or advancement shadowed by a practice of accumulation. There is no purpose, no socially sanctioned function related to accumulations—or social norms—present.

If death is associated with joy, not anguish, and doesn't collapse into the strictures of the social world shaped and limited by reasonableness and alignment with the logic of whiteness, it is also the case that nonhistorical figures, or mythological beings, might further explicate death viewed as joyous, meaning nondistinguished, expression.[106] For both the Marquis de Sade and Tyler, the Creator, the erotic plays out in violence and demise in the form of fantasy, as an open narrative of the fantastic that speaks to those orientations that whiteness seeks to closet. There is a mythic quality to their expression that might be further explicated through a direct turn to mythology of a similar figure. I have in mind one who came up in chapter 1, in connection to the Orphic hustler: Dionysus, here in the form of Bacchus.[107]

I find useful the manner in which thinkers like Bataille enhance the erotic quality of the bacchic mood and morality.[108] How could it be otherwise, when he references the erotic as "the death impulse"?[109] I am not arguing that hip hop artists like Tyler, the Creator are "inspired" directly through an appeal to bacchic sensibilities.[110] In fact, whether the bacchic move is intentional or not doesn't concern me. Instead, I am interested in how the bacchic impulse serves as a useful structure for understanding what is taking place in certain hip hop quarters regarding notions of death (i.e., the freeing from fear and oppressive paradigms that Bacchus represents).[111] What I offer is a reflection on hip hop as both strategy of exploration and content of that exploration. My read of bacchic hip hop is multidirectional to the extent it brings into play sociocultural, political, psychological, and economic considerations without privileging any one code. And what gets highlighted is "consumption"—taming or using up the fear, which entails a "wasting" of the intent behind fear—of death that seems to reflect (intentionally or not) dynamics of the performativity of bacchic sensibilities and strategies of joy that the social world deems "madness." By this approach, the complexities of hip hop—its multifaceted and layered relationships with social realities—are mirrored in its interpretation of and commentary on *deathlife*.

At least in passing, Bataille links (genealogically) his discussion of the erotic of death to the orgiastic violence associated with Bacchus, and this connection is worth considering here.[112] Yet I make no effort to track Bacchus (and Dionysus) with the concerns of a Hellenist or with the strategies of a philosopher determined to arrange a new pattern of life based on Dionysus.[113] Nor do I pretend to treat this material as a classicist would. My aim isn't to provide a full discussion of Bacchus. Rather, I wish to demonstrate—in relationship to another use of bacchic sensibilities in the work of Nella Larsen, and specifically her novel *Quicksand* (1928)—a way in which the language of the bacchic encounter expresses sensibilities and patterns of ethics-morality framed in terms of an expansive sense of the freeing (lucidity-rendering) connection of death and life. I offer no prescriptive commentary on the plausible moral-ethical moves of Larsen's protagonist Helga Crane, and I am not suggesting I have a sense of the particular gender, sex(uality), parental demands, and community animosity articulated by Larsen and responded to by Crane. Nor am I suggesting the performance of bacchic sensibilities is identical for Crane and Tyler, the Creator—rather, they constitute bacchic personalities along a spectrum of examples productively viewed through a Bataillean lens. They engage death without seeking to sanitize and isolate it, as whiteness is wont to do, and instead maintain its presence as life expression. And in this is a type of freedom amid bondage. I understand the geography of my life, and that of Tyler, the Creator's, is far from Larsen's depiction of real-world conditions. Mindful of how Larsen's characters and Tyler, the Creator are socially coded differently as well as the ramification of this difference, I turn to Larsen's *Quicksand* in part because I want to suggest that

Tyler is part of a canon of bacchic framings of Blackness housed in cultural production. Furthermore, I want to use *Quicksand*'s protagonist, Crane, to suggest and amplify some of the dynamics of this bacchic project defining Tyler, the Creator's music. Bacchus/Dionysus, like Orpheus earlier in this book, functions as a trope by means of which I aim to explore and describe a particular vision of death housed in hip hop that disrupts whiteness's effort to distinguish it from life through an imposition of fear. I am suggesting here the utility of a turn to Bacchus as a way to read an underexplored (and undoubtedly troubling) depiction of death within a particular example of hip hop culture that finds death an expression of erotic joy (i.e., free from fear and the utility demanded by whiteness). In this way, hip hop challenges efforts to hide whiteness's intent vis-à-vis *deathlife*.[114]

Bacchus emphasizes manic energy or the erotic dimension of madness ritualized.[115] There is a tension present in this figure—Marcel Detienne proposes he is a "double god"—and this tension harnesses life (the god of harvest) and death (the god whose rituals are marked by frenzy and demise). More precisely, "Dionysos," Detienne remarks, "is the god who snatches his victim by surprise, who trips his prey and drags it down into madness, murder, and defilement; yet he is also the god of vines that ripen in a day."[116] Viewed through popular presentations of Bacchus/Dionysus, one finds the former (Bacchus) associated with a harm that heals: "The more insanity is unleashed, the more room there is for catharsis."[117] Here, one finds mediation of life and death by means of which destruction and consumption are kin. And by means of this blending, chaos takes on a compelling and intense quality of Otherness—of presence outside social categories of moral-ethical confinement, which is a type of "strangeness" taking hold.[118]

The literary world of the United States is marked in certain ways by a turn to Bacchus/Dionysus for discursive expression of a cultural awakening shadowing protest and rearrangement of embodied encounters in the world. "The god of intoxication, madness, ecstasy, and metamorphosis," writes John Carlevale, "seemed to be everywhere as intellectuals sought apt symbols for the appetites and anxieties stimulated by what came to be called the 'New Sensibility.'"[119] But this is a narrow depiction, in that this figure's influence in the contemporary United States extends beyond academic and artistic letters, instead speaking to and through the diversity of encounters with and naming(s) of the world. As Richard Schechner reflects, Bacchus "is present in Today's America—showing himself in the hippies, in the 'carnival spirit' of black insurrectionists, on campuses; and even, in disguise, on the patios and in the living rooms of suburbia."[120] The period of US history sparking this turn to raw celebration of earthiness comes on the heels of World War II and the wounds of the Vietnam War as well as the exposure of racial hate acted out in violent response to demands for justice. It is into this world that literary figures plunge. They engage in an orgy of possibility while surrounded by signs of an inhospitable world. The turmoil of the social world, no longer deniable qua shifts in ideological platforms, was embraced and filtered through a type of (metaphysical and) moral excess.

It isn't simply white writers and thinkers who find something of existential, if not metaphysical, value in a retelling of this Greco-Roman mythic figure's balancing, if not blending, of worlds (i.e., death and life). The times not only made uncomfortable demands on those of European descent but also pushed against the existential and ontological standing of those who'd been reified by sociopolitical forces over the course of centuries. This turn to Bacchus points to anxiety over the restrictive dynamics of society after World War II and the uncertainty of existential and ontological assumptions in light of various social justice movements. Appeal to the trope of this figure speaks a yearning for the sanction of explosive behavior meant to affirm joy and self-interest. To be precise, guided by a very different relationship to sociocultural mechanisms of meaning and being cut deeply by racialization, there is a long-standing practice within Black arts and letters to use Greek (and Roman) signifiers and mythological poetics to unpack dimensions of experience in the US context—to rethink what whiteness projects in various forms of Blackness.[121] As should be clear, such works did not seek to simply transplant Greek sensibilities or to assume the superiority of Greco-Roman (hence "European") frameworks for depicting the workings of collective life; nor does this use entail an uncritical embrace of a certain modality of optimism and individual pleasure-pain disconnected from ideological and material circumstances. Instead, this move circumvents—if it doesn't signify—European intent and makes Greco-Roman structuring(s) do counterwork by serving to assert the deep value of Blacks over against the dominant social narrative. And this is in direct opposition to any effort to reinforce the "Greek Ideal," as Cornel West describes the normative gaze by means of which white supremacy and its offshoot of white privilege are rendered powerful (i.e., having the ability to shape what is socially assumed and what is socially acted on) and worthy of life with the means to bracket off and control death, or existential and ontological chaos.[122] This normative gaze seeks to safeguard those of European descent by Othering (i.e., framing through Blackness) populations and projecting onto them—because of their difference—death in an expansive sense. The Greek ideal is turned on its head, signified, and made to support the Black confrontation with whiteness's narrative of death and dying hidden in *deathlife*.

In some cases, the appeal to Bacchus, for instance, depicts a bacchic performance as angst-producing—a turn away from comfort and a push into raw sensuality that holds the potential to damage, and through this violent alteration produce new possibilities otherwise hidden. This is certainly one plausible way to read, for instance, what Larsen describes in her novel *Quicksand*, in relation to Helga Crane. At one point, in her effort to recast herself over against the social (death-dealing) demands of gender and race, Crane leaves the United States and lives in Denmark with (distant) family members. In this move, there is a refusal to be bound by the performance of Blackness as intended by the workings of whiteness, and a celebration of deep immersion in the workings of the erotic's performance of joyful demise (e.g., a "death" of social obligation). She seeks to rebel to damage stifling circumstances, but in so doing she seeks to gain the treasure denied her. There is an erotic quality (a type of pleasurable abandon) to this, as one sees with her relationships in Europe. For her, this pleasure is an ownership over herself, a determination of how she occupies space and how she "feels" in that space. But, for whites viewing her through whiteness, Crane remains—as the character Axel Olsen tells her—a figure with "the warm impulsive nature of the women of Africa, but, my lovely, you have, I fear the soul of a prostitute."[123] Crane will leave the Danes to their whiteness and return to the United States to tackle whiteness cast a different (and familiar) way.

It will be of interest to readers to consider what follows in light of the manner in which contemporary reminiscence on bacchic performance at times speaks to how music and sex(uality) of a variety of expressive modalities serve as alternate pathways through the modern dilemma: life and/in/as demise.[124] Before continuing my discussion of Tyler, the Creator in relationship to Larsen's *Quicksand*, I want to consider briefly another take on Tyler's alteration of gender-sexuality performance as additional context for thinking about his take on *deathlife*. We are reminded by Moya Bailey that one can understand "queer" as "the abnormal, the strange, the dangerous. . . . Queer is a total rejection of the regime of the Normal."[125] And while this shift is helpful, it isn't complete. There is more, another turn, that extends possibilities. While the death impulse aggressively acted out through his bacchic joy in demise isn't what Bailey has in mind, there is something about the disruption of sexuality tied to Tyler's presentation of *deathlife* that might be engaged through her framework of the "homolatent," which, "unlike 'queer,' 'homosexual,' or 'same gender loving' . . . attempts to address the abjection of desire." Bailey continues, "I offer the term homolatent: 'homo' to foreground the same gender orientation of the behavior and 'latent' to foreshadow the 'pathological' potential of queer desire's rupture into the real."[126] In this sense, there are potential connections between what Bailey labels homolatent and what I reference in terms of the bacchic. However, while Bailey highlights Odd Future Wolf Gang Kill Them All, I limit consideration to one figure from that group, Tyler, the Creator.

As Bailey rightly notes, the work of Odd Future speaks "to a grandiose performance of pain and violence that is inextricably linked to masculinity."[127] There is "anti/social-social" interplay between gender and sexuality frameworks with a consistency that is defined only in terms of its repeated attack on social identities. Gender and sexuality are rendered both visible and opaque (e.g., both stereotypically heterosexual and also "homosocial") while becoming a mechanism by means of which lyrical performance disturbs distinction between sexualized joy and demise. One might call this a mode of queering or contravention that challenges the nature of life-death relationality—but one given a more graphic dimension through its homolatent quality that involves a "perverse" playfulness with/in the structures of gender and sexuality used to capture the erotic quality of the desire named by this destructiveness. There is an aggressiveness, a violence that captures the demise expressed with such pleasure in the lyrical images offered. Tyler's smile isn't simply for the camera. Yet neither *queer* nor *homolatent* sufficiently captures the underlying impulse or social rationale for the lyrics expressed to the extent that neither term can account adequately for the thanatological quality of Blackness undergirding and informing the lyrical content. Embedded in his lyrics and performance is an effort to display a vile posture of contradiction (e.g., violence allows for a type of fluidity of identity), leaving listeners anxious and hyperaware of pain—or, perhaps, open to a futureless future. To miss this point is to miss the particular need (e.g., Blackness as a safeguard against white death) that fuels the nihilism—the "I don't give a fuck" as a radical individualism and not a call for community— that Bailey critiques.[128] In fact, on second thought, it isn't really nihilism in that nihilism assumes an option (e.g., better relationships, healthy gender and sexuality conversations), when what artists like Tyler recognize is the inability to distinguish such a life option from its negation. Bailey wants to find through homolatent relationships in hip hop a source of optimism and a means by which to construct future. However, Tyler's queering of circumstances (even when further read through homolatency) offers no grounds for optimism—if by optimism is meant a source of life outside the grasp of death—which is to say death is ever present.

Bailey discusses latency—for example, an expressed interplay of masculinity, heterosexuality, and queerness—in terms of dynamics of engagement within the realm called life that cause pain and death. There is, with that scenario, something recognizable as life that is lost. One might say homolatent aggression is an effort to produce a context for life, to resist what serves as symbols of incomplete status. However, the framework can't be pushed too far in relationship to Tyler in that his aim, his aggression, is meant to produce demise not over against life but rather as indistinguishable from life.[129] With Tyler's enactments, there is slippage with respect to identity (a celebration of contradiction), but there isn't a way to conceive the self or others that can serve to detangle life from death. Rather, his employment of the homolatent is a stylized performance of violence that ends any distinction between life and death. In this case, application of homolatency, over against how Bailey draws it from Octavia Butler's work, involves not a reactive measure born of frustration but rather a determined act complete in itself—that is, destruction not as a consequence of unfulfilled aims but rather an act of demise as joy.

My argument is that the bacchic, as Larsen phrases it and Tyler, the Creator enacts it, appeals within hip hop as a positive depiction of demise as the ultimate erotic act against the nature of death hidden by whiteness. While the circumstances are far from the same, there is with Tyler a similar push toward the pleasure of destroying what the social world intends. For Crane, this is a destruction of the social coding that renders Black women tamed by a whiteness that demands a certain utility be assigned to them—a utility that involves a controlled consumption of Black pleasure safeguarding white life. Crane sees this graphically with Europe, but there are ways in which the "tragic mulatto" figure she represents is also defined by a shadow whiteness that is visible to Blacks. It's a double bind that serves to simply reinforce the dictates of the social world. Even the desire to "give herself" to someone who also suffered the social world's framing of Blackness couldn't address the fundamental issue: a "feeling of ridicule and self-loathing remained." As Larsen describes the situation after Crane's failed attempt to connect with Dr. Anderson—who represented an exercise of Black being within the constrictions of whiteness's dedicates of respectability, "Almost she wished she could die. Not quite. It wasn't that she was afraid of death, which had, she thought, its picturesque aspects. It was rather that she knew she could not die. And death, after the debacle, would but intensify its absurdity. Also, it would reduce her, Helga Crane, to unimportance, to nothingness. Even in her unhappy state, that did not appeal to her."[130] As the story develops, the narrative reaches a turning point in which the erotic signals not white ownership but rather a mode of signifying Black self-expression that engages pleasurable movement assumed to be for a purpose beyond the limits of the social world.

Crane stumbles out into the rain and enters a Harlem church service where worship takes "on an almost Bacchic vehemence" through a deeply embodied play. "Behind her, before her, beside her," writes Larsen, "frenzied women gesticulated, screamed, wept, and tottered to the praying of the preacher, which had gradually become a cadenced chant. . . . It went on and on without pause with the persistence of some unconquerable faith exalted beyond time and reality." It was an event that urged both intrigue but also disgust from Crane. Ultimately, she was captured by the energy: "She felt an echo of the weird orgy resound in her own heart; she felt herself possessed by the same madness."[131] It is not a crude drunkenness. Rather, it is a "taste" of Bacchus's wine that opens one to a type of embodied joy—a moment during which whiteness is reduced in power and scope. It is a certain modality of the ecstatic meant to contour the imposed rigidity of the social world. It is a ritual movement through death that pushes beyond death. It is for Crane to be, like Bacchus, both dead and alive. Yet when one places this church scene within the larger drama of the social world, this for Helga is an effort to escape death (i.e., irrelevance), which ultimately leads to the strong potential for both irrelevance and physical demise—those very things she has worked to safeguard against over the course of an expansive geography: the South, the Northeast, Europe, and back.

Of importance here is how the bacchic exposure to Blackness ritualized and expressed as a cipher for a reality opposed to the social world (i.e., the Black Church as counterpoint) signals a shift in Crane's thinking on the nature and meaning of demise. This altered epistemology doesn't end the dilemma of death but rather positions her differently by opening her to greater awareness of the mechanisms of dominance that whiteness seeks to hide. It is Bacchus's assistance with a moral conundrum by "aiding . . . ascent towards God through 'divine frenzy' or 'divine madness'" that matters within the context of this Black Pentecostal quaking encountered by Crane.[132] As scholars have noted, Bacchus provides a terrible point of access between frenzy and control, "animal" instincts and "higher" ideals, between wild abandon that rips apart and displays demise, and passage to new and profound modalities of presence.[133] Theologically speaking, it is death of an "old self" and birth of a new "self," a new self that isn't free from the threat of demise. Even in this religious ritualization, death and life merge, and the practice of the "righteous" is meant to tame the implications of this merger. Crane would reflect on religion that it was "an illusion. Yes. But better, far better, than this terrible reality. Religion had, after all, its uses. It blunted the perceptions. Robbed life of its crudest truths. Especially it had its uses for the poor—and the blacks."[134]

The bacchic challenge for Crane is posed in terms of states of being, metaphysical locations within the context of a troubled social world in which a cruel tension exists between life (e.g., salvation) and death (e.g., sin) that pitted theological framings against sociocultural materiality. Such is the dilemma, cast in sociocultural and theological terms: the display of Black bodies performing themselves, while also pointing out an energy that dismantles the character's ontology and sense of space (read as belonging).[135] The link between life and death pervades this book, but it is with this bacchic framing that this presence of death entails a rugged but short-lived joy—a modality of the erotic expressed through the intoxication of lucidity regarding circumstances. Near the end of the story, when her physical body displays graphically the merger of life and death, Larsen speaks to Crane's lucidity regarding circumstances. "The neighbors and churchfolk," Larsen writes, "came in for their share of her all-embracing hatred. She hated their raucous laughter, their stupid acceptance of all things, and their unfailing trust in 'de Lawd.'"[136]

There is difference in the contextual dynamics (some of which, no doubt, is built on their different socially coded circumstances, such as the ramped misogyny within his lyrics and a lingering challenge of respectability within Larsen's story); still, one finds with Larsen's Crane a bumping against the restrictive enterprise of the social world and its stranglehold on desire, and there is with Tyler a rejection of this enterprise. Significant differences recognized, there is a shared defiance that labels both Crane and Tyler as social outcasts and misfits—by both whites and Blacks who adhere to the logic of the social world. There is a shared and troubled refusal to think the "self" using a metaphysical standard of excellence that simply hides under its pronouncements a commitment to the status quo above all else. This acquaintance with the Black Church that transforms her social circumstances (e.g., now a preacher's wife, in a small town, with children) doesn't free from the markings of Blackness intended by the social world. Crane surmises that "what ailed the whole Negro race in America, [was] this fatuous belief in the white man's God, this childlike trust in full compensation for all woes and privations in 'kingdom come.'"[137] And something of this epistemological rebellion surfaces in the raw lyrical rant of Tyler, the Creator:

Fuck your traditions, fuck your positions
Fuck your religion, fuck your decisions
They're not mine, so you gotta let 'em go.[138]

With Crane, the reader is met by death, for example, the birth of children consuming her well-being, a community devouring her sense of self, and a husband whose company troubled her, all leading to her physical and on-tological demise to be recognized and struggled against as a dimension of life. I find a hint of this posture when Larsen describes Crane's self-reflexive moment at the end of the novella. Thinking about how to get out of her cir-cumstances, Larsen writes, "How, then, was she to escape from the oppres-sion, the degradation, that her life had become? It was so difficult. It was terribly difficult. It was almost hopeless. . . . [F]or a while—for the immedi-ate present, she told herself—she put aside the making of any plan for her going. 'I'm still,' she reasoned, 'too weak, too sick. By and by, when I'm really strong.'"[139] Death and life are held together and expressed as such through her plotting and planning.

A social position that allows distinction between the two and provides the resources to "think" this distinction isn't available to those who can't claim whiteness, and this is despite the effort of Black Church theology and ethics to claim otherwise. Crane uncovers these mechanics of the social world and denounces the delusion of the Black Church's faith in a distinction prom-ised in the "by and by." The ethics demanded by whiteness and the ethics promoted by the Church are both without satisfaction in that both hide the nature of death. Neither Crane nor Tyler occasions such deception. In Tyler's words, religion "keeps people in a box and won't allow them to do what the fuck they want."[140] What I mean to point out is simply a particular perspec-tive on death that is cast through an exposing of whiteness's intent played out through Blackness. Crane knows death and seeks to manage it as life through a continuing longing for transformation of circumstances allowing for a greater fullness through "freedom from" (i.e., she wants to escape all the trappings of her small town and her patriarchal, economically repressed, and culturally monotone life). In so doing, she seeks to gain for herself a life as it is intended for those shrouded by whiteness. Yet, as Crane knows through her rejection of whiteness's projection of divinity, divinity does not deny or destroy the presence of death.[141] As Larsen recounts,

With the obscuring curtain of religion rent, she was able to look about her and see with shocked eyes this thing that she had done to herself. She couldn't, she thought ironically, even blame God for it, now that she knew that He didn't exist. . . . The white man's God. And His great love for all people regardless of race! What idiotic nonsense she had allowed herself to believe. How could she, how could anyone, have been so deluded? How could ten million black folk credit it when daily before their eyes was enacted its contradiction?[142]

The preacher and the "faithful" alter nothing for Crane, and "therapy's been sinning and niggas getting offended," Tyler writes, because "they don't want to fuck with me 'cause I do not fuck with religion."[143]

Tyler (at least certain iterations of his persona) embraces the pain and pleasure tied to death (i.e., the blending of the possible and the impossible). Death, in a graphic sense, isn't feared. It's consumed, brought into life to, in a bacchic sense, produce a deeply erotic poetics of pleasure without inhibitions that "kill" distinction: is he gay or straight, imagining or advocating, insane or not, and so on. This isn't to say that artists such as Tyler (in certain modalities) entail a firm transfiguration of Bacchus. Instead, I mean to suggest Tyler, the Creator's framing, as is also the case with earlier narrations such as *Quicksand*, entails qualities of a bacchic mood or sensibilities played out through a range of imagined thoughts and activities that run contrary to the social world's attended bracketing off of death.

ZOMBIC HUNGER

> All I see is Zombies
> Feeding all around us.

These lyrics from Childish Gambino's track titled "Zombies" (2016) point
to the overwhelming presence of the living dead, the un/dead, the walking
dead, or any of the many other ways of naming those who constitute death.[1]
What these lines hint at is a strategy of demise that troubles the social world
and that, because of this challenge to the narrative of order, is never far from
consideration within cultural narratives.

If these narratives reflect the social world back on itself, then, there would
have to be death. According to Brad Evans and Henry Giroux, there is a climate of violence—a history, really, and "beneath the surface of every sem-
blance of peace, it is possible to identify all too easily the scars of sacrifice
and the bloodshed of victims whose only error was often to be born in a cruel
age."[2] Stories concerning the US preoccupation with death (even when this
involves avoiding death) are often played out in literary terms, through the
characters of writers such as Richard Wright. For example, there are efforts to

read murder in gangsta rap through the trope of Bigger Thomas, yet for this figure murder is unintentional; it isn't an act but rather a reaction.[3] There is not for Thomas a sense that murder constitutes a relationship to death; rather it represents the consequences of social arrangements. Thomas denies the act but embraces the punishment, whereas the gangsta rapper embraces the act but denies the punishment. The other murder, the other taking of life, for Thomas is nonconsequential in that it involves an effort to escape conditions.[4] Murder framed this way, however, doesn't account for all presentations of demise. Think, for example, of hip hop. "The beautiful murder, the murder lifted into the mind of 'winged words,'" writes Michael Collins, "is in many ways the heartbeat of American culture—indeed, of all western culture. . . . Hardcore rappers rhyming about blowing away their foes with 9-millimeter pistols are in a sense part of a grand and troubling tradition."[5] Or, as Nick De Genova frames it, "Gangster rap is the expression of an urban American 'culture of terror' and 'space of death.'"[6] Put yet another way, "Everywhere history has been written in blood."[7]

Here, however, I argue that the zombie is an existential and ontological step beyond the "natural born killer," "thug," and "bad nigga" personae found in cultural narratives of rough existence.[8] While recognizing this perspective on demise framed in terms of the gangsta persona, my interest is in a different take—one where the moral and ethical codes of the social world are without bearing and when death isn't framed over against life. Gangsta narratives assume life-taking life, death as the product of active life. Here death as distinct from life is normative.[9] While certainly akin to this personification of violence, what I speak to in this chapter is a different arrangement—a larger description and discussion of performance of death consuming life. What I have in mind is more consistent with the imagery presented by Jay-Z in his verse on "Monster" (2010)—the creature, "a zombie with no conscience," or the "motherfuckin' monster" claimed in that track and forcefully presented in certain aspects of horrorcore rap.[10]

This style of rap confronts death, shepherds it, and forces proximity. There is no safe distance, no ability to bracket it in that its agents are legion and reflected in the troubling persona of the artist beyond what the social world intends. There is a distinction here with respect to the image by means of which violence is understood and performed. For gangsta rap, as I understand it, the image is the crazed, antisocial human operating at the margins of society; but with horrorcore I am pointing to a differently arranged presence—the type of existence in line with Gravedigger's self-description on "Flatline": "I'm not a human being; I'm a walking poltergeist."[11] These zombic artists envision the world of death in a particular manner—a way that can't be easily explained away or absorbed by the narrative of white life, and such is the terror for whiteness. This is the point: death in this context eludes rationality; it escapes the social structures of behavior meant to serve as boundaries between death and life.

Zombies are unleashed on the world. As the Flatlinerz offer by way of warning, "Run, run, run for your life; Flatlinerz coming to kill in the night."[12] What is to be made of a graphic alternative—one that highlights death but disrupts certain dimensions of death according to the social world's normative tale? Whiteness projects Blacks as the embodiment of death, a lifeless "something" that takes life and produces death. And the taking on of the zombie persona by hip hop artists might be said to avoid a denial of death through a death that renders life a mode of thanatology. This is the consumption of life by death, making the two indistinguishable through the act of taking—or, better yet, in this case, through zombic hunger. As one line goes, "turnin' niggas into zombies."[13] In videos for the Gravediggaz, whose line this is, sometimes faces are painted and in this way push against an aesthetic defined as resembling the "human," and this provides some distinction regarding the embodiment of death—an openness to behave outside the grammar of societal moral and ethical codes.[14] The tools for destruction, for death, might be the same as those found in gangsta rap (although more commonly they go without detailed description), but the meaning isn't the same. Rather than the consequence of the marginalized seeking retribution (e.g., wealth and status), death with the zombie *is* the nature and purpose of existence. When the narrative of whiteness is unchallenged, Blacks are the wildness of death tamed. As the agent of death, however, the zombic artist marks a different perception—the inability to bracket death.

Scholars such as Charis Kubrin seem to suggest rap speaks to and about a cultural code, a mood of sorts shaping a collective ethos of conduct and perception that varies from a more normative stance or arrangement of life.[15] Here's where I think the discussion of zombic death fosters a difference. The ontology of death, the reality of death as layered and already always performed as life, cuts across various lines of cultural demarcation.[16] The connection between death and living, embodiment and the dynamics of death, is consistent. The living dead, the zombie, can be thought of as marking something along the lines of what Lauren Berlant and Lee Edelman label "negativity," which is meant to name "incoherencies and divisions" that disturb the effort to fix identity and that disrupt the pretense of control and autonomy.[17] There are also ways in which this performance of death means what William

Pawlett labels a "structure of difference," which entails a "socially-designated identity position of difference or otherness in relation to another socially-designated position."[18] In this case, the performance—the consuming of death—involves an overdetermination, which obscures any distinction (i.e., boundaries of enactment) between what are considered in normative social terms the dead and the alive. Traditional modality of explanation—the standard grammar of existence—does not rectify this situation. The accepted modeling of ontology fails to fully capture the nature of this encounter.[19] This is more than projection of the "unhuman" in that the grammar of humanity (read whiteness) is out of bounds, nondescriptive in this context because the zombie isn't simply a reconstituting of life as less than life.[20] It involves the uselessness of such considerations because the zombie constitutes nothing that can be so demarcated. Zombies, then, represent a failed geography of distinction—an expanse toxic and marked by the failure of moral and ethical codes to signal order.

While zombies are best known in terms of Haitian Vodou and often used as a cautionary tale against Black independence and personhood, the Western attention to and production of zombies coincides with the creation of modernity's "negroes."[21] Whiteness is a social construct that constructs. The zombie is meant to be a trope supporting the heavy weight of the social world and its various narratives of white superiority, or more generally white life. However, the fiction of the zombie as the safeguard against the death of whiteness is challenged by the very weight of that narrative. Hence, the zombie, it seems, also marks the destruction of whiteness's work—the end of space and time as confinement—as the framework for white life and its ontological tales.

What Zombies Do

While marked with a variety of meanings, the idea of the zombie would capture popular attention and would do so typically in the form of religious practitioners harnessing labor and service by bringing people back from the dead in the form of will-less, agency-denied zombies.[22] While the actuality of such beings is and has been debated, at least as metaphor, the Haitian zombie provided a cautionary tale of cultural chaos, social disorder, economic confusion, and political trauma when Europeans aren't in control: life bleeding into death.[23] The term *zombie* isn't of European origin but is more properly associated with West Africa; from that location it moved, as did African bodies, across the Atlantic Ocean. To the extent zombification marks the emergence of modernity, it has something to do with Europe's reconstitution of

African existence through the process of enslavement. In this manner, as the field of zombie studies tends to recognize, the grammar of the un/dead performed as the zombie has its beginning in the slave trade and the language of slavery—and by extension is often explored in relationship to categories of race and economics.[24]

Borrowing from Orlando Patterson, Afropessimists think of this process of enslavement, its production of Blackness, in relationship to "social death" as an ontological transformation whereby the enslaved (and their descendants) are objects who exist for the benefit of subjects—and this arrangement is in lieu of physical death.[25] According to Frank Wilderson, the enslaved isn't "an oppressed subject, who experiences exploitation and alienation, but . . . an object of accumulation and fungibility (exchangeability)."[26] From this situation two relationships to being are established: whiteness is couched in the language of humanity and expressed through a positive ontology grounding what I call white life, and Blackness (the existence of the enslaved and their descendants) is made to connote a position of anti-ontology, the nonhuman, or what I would reference as death. In other words, the enslaved and their descendants are not recognized through the grammar of identity and agency tied to a narrative of freedom. Rather, they are objects constituted in relationship to an anti-Blackness that holds together the social world and maintains the centrality of whiteness—of a limited and limiting structuring of the human as over against Black existence. This is the nature of "social death" as a position defined by anti-ontology, or what I would call the irrelevance of Blacks as dead.[27] In either case, there is something about Black existence that is captured through death—through a limited movement in the world as mobile substance, but not humans living. Death that names the zombie is given sanction and epistemological force resistant to logic and reason and other modalities of interrogation.[28] All this placed the zombie within the story of enslavement and continued anti-Black mechanisms of collective life in the Americas—that is, in the service of whiteness's privileged logic of life.

By the early twentieth century, stories of zombies had infiltrated the US popular imagination through literature and then movies and, pushing beyond limited religious practices, provided a more general depiction of the un/dead who threaten the very grounding of collective *life*. They are those who, in a word, expose demise and threaten the logic of white life as distinct and bounded against death.[29] Literature spoke of a different mode of existence, one devoid of all the traditional markers of life, and the films projected the possibility of contamination: "They're coming to get you . . . there's one of them now!"[30]

The timing of attention to the zombie in the United States is telling. The push beyond the Caribbean speaks not to a shift in epistemological and ontological considerations regarding the Americas in general and the zombie in particular. Rather, anxiety over an expanded geography, infected by what the zombie represented beyond religious-theological practices, was at best difficult to control and marked a growing awareness of the pervasiveness of death as uncontained and destructive on every level. Blackness posed a "darkening," so to speak, of the social world that threatened the "natural" state of whiteness. And the trope of the zombie served as a satisfying mechanism for indirectly naming and rehearsing this challenge. The "creation" of the zombie comes about through a manipulation of cultural frameworks and language—including the construction of various environments and the nurturing of particular existential conditions—by means of which the status of the victim is altered and the "other" put into clear and terrifying focus as "emptied of being, a receptacle of nothingness, wholly other."[31]

On the heels of a failed effort to colonize Haiti, and as the United States entered the Great Depression, the zombie became in the US imagination a geography of marginalized beings.[32] A sociocultural misstep is tied to economic failure, and so "many Americans were made aware of just how powerless they were in the capitalist system. Identification with zombies, then, may have been particularly resonant in the 1930s United States, as zombies became an ideological critique of modernity. . . . Furthermore, the depression exacerbated racial tensions, and stereotypes of people of color thrived. . . . They became the monsters, so to speak."[33] The zombie marked, then, both the presence of death as physical demise and also a loss of meaning or irrelevance as an even greater threat to the logic holding together the social world and the significance of whiteness it is meant to safeguard. As this need to maintain a narrative of meaning increased, the aesthetic and aim of the zombie shifted: more gruesome, more evidence of physical decay, and a growing hunger for human flesh. Zombies decay, but only to a point. They are residue, or what remains when humanity isn't present—an animated void of a kind when markers of robust meaning aren't possible. As writers have noted, the metaphorical significance of the zombie can't be overstated in that "the true horror in these movies lies in the prospect of Westerners becoming dominated, subjugated, symbolically raped, and effectively 'colonized' by pagan representations."[34] In this way one might say there is a fluidity of representation marking the zombie tied to various cultural connotations and expressed in relationship to various modalities of ritual enactment—religion, politics, economics, sociality, and so on—impinging, shifting, changing, and reflecting the challenge to the distinction between life and death.

To call zombies "Americans," or "citizens," would be to lose sight of their significance and to misname a trope. The un/dead wandering the earth often functions as a trope meant to reflect problematic socioeconomic and political arrangements (i.e., neoliberalism) of a collective life gone wrong—the manner in which systems of production and display are so troubled and troubling as to remove a full sense of humanity.[35] For example, as the United States struggled with social justice during the twentieth century, zombie depictions took a turn with the work of George Romero, whose film *Night of the Living Dead* (1968) was meant to wrestle with issues of capitalism and racial injustice.[36] The zombie, at times a slow-moving and flesh-eating creature, stood for a variety of marginalized populations and, through its destruction of social arrangements and boundaries, spoke an unspoken word against socioeconomic and political constructs (e.g., ethical and moral stipulations) that shaped and consumed and left in their wake only a fraction of the being that once was. As Sarah Juliet Lauro makes clear, there is a link between the nineteenth-century and twentieth-century presentations of the zombie, a binding together based on a shared logic of opposition. In other words, if the zombie of twentieth- and twenty-first-century cinema can be said to be "about" capitalism, this is only because the much longer-lived zombie myth that the film industry attempts to absorb is "about" colonialism. And the zombie myth is not just concerned with the disempowerment of the colonial subject but equally the dialectical exchanges between masters and slaves, between the colonized and the colonizer; and as such it is also about the cultural powers of the entirely real domain of the imaginary, as retained even by those who are described as socially dead.[37] Related to this, "Romero's films," writes David Pagano, "involve the . . . paradox that the world must end in order for there to be any future for the world."[38] Where I differ is not with the apocalyptic tone, but rather the sense of future within Pagano's comment. I suggest instead that the threat of the zombie is the perceived enveloping of the world ended—the end of the world as final and with it the end of the logic securing white life: "There's no escape, there's nowhere to run."[39] Some are left behind, not consumed by death, and what remains is only the possibility of a grammar of death—a descriptive process incapable of including life. What remains is "nothing" in a certain sense: "Nothing will brace you, nothing prepares; for all the pain that might be out there; Life is but a dream, no, it's a nightmare."[40] In short, it is the end of future because the zombie consumes the logic of life (as a distinct and "safe" reality), thereby exposing the hidden meaning of *deathlife*.

Various scholars in zombie studies have noted the zombie as troubling the category of being to the degree the zombie is both human and not human, but I want to take that further: the formula of white supremacy mutated the condition of the African and transformed "it" into an irrelevant reality—hence the zombie marked out as a cautionary tale the "place" and movement of death.[41] The zombie's presence poses a threat (perceived ontologically through whiteness) in the form of a question: "Is there the possibility that [whites] could be absent from [themselves], that [they] could look into the body and find only an absence?"[42] Such a question "is ontologically terrifying because it denies humans that which makes us human . . . a physical body occupied by nothingness—a human shell lacking whatever properties are presumed to constitute self to our consciousness."[43] In effect, one might say the zombie presence is an apocalypse necessary for the (dis)ordering of the United States around the logic of whiteness and its demands regarding the nature and meaning of (white) life.[44]

Death shapes the "American imagination" and comes to define the structuring of what constitutes life and, by extension, what must be bracketed off—with Blacks as a prime example of the uncertain Other who threatens. Or, one might say, "Black death [is a] predictable and constitutive aspect of democracy."[45] Whether a critique of collective infrastructure or a cautionary tale against the loss of the Western way of life, the zombie is saturated with death. It is overdetermined with respect to its connection to death by being death; but the form in which this is communicated varies over time and depending on context. What is more, Blackness as death is a complex epistemological and ontological determination constitutive of the world. Christina Sharpe theorizes this embodied practice of Blackness (i.e., death) as the "wake" involving the continuing disruptive nature of a past that isn't subdued, controlled, or ended but instead "produces death and trauma."[46] This, I would add, isn't just the negation of ontology by means of which the structuring of demise still requires and utilizes the grammar of ontology in reverse. No, what I propose through the zombie is an analytic by means of which I want to emphasize a state not describable adequately using this grammar of ontology as such (the effort to use this grammar serves only to reinforce the problem)—i.e., anti-ontology. Rather, it is a state outside ontology in that it entails death (i.e., nonbeing) and life (i.e., being) at the same time—and as such it doesn't allow for the type of "boundary between" I perceive as present in the ontology/non-ontology dichotomy.[47] So, I seek to further clarify the lack of coherence through the category of *irrelevance* as the inability to read or measure Blackness through a sliding scale of ontologies.[48] In other words, what if Blackness is equated with death and life—over against the objections of whites? The logic of whiteness is troubled by this disruption and actively seeks to destroy through a quarantine of Blackness as object for use. The zombie is both a marker of physical death and a symbol of irrelevance that marches toward the contamination of human life through both modes of death. Whether called a "symbol," a "metaphor," or some other abstraction, the zombie speaks about and from death and in this way already and always forces confrontation with the reach of death into life.[49] They are dangerous entities regarding whom the grammar of (white) life is inappropriate, and they are entities of destruction without the social boundaries produced by storied ethical and moral obligation. While death is present in the various depictions of the zombie, Kevin Boon has argued that the zombie is a flexible symbol in that depictions change over time and in light of cultural need, at times even contradicting or competing with the optics and "staging" with earlier framings of the symbol—offering a variety of messages concerning the nature and meaning of life and death.[50]

The zombie is a particular blurring of Blackness and whiteness in that it is an existence marked and recognized only to the extent it spreads death and entails a profound threat against white life as a form of safety.[51] This is death that can't be bracketed or captured by traditional moral-ethical discourses of contact and conduct. It eludes a sense of death as distinct and "personal" in that it maintains the unpredictability, the inconceivable consumption of embodied life. This is the source of ontological paranoia to the extent death by zombie involves excess of death—death by the dead exposing the lie of distinct life. This is death beyond what the system needs to preserve itself and its logic. It is indiscriminate, wild, without remorse and without apparent narrative of acceptable purpose. Encountering the zombie is not to risk death from a distance, but to have life consumed by death. In this way, zombies prompt catastrophic anxiety in that the presentation of death raises questions concerning the inevitability of death, which forces whites to think death when their privilege of whiteness is meant to safeguard from that need.[52] In a word, zombies are created to offer a narrative of life over against death—to name and position "the" threat against the social world. However, in so doing, the zombie points out the illusion of distinction, exposing the lie of boundaries between life and death because it makes apparent the hidden nature of *deathlife*. Once "created," the zombie can't be controlled. In a sense, the zombie kills not other zombies but also whites (i.e., those assumed by the social world to be alive), and it seeks to do so until there are no more, until the world ends.

I want to think about killing, murder, demise as a mode of infection, and by this I mean to name the manner in which death is spread as social disorganization, or to borrow, again, from Berlant and Edelman, a "negativity" that disrupts a fixed and total identity through the specter of death.[53] There isn't the possibility of a fix, of a boundary that walls off discomfort and demise—there is only the ongoing specter of death. From 1619 moving forward, the fear has been that zombies might kill—the not fully alive enslaved and free Africans might not simply be death; they might cause death. The zombie is a "sticky" metaphor, or one might call it a fundamental curse "that follows the oppressor home"—if one reads the "oppressor" as being the protectors of whiteness deployed to attempt a short-circuiting of death.[54] This is not simply a metaphor for chaos, although it is certainly that; rather, it is also literal death and demise of meaning by way of which both physical end and irrelevance are a threat to the population charged with avoiding death/the dead. They might become like the zombie and lose their whiteness as a marker of life. It is the "bleeding edges," as Sharon Holland describes the penetrating nature of the dead that is feared.[55]

One might say, along with Jane Anna Gordon and Lewis Gordon, the zombie constitutes a dilemma, self-made but terrifying nonetheless. The zombie in this way isn't a closed system but rather reflects its creator (i.e., whiteness) and the creator's anxieties regarding death. But rather than understanding zombies as "symptomatic," as Gordon and Gordon describe monsters in their marking out that "something has gone wrong," I would suggest the zombie constitutes despised potentiality—that is to say, something can or will go wrong.[56] To put it more explicitly, death will happen and relevance (life) isn't identical to whiteness. The terror in part rests in the fact that, just as the zombies continue to impinge upon space, this questioning or exposing of death continues. Whites shouldn't think of escape from this metaphysical dilemma as tied to the destruction of zombies. They can't be destroyed in this way in that whiteness will continue to need Blacks in an effort to keep its organizational logic intact. And it will continue to project Blacks in such a way as to justify the violent restrictions demanded by whiteness. The zombie can't be scapegoated.[57] Ending a zombie does nothing to end the terror; it does nothing to bracket off and confine death; and it doesn't safeguard whiteness against its enemies. No appeal can be made to zombies, and by extension whiteness can't justify the production of zombies without exposing its shortcomings. Traditional grammars of exchange and organization of energy fail to the extent Blacks (because of Blackness) can't be incorporated into the schema. This status is tied to a narrative of dangerous difference whereby the language of human community, of values, of citizenry does not apply—and therefore can't be used to establish a robust sense of life for Blacks.[58]

One might call Blackness a type of "undoing."[59] With the modifications I suggest above, as Calvin Warren notes, "The boundaries of the human are shored-up by this antagonism and without it, the human, and the world within which it lives, would cease to exist," so "the non-ontology of blackness [what I have labeled anti-ontology, or would call the irrelevance of Blackness] secures the boundaries of the human; it delimits the coordinates of the human."[60] In a certain sense, one might say, to borrow from Frank Wilderson, "From the incoherence of Black death, America generates the coherence of white life."[61] Even the depiction of the aesthetic of zombification gathered from film speaks to this incoherent destruction. The zombie so depicted typically is not without the destruction of flesh—decaying flesh, oozing openings, pieces of skin and muscle ripped off. One might view this in relationship to the destruction of flesh, noted by Hortense Spillers as the mutilation of the markers of meaning, which leaves only the body manipulated by anti-Blackness—what others might call the corpse, or what I reference as the zombie.[62] Despite the difference in the technology used to do it, think of Spillers's description of this flesh ripped away and do so in relationship to the zombies as I've described them and, perhaps, as you've seen in movies and on television: "The anatomical specifications of rupture, of altered human tissue, take on the objective description of laboratory prose—eyes beaten out, arms, backs, skulls branded, a left jaw, a right ankle, punctured; teeth missing, as the calculated work of iron, whips, chains, knives, the canine patrol, the bullet."[63] The decaying of flesh through a mysterious process without proper genealogical narrative produces, on one hand, a body fit for extreme labor and other modes of abuse; on the other, it produces the body as the dead/undead who both represent and produce the terror of demise. In either case Blackness is, to borrow from Saidiya Hartman, projected as "abject, threatening, servile, dangerous, dependent, irrational, and infectious."[64] What is left is body—the form, the container, metaphor, or marker of death performed. The zombie is without flesh to the extent it is without meaning—cannot be read through a grammar of significance—or perhaps what Brotha Lynch Hung applies when saying "somethin' 'bout the brain is aimless."[65] This body, then, "has no corporeal integrity. . . . [I]t has no depth, no repressed wish to be revealed or decoded. In a way the zombie body is not a sign, but rather a sticky surface that signs cling to."[66] One might call the zombie a cipher or a containerlike trope.

This is how whiteness imagines it and how the logic of the social world needs it.[67] The zombie is meant to be a receptacle holding the anxiety of whiteness, all that whiteness can't bear and also maintain its perception of humanity.[68] While the zombie represents (white) necessity, it also constitutes a threat to the logic of utility, or the production of Blackness without relevance but instead with the function of an object.

Attempting to think with Spillers, it is the flesh we see falling away, decaying, rendered putrid and disgusting. Instead of the enslaver or other forms of anti-Blackness tearing at it, death dismantles it, pulls at it, discolors it, and renders it nauseating. This flesh, this "primary narrative," as Spillers calls it, falls away, littering the philosophical and physical geography of space or engagement with death. It trails away (a trail followed by whiteness), and with it that which might suggest a substance to this "container"—a meaning to this form beyond the work it does for/against whiteness. The decay—broadly considered—or the compromised state of fixity speaks to the assumed (but false) distinction between geography of death and the human as alive. In either case, whether Spillers's destruction of flesh (i.e., "primary narrative") or zombification, the intention is this: meaning and agency are destroyed, and what is left is a capsule of otherness.[69]

The flesh is forgotten: Who knows how the zombie has come about? In response to this question, one might say that the zombie "doesn't generate historical categories of entitlement, sovereignty"; that is to say, they "are 'off the map' with respect to the cartography that charts civil society's semiotics," and so, the zombie has "a past, but not a heritage."[70] The zombie is made as such—as porous, degraded stuff, oddly serving as a somewhat safe receptacle for death, but only if it can be so named and confined. Tim Lanzendörfer argues that the function of the zombie is less significant as metaphor, and what is more important is "the worlds it enables."[71] I twist this a bit and instead highlight the manner in which the zombie signifies the capacity to destroy worlds and, in this way, heighten the sense of an "end" to (white) life. The process of this creation is hidden (if not forgotten) of necessity. It must come across as natural; the zombie must "just happen" without clear antecedents, and the terror it produces must be such that it overcomes any sustainable effort toward construction and purpose. They are present by negation; they matter through function. The narrative of irrelevance manifest in the zombie is too "fantastic," too bizarre, and too unreal to carry logical interrogation.[72] The utility of the zombie is pure threat, pure warning, and pure caution: stay at the ready against Blackness (that is, irrelevance and physical death). Warren, Spillers, and others speak in terms of responses to Blackness (e.g., torture, punishment, rape, and so on). Do such approaches to pain work on zombies?

The zombie isn't necessarily real in a historical sense; but it has "substance" if one considers the influence and impact of the zombie as a tragic trope—as a cipher by means of which physical death and anxiety over irrelevance are played out. The zombie represents death as an attachment, as a strangling device that ever threatens demise because "attack seems already past and always impending, always . . . behind and in front of you, marking an expansive temporal horizon of violence and terror."[73] The zombie occasions demise without falling victim to it. It brings punishment to which it isn't accountable or vulnerable. This is a state of suspension—a condition marked by a moral and ethical void that means only death as life / life as death. Perhaps this is in part the fear for whites: the zombie as constructed doesn't fall victim to the usual strategies of confinement. What must be taken from them is the thing the social narrative denies them: a functioning reasonableness associated with the human mind. For example, according to popularized cultural narratives, a bullet to the head stops a zombie, but this isn't the destruction of its center of reason ("I think, therefore I am," for instance), but more along the lines of turning off a "motor" for locomotion.

The zombie has the potential to destroy whiteness and the social world housing it, without whites having recourse to the standard practices of containment. Zombies destroy both the social world and any system by way of which meaning can be assessed and the distinctive quality of the human gauged. The zombie functions outside the grammar of world-building; it moves without concern for the history of personhood and any markers of meaning so sacred to whiteness. It is mobilized disregard, destruction without will or insight. The zombie exists outside the structure of accord that marks the boundaries of the world. The zombie has only a shadow, a glimmer, of familiarity that quickly falls away. The production of equipment for the performance of death is dangerous business because it exposes something about the whites doing the making: Why the need for this object of annihilation? What is the weakness of whites and their whiteness that demands this display of death?

Horrorcore and Eating Life

"Zombie runs" and "zombie walks," so popular in recent years, may seek to signify the terror, to mitigate the exposure to death by taming the contact.[74] However, they serve really to perform a preoccupation with death that can't be subdued. In the words of the hip hop group Flatlinerz, "It's a good day to die, today's your day."[75]

David McNally speaks of "zombie music" as a way of naming an expressive struggle against the racist structure of collective life. In other words, "As new practices and cultures of resistance formed," McNally asserts, "music became a key register for expressing discontent with racism, menial jobs, unemployment, poor wages, and military inscription."[76] Highlighting the compositions of Thelonious Monk, whose music was called "zombie music" because it reminded some other musicians of what one might hear in a horror film, McNally describes a particular formulation of this protest music similarly as "zombie music." For McNally what matters isn't so much the particular association with the sound of horror film scores, but rather the manner in which jazz "kills" music in order to reconstitute it. This creative reconstituting of music—by dismantling the grammar and vocabulary of early musical formats—gives jazz a zombie quality, or "rhythms of zombie rebellion" and "the ferocious sounds of the dance of the living dead."[77] This aspect of jazz gets read as a push against dehumanization tied to anti-Black racism. And so "the living dead come to life, dance across a landscape of corpses and ruin, and affirm the irreducible beauty of their freedom song."[78] I agree with McNally that something of the nature and meaning of the zombie is expressed through the cadence and content of music. However, rather than pointing in the direction of transformation, against the idea that this music speaks a strike for the humanity of a despised population, I argue hip hop, in this case, demonstrates the sound of the zombie. Hip hop provides a view into the eternal workings of death without escape into life. If W. E. B. Du Bois's notion of the "Veil" were applied, hip hop would be that which shows the dimension of *deathlife* hidden from whites in their social world.[79]

The creative impulse stemming from and really constituting whiteness involves construction of a narrative that refuses a distinction between the social code of Blackness and Black people. Both constitute death simply performed in two modes. Again, the zombie becomes a metaphor, a cipher for this conflation. From this vantage point death's movement marks rejection of the boundaries that whiteness seeks to impose. One can draw something of this perception in a verse by Gangsta Boo:

> Bloody bodies in the yard like a zombie apocalypse
> The Walking Dead I'm so so scared
> And I don't know how to get up out this bitch
> as I creep these ghetto streets looking for a feast.[80]

Extend the geography of performance, and one finds with Esham something along the lines of this dynamic of profound alteration—a change to circumstances and perception generated by hip hop:

> Here comes the voodoo
> What you going to do when my crew
> Back from the dead once more again
> Fucking up the flow again
> Fuck it here we go again.[81]

The zombification of Blacks is an epistemological fantasy projected out and driven by a structural necessity: the preservation of whiteness and its social world. What if zombified Blacks become active within this fantasy, spilling outside the boundaries of secure Blackness and outside the hidden intent of their creation? There are modalities of hip hop offering an answer to that question.[82] Think, for example, in terms of horrorcore and the manner in which it rehearses death bringing death—and in this process exposes the construction and the "end" of life performed against life (i.e., rejection of death).[83]

According to some accounts, this subgenre of rap music is first mentioned in the early 1990s and involves an intensification of gangsta rap and its graphic depiction of violence and death.[84] It, in this sense, is a language describing the undead in amoral and de/ethical movement.[85] Or, as Tech N9ne proclaims on "Misery" (2007), "This is merciless; this is musical massacre." Horrorcore speaks a moment of total demise. The Flatlinerz present this relationship when in their hands the microphone becomes a means of movement bringing together life and death. In their words, "My mic is the passageway to the land of the living; unforgiving and the realm of death."[86] Here, the primary concern is the visibility of the signified, the presentation of the metaphor vis-à-vis linguistic performance, and in this way death travels through articulation and demonstration, making it the same as life. In the thanatological narratives of horrorcore, the zombie is meant to introduce violence and destruction as a performance of the social world's total annihilation. Safety isn't available. As Tech N9ne remarks,

> I'm your worst fear, I'm your favorite . . .
> You cannot escape me, I'm your last resort.[87]

The zombie is a no-body in that there is little need to distinguish, to mark as different, various presentations of the zombie. In a sense, they are all the same. They are known only through their acting or performance. And they aren't considered subjects as such but mobile objects of death—with only the ability to destroy and defect. Turning again to Tech N9ne, one gets a sense of this mayhem:

> Wake this hatred and make this place get apeshit!
> No kinda way you stopping this
> Flow gonna make apocalypse
> Power's stop lots of mocking shit
> Lot of us often is blocking this, optimist
> Positive, hope for the future's loss of awesomeness.[88]

The zombie is overdetermined by death so as to be only death because the body is unable to bracket death, to step aside, rendering it a some/thing rather than human. In this state, it is without sensitivity or adherence to codes (either by embrace or by explicit subversion) that structure thought and activity with the social world. The *un* in *undead* for the zombie re-fers to locomotion, which is movement, continuation, persistence of death threatening to expose the lie about life. The zombie displays in this regard an economy of devastation by means of which no element of being is spared. Rap speaks this status in a graphic manner when one considers, for example, Brotha Lynch Hung's "MDK" (2013):

> And I got bodies in the trunk, some of that cayenne pepper
> Midnight just passed, better keep your eyes on Lector
> I'm hidin' in your closet with a machete and trash bags
> Spaghetti your insides, get ready, I been died
> Dead like a zombie.[89]

The zombie's "work" is death. "I kill and massacre and burn away all the body flesh," as the Flatlinerz describe the purpose of their existence.[90] In this way, the zombie signifies more than "the space between symbolic death (the decay of meaning in one's life) and physical death."[91] Instead, the zombie means something more crushing than that, more than a decrease or decline in personal significance and weight in the world. The zombie is death and the barrier of death—the end of all that defines life. It threatens (through a type of exposure therapy) the safeguarded boundaries, the logic, the as-sumed necessity of the social world and its rules. For example, on Brotha Lynch Hung's track titled "Return of Da Baby Killa" (1995), without a sense of remorse, without distance from the act, he becomes death consuming the most vulnerable and presenting the body as indistinguishable from "meat":

As I creep, picture every human that I see
Slabs of human meat cause my kids gotta eat
I lives kinda deep, dark, up in the cut . . .

Nigga, what? You ain't even seen me in my prime
Eatin' baby brains, baby veins, baby spines
I know they be cryin' when I'm cuttin' off the neck.

As Lanzendörfer writes, "In almost all instances, the zombie is a monster of the apocalypse. . . . The zombie then, is a form, one that requires the destruction of the world that is and the imagination of a world to come."[92] The world to come, I would add, is simply emptiness in that the structuring of life over against death is lost. The very construction of the zombie holds within itself the possible destruction of the (white) world in that the zombie (i.e., the irrelevant "derelict object") seeks to devour white flesh (i.e., the alive "liminal subject").[93] It seeks to consume the logic of life (i.e., the "prime narrative") by focusing death on those perceived to be alive. Such denies the distinction between life and death, in that "bodies without flesh, without the narratives of life, movement, and futurity that the flesh presents to the world, cannot be said really to exist at all—they are specters of ontology, socially dead bodies, stripped of flesh and existence." This is undifferentiated death—an irrelevance that can't be explained using the traditional grammar of life in that it is the very negation of such life, such relevance.[94] Or, in the words of Zigg Zagg, "This time the inside of me is empty, outside I look like the Devil."[95]

While not speaking in terms of zombies, there are ways in which Calvin Warren addresses the larger concern of world-ending as it relates to irrelevance. He writes, "Pressing the ontological question presents terror—the terror that ontological security is gone, the terror that ethical claims no longer have an anchor, and the terror of inhabiting existence outside the precincts of humanity and its humanism."[96] Yet he turns to "spirit" as a resolution, as an effort to think beyond the human, post–end of the world.[97] With regard to the work of the zombie, I simply want to linger over the end of the world without offering an alternative—that is, a "period after" as "spiritual practice"—or attempting to think the end within the grammar of life.[98] Instead, I want to think about the end through the grammar and vocabulary of death. Esham, after recounting his performance of violence, gets to this point:

Plus you don't understand
You can't kill a dead man.[99]

The zombie marks a bizarre existence unrecognizable through the grammar of life. It isn't simply that zombies aren't human any longer. No, to say "no longer human" tells us nothing about the placement of the zombie. It is more accurately described as embodied, animated demise. Toxic capitalism and other markers of twenty-first-century society may be the context for zombies, but what they constitute—what the trope is meant to signify and express—isn't captured by simply pointing to these material mechanisms. For some within zombie studies, there is the possibility of renewal even within this narrative of demise. For instance, Steven Pokornowski hopes "recalibrating the ways we imagine monstrosity, alterity, and violence in popular cultural texts, like zombie narratives, will help facilitate a shift in the way imaginations are policed, and violence justified. Zombie fictions need to recognize race and racial history, and show us not how the exceptional man survives, but how when some life is made vulnerable, all life is put in danger."[100] In making this statement, Pokornowski fails to recognize sufficiently the degree to which the social world depends on the production and performance of zombies, even as these zombies threaten it. The illusion is this: the social world—through the delusion of white privilege—assumes that the zombie can be controlled. The configuration of the world (e.g., the social world), then, is intended to present boundaries against physical death by means of which it is contained and managed as well as metaphysical structuring of whites so as to safeguard ontological identity over against irrelevance.

What is done to the zombie, by consequence of its condition, from the vantage point of whiteness doesn't constitute violence per se in that violence at its extreme is meant to produce death; what, then, is action against the embodiment of death? What whiteness fails to grasp is how, by extension, the activity of the zombie—because of its existence outside the moral and ethical frameworks of the human—can't be judged by those rules of engagement. Again, violence is to end the living by the living; it is human impulse fulfilled against life. Whiteness produced the contagion. It produced the zombie, again, as an ontological necessity—a buttress if not foundation for the social world, or a point of pedagogy, a way of saying: "Play by the rules or this can happen to you."

The zombie is a substance without *substance* measurable using the rubrics of the living. Talk of the undead, the living dead, or zombies nullifies the logic of certain linguistic codes of life (e.g., independence, agency, revolution), a grammar sparking conceptions of political and social life as structured. In some cases, authors seek to humanize, as it were, the zombie by reading it using a human vocabulary of freedom, liberation, rebellion, and other conceptual and practical markers of personhood. But to do so is to miss the point: the zombie is without agency, without an ethical and moral framework and without the metaphysical grounding necessary for such historically situated mechanisms of communal life and personal space. The goal of the zombie is death through a consumption of life, or as Brotha Lynch Hung says in "Look It's a Dead Body" (2011),

> Look it's a dead body over here
> Blood all over the place like motor steel
> Niggas ain't fucking with Lynch
> You know the deal
> I eat 'em when I am done with 'em, nigga
> That's overkill.[101]

Zombies gather, according to popular depictions, but this is without any intentional mapping of relationship. Zombies simply share space, but this doesn't constitute the forming of community. The zombie is the metaphysical counterpoint: in constructing the human, the counterpoint is also developed to safeguard the distinctive and vital nature of the human as ontologically relevant and, through its technological advances, as master of death. This, in part, is, to borrow from Lauro, "the psychic load" placed on the zombie—the "figural tool wielded by those who would make it signify what they would."[102]

Films and stories depicting whites as falling victim to zombification speak to the same concern (the loss of whiteness over against Blackness), with the imposition of death outside its "natural" borders and boundaries as a means of containment. The threat of death is ever present and can consume whites.[103] The trope of the zombie through which horrorcore is filtered is a complex signifier, and performance of/as death in this context has a mystical quality—an ecstatic-like experience that brings into the material realm a certain contact with, connection to, more metaphysical considerations. It is a performance that points beyond the performance to more fundamental, more awful considerations. Although speaking regarding how a zombie's observation is similar to technological "information mining," Christopher Flavin captures some of what I have in mind when saying, "The ceaseless observation of the living by the dead and the unblinking assessment and interpolation it suggests . . . gives the zombie its power to horrify and fascinate. . . . The living must watch themselves as closely as they watch the dead, and as closely as they are watched by the dead."[104] The activity of the zombie isn't about utilized intake, but rather mere destruction, demise, death—an unending ending, which is also a beginning.[105] The zombie doesn't subdue death, doesn't outsmart and avoid it. The zombie, instead, is death and poses contamination by death that destroys the illusion of life as safeguarded. In "MDK," Brotha Lynch Hung expresses the kind of perpetual "hunger" this entails:

> Murder, death, kill, we hungry
> Murder, death, kill, we hungry.[106]

Rehearsal of the zombie, the ongoing projection of the zombie as a societal trope of dangerous difference qua death, entails something of a thanatology exercise meant to produce vigorous protection of ontology against the Black threat—the dead Black body that threatens the life of whiteness. Even when the Hollywood zombies are white, there is an "unnatural" nature to death, and typically there is a way around, a hope against, demise. In this case physical death by means of zombies won't impact most, but their very existence keeps "alive," so to speak, the threat of irrelevance. What zombie fighters (e.g., white supremacists) seek, it seems, is really metaphysics by means of which to resist the slow push toward ontological demise. Yet the zombie persists and its numbers grow in direct relationship to the narratives of anxiety meant to manage death through them.[107] In a sense white culture is contiguous with the manufacturing of zombies.[108]

This in part is the terror, the already and always nature of the end, or as Zigg Zagg puts it, "Night after night, I had another thought of destruction."[109] The activity of the zombie is destructive in a fundamental sense: it consumes the social world from within and without. After all, even in the movies, a majority of the zombies pursue but do not overtake humans. Instead, viewers are left to ponder the possibility of loss. In other words, the threat of disruption—of an unrecoverable loss of being, or of the end of the world—is sufficient. The eating of humans (i.e., the living), by extension, need not be overthought in order to understand the significance of their menace, although consumption of human flesh as a marker of demise is evident in rap. Take, for example, Gangsta NIP, whose "Horror Movie Rap" (1992) contains these lines:

> A tisket, a tasket, a bloody, bloody basket
> Cut his head and ate his leg, now he's in a casket.

To kill is the destruction of life and the world it inhabits, not the securing of social rewards and other material markers of meaning. Put another way, as the Gravediggaz proclaim, "I chew and attack; like Crest on plaque; after that, your world is black; you drop into a hole."[110] The zombie in hip hop points out fearful realities: physical death is inevitable and it changes the texture and content of the human form. That is, it destroys the integrity and perceived boundaries of the human form. In addition, it points to the deceptive nature of irrelevance by turning to the problematic composition and function of memory. It links physical demise and irrelevance through the decaying body and the decay of memory. The destruction of the human form in the lyrical content of zombic hip hop only serves to render this dual process poetic.[111]

Whereas Afropessimism tends to critique approaches to Black freedom because of the essential nature of anti-Blackness, there remains a sense in which the sentient Black wants a difference, wants more; my argument is the zombie doesn't involve this dimension of reflection. The zombie destroys. And more important than speculation on what the zombified figure might want is the manner in which the zombie speaks to what whites can't have. To attempt to change the zombie—whether the "living" dead, a mutated humanity that can be redeemed through scientific innovation, or some other form—is to question the structuring of life that produced it in the first place. On this point, listen to Tech N9ne:

> Life designed you
> To try and blind you
> From that Boogieman.[112]

In a similar vein, Gordon and Gordon describe "postmodern monsters" that "force those around them to imagine predicaments in which meaningful social worlds were destroyed by creatures that function as mere mechanism."[113] Still, they suggest that the type of nihilistic vision represented by the march of zombies isn't the last word. As they see it, "Monsters always mean that there is something that the human community can do, that things have not gone too far."[114] I am not persuaded: the nihilism, irrelevance, and the end of the world all persist. Afropessimism, for instance, short-circuits any quick movement in similarly ontological circumstances to the possibility of resolution; it highlights instead the urge toward total destruction beyond dominant moral and ethical sensibilities (beyond a grammar of "right" and "wrong" sanctioned by current rules of communal relationships)—or even the "death of values, including the values of knowledge."[115] The resolution, in fact, might entail no world capable of supporting (white) life.

> If you come with me then I can show you;
> Where we'll take you, where you dare not go to;
> Follow me and let me mind control you;
> We'll rebuild this world that will destroy you.[116]

Going back to the zombies of hip hop, the resolution involves destroying markers of whiteness, and this requires the end of the known social world. It is the plausibility and the optics of such an end that the horde of zombies, the hip hop horde of zombies, represents. Again, one might think of the zombie as representing the possibility of destroying death's assumed distinctiveness. This is accomplished by ripping apart the social world supporting whiteness without using the ground rules established by that social world, in particular, the moral and ethical framework and language defined by white privilege and a sense of hope meant to preserve the structuring of life. The zombie in action expresses an indiscriminate effort to destroy whiteness and the life it seeks to name and preserve.

Wilderson's argument works here. When discussing a way to end Black suffering (do zombies suffer?), he notes that only the end of the world can produce this result: "The Human need to be liberated *in* the world is not the same as the Black need to be liberated *from* the world; which is why even their most radical cognitive maps draw borders between the living and the dead."[117] To rethink or reconstitute the zombie "otherwise" is to welcome death, and (white) life can't accommodate such a move and maintain its assumed distinctiveness. The illusion of (white) life as bracketed off from death is broken. As the Gravediggaz make clear, "Walking in the shadows you realize; that life is nothing but a form of animated death."[118] The zombie performs the human's undoing by pointing out the unlikely nature of the human, to the extent that the "'human' is a repository of violent practices and technologies that has crystalized over time."[119] That is to say, the human (read white) is constituted through and dependent on violence against the Other constructed as Black—in the extreme as a zombie. However, herein is the distinction between the zombie and the human: while both are constructed through a network of violence, the former is configured as the embodiment of death acted out, and the latter is configured over against death. The zombie is both the source of contagion and a contagion. Structuring of Blackness within the social world marks it a contagion; indeed, the zombie also works to destroy not simply through its "consumption" of bodies but also through the contagion (e.g., hip hop) it unleashes on the world.

The destructive, or poetic, quality of hip hop, by means of which language is subverted and made to function against social interests, is taken to the extreme. Language, if one takes also the sound of language, is a trail marking out the dynamics of a Blackness operating to both destroy and safeguard the world. "The zombie's status as undead—immortal in its mortality—exists in its being as sign," write Edward Comentale and Aaron Jaffe when reflecting on the nature and meaning of the zombie, "but only as it wreaks havoc on signifi-cation. Its weird temporality—the ideality of its repeatable form at odds with its corrupt moment-to-moment becoming—mirrors as it mocks the sign as such."[120] The zombie is said to be without language but is sound transformed and embodied. It is sound against sound, sound not guided by or pulled into moral and ethical frameworks of recognized description. This is accurate but not entirely true. The zombie horde doesn't have language, if what is meant is a grammar and vocabulary that harness and express experience in line with whiteness, by which is meant white ways of being. But it has language, if what one means is a poetic expression that makes visible the nature and meaning of death imposed and the lie of life exposed. This language, then, is hip hop. The "sixteen bars" are the sonic reach of these zombic artists that pushes and causes the panic. To the extent the moral and ethical markers of white life do not apply to them, their narration is that much more startling as it exposes what is meant to remain hidden. In so doing it threatens the end not by means of unrecognized action (i.e., whites "eat," whites kill, and whites move), but through shifting the focus, aim, and target of such activities and thereby rendering them a threat to the stability of whiteness and the social world.[121] As Insane Poetry frames this performance, "We live to die."[122]

The work of whiteness brings about its own demise, and irrelevance is wed to white ontological significance: it is the significance that dis/regard produces. Hence, there is something about it that is (in)significant to the ex-tent it depends on narrative illusion. What whites come to find is this: once created, zombies are hard to control. Zombies kill, and in so doing they ex-pose the lie of whiteness because they kill without moral and ethical denial. How does one "kill" death without exposing something about the category of life? Such a dilemma speaks to the potential end of the world that the zombie horde—or what the group Insane Poetry might call "stalkin' with the nightbreed"—represents.[123] One gets a sense of this impending destruc-tion when reflecting on the mayhem that Gangsta Boo says she will unleash: "There is no tomorrow, Armageddon is gettin' closer."[124] Another way to con-ceive this ultimate destruction is to linger over the substantive markers of this social world. The omnipresence of death and its performance through the zombie can be conveyed in the form of a question: "When the living are now the undead, does anything like society survive?"[125]

TWO TYPES OF MELANCHOLIA

A question remains to be addressed before closing out this book: How does one conceptualize the acknowledgment of (or perhaps response to) *deathlife* suggested by the hip hop artists discussed in these pages?

To explore (but not ultimately answer) the question, this epilogue presents two modes of melancholia. The first, theologically inflected melancholia, is presented as a standard approach out of line with what this book highlights. For context, I provide a few examples of theologized melancholia as a sense of mournfulness over loss projected outside time and space. I argue what some artists offer are modes of sorrow, real and intense, but distinct from what is meant by the second type of melancholia—moralistic melancholia, which is a naming of the "posture," or structuring of awareness associated with *deathlife* as I've theorized and discussed it.[1] Because this structuring of awareness is more tacitly present than explicitly stated, the category of "posture" provides a useful schema for mapping this acknowledgment of *deathlife*. In other words, *posture* provides a method by which to capture the implications of hip hop thanatological narrations by moving from stories to a general naming of and response to the ethos re/presented. Obviously, this is not to suggest that this is the only narrative concerning death or that it is the dominant perspective represented in the corpus of the artists highlighted in the previous chapters; rather, it is present in some of their songs and constitutes an underexplored and underappreciated perspective within hip hop culture, yet one that, in light of our existential circumstances, is worthy of some attention.

One might think of moralistic melancholia as a response to *deathlife* defined by *peristellein*[2]—a kind of consumptive "contracting around" that reduces the utility of ethics of distinction: doing (life) and done (death). This moralistic melancholia—characterized by *peristellein*—involves a type of "harmonious" movement (a balance between as a means of mapping experience) by which the distinctive nature of the elements involved is lost through the determinative (involuntary) nature of the balanced impulse— the "rhythm" produced by both death and life is the same. Through moralistic melancholia, the artists presented do not appeal to a future free of this bond, to a possibility of distinction; so, there is no sense of loss running consistent with the story of whiteness.

Melancholia I: Mourning Death, Celebrating Life

Hip hop is not the first cultural form to wrestle with trauma and anxiety—the difficulties and limits—marking the social world. Still, it does so with a type of appreciable rawness and through paradoxes not so easily found in other forms of cultural production.[3] The angst that produces/conditions certain dimensions of the social world is expressed in graphic form and in ways that shift the meaning and connotation of conventional linguistic signifiers and signs. In this sense, hip hop culture (particularly rap) offers a new language, an alternate grammar and vocabulary, for articulating the nature and meaning of life. The various genres of rap—which might be described as status rap, socially conscious rap, and gangsta rap—offer perspectives on this basic question: How does one make life within a world marked by the ongoing presence of death and decay?

If one considers the first articulation of "death or life" discussed in the introduction, one might argue that mourning is the affective presentation of the past and future as having possibilities unfulfilled. To mourn is in essence to yearn psychologically for enactment of what is assumed plausible in terms of a separation, or bracketing, of death *from* life as affirmation of the integrity of life despite all. To mourn is a "spatial" (or relational) wish seeking to arrange a more comfortable presentation of presence across temporal dislocation. Certainly, there is some of this in rap music; in fact, a great deal of rap involves this mourning in poetic form.

Joseph Winters notes this turn to melancholia as mourning of loss when suggesting that hip hop has a relationship to the "sorrow songs." Like this early form of Black musical expression chronicling sociopolitical and existential circumstances filtered through a theological framework, rap music in certain forms offers pronounced attention to "sorrow" and "hope," as well as a nostalgic relationship to an assumed past of creative expression over against the current social world.[4] It is important to remember the original spirituals or sorrow songs are lost to us in large part—what W. E. B. Du Bois and others drew from involved the corpus that survived and that, in a somewhat significant sense, had been sanitized.[5] Hence, the modern understanding of the spiritual is something of a fiction that speaks as much to our theological-social need as to the actual content of that musical form. I would argue "loss" as the ground for melancholia is an epistemological stretch in that it requires an initial object, an initial situation, an initial something against which the new object, situation, or something is measured. What would this be for Blacks, so far from the arrival on boats and in the aftermath of a failed experiment in expansive democratic coverage? A feeling of loss assumes integrity of past experience, when—borrowing from Albert Camus, the idea of an unresponsive universe—a type of emptiness seems more consistent with the predicament of Blacks from their initial presence at least to the start of the twentieth century. Writing of the sorrow songs from that historical vantage point Du Bois says, "They are the music of an unhappy people, of the children of disappointment; they tell of death and suffering and unvoiced longing toward a truer world, of misty wanderings and hidden ways." Also, "In these songs, I have said, the slave spoke to the world. Such a message is naturally veiled and half articulate."[6] The spirituals are premised on a wish against history. It is a wish—an effort, as Jonathan Flatley names it—to bring "the now and then together."[7] Or, one might call it a loss of perspective.

Through this connection of temperament he seeks to point out that both musical forms (spirituals and rap) arise from contexts of absurd suffering. And they use that existential situation to speak an alternate path that doesn't deny this pain but instead articulates it, using it to envision the possibility of a different life in the absence of what (on both the individual and collective level) has been lost or taken.[8] In a sense, the sorrow songs offer a strategy for en/fleshing these circumstances and, often through a turn toward the transcendent, forging new meanings and possibilities.[9] Turning to Grandmaster Flash and the Furious Five's "The Message," for example, Winters points to a wrestling with historical circumstances—naming suffering as a way of countering misery. Referencing the song's hook—"Don't push me, 'cause I'm close to the edge"—Winters argues that being on the edge "enables one to see possibilities, to discover new ways of being in the world that lie beyond that limit."[10] He suggests there is here a narrative of lament, of melancholia, that is, a recognition of loss that opens to new possibilities of being over against the death-dealing circumstances of inner-city life. Which is to say, death can be detangled from life in that there is promise expressed that signifies misery.

In discussing the sorrow song, Winters notes its influence on hip hop: "The sorrow-song tradition, which artists like Jay-Z occasionally draw from and participate in, inspires hope for a different kind of world, a world in which our relationships with others are marked by a recognition of our shared vulnerability and a heightened sensitivity to the suffering of others."[11] This, he argues, entails a type of "creative mourning"—cathartic in its performance, potentially transformative in its practice, and representing what some might consider existential naiveté—perhaps akin to speculative pronouncement as contrary statement.[12] With this perspective there is a degree of distance: death comes by other means and stands against what is desired. Death, then, in this case exists and makes claims over against Black personhood. It, demise, is other than Black personhood as it consumes Black persons. Death is vicious in its distinctiveness over against specified (or traceable, within the context of time and space, using mundane measurables) Black personhood—known also as historicized life.

This is far from a desire for death as one finds in some rap. As an existential statement it is the opposite. It is an effort to deny life ended by death. Such a move serves to proclaim at least in soft terms that life is simply transformed by death—rendering it a vague *after*-life discussed using the language associated with what is most valued about human relationships. Here, death is perceived as a type of exhaustion, a depletion of a certain modality of life that exposes access to other modalities just as meaningful. Think, for example, in terms of artists who project dynamics of thug life into new realms of engagement. Or, as Tupac Shakur reflects,

How many brothers fell victim in the streets?
Rest in peace, young nigga, there's a heaven for a G.[13]

Death is ever present—always shadowing possibilities of living and therefore always a point of conversation and reflection; hence, a type of coded nostalgia is in play. This is death as verb—to do something against personhood through the workings of Blackness constructed by whiteness. But it can also be a noun, as in what is left after Black personhood chronicled by those who mourn. Those for whom it is a noun desire to grant the past a particularly intense significance that propels it into the future by reconceiving the present as not-death.[14] Progress, on some level, has promised (falsely) ease with demise through the ability to bracket and subdue death, to see life as over against death. In this way, melancholia as sadness due to loss is a misplaced lament for a constitution of Blackness that isn't—to the extent Black personhood is a false projection. If anything, it is a wish, a mode of misplaced nostalgia. What emerges is a situation in which the deceased is believed to enter a memorialized state beyond freedom, to the extent it has an alternate and sure reference point. This is not simply unlike embodied movement through a socially poisoned world. There is here an effort to normalize death through a process of distinction articulated by forlonging—death as event that disassociates rather than a blended state of being as *deathlife*. Forlonging is a sense of grief that tames language through an overwhelming sadness as a form of ongoing corrosion.[15] Death and life are understood in this way as a matter of disjunction—a distinguishable arrangement of circumstances, with one to be embraced and the other lamented.

Something about this particular mode of melancholia assumes the ability to "die well"—a "right" time, "right" circumstances, "reasonable" conditions—as well as modes of respectful acknowledgment of departure complete with ritualization of memory and performance of hope for those who remain.[16] And what is lamented as loss is the opportunity to die well, so to speak. It notes embodied life as fragile (i.e., vulnerable to social circumstances) but held together beyond its own temporality by means of memory, or what Pete Rock & CL Smooth call "reminiscing." In "They Reminisce over You (T.R.O.Y.)" (1992), they move through a series of performed moments of re/membering by reflecting on the fragility of existence through the brutality of social conditions and the comforting quality of relationships. In this way they seek to distinguish life from death by pulling those loved from the past into the present. Memory serving as a substitute for physical presence, as confirmed by CL Smooth: "I reminisce so you never forget this."[17] Such is a moment of melancholia in the more widely recognized form: sorrow, loss, and emotional pain. The energetic beat, the pounding and rhythm, is combined with a sorrowful recalling that marks out the sonic power of rap guided by a narrative of trauma. One finds reflection on the tragicomic quality of life transformed into death and back into reminiscence as life reconstituted. Such reminiscing plays out a mode of mourning, of loss, enacted without losing the stylization (and defiance) that has marked hip hop culture. The activities of the one lost—in this case, their friend Troy Dixon—are narrated or linguistically performed and felt sonically and brought back to life, so to speak. Even the sample from the song "Today" speaks to a sonic effort to pull the past (death) into the present (life)—to nullify (at least musically) a sense of death as final and as the complete severing of relationship.[18]

The ability of memory to push against the finality of death is expressed in more recent songs, like Jay Electronica's "A.P.I.D.T.A" (2020; meaning "all praise is due to Allah"), in which he reflects on the death of his mother. Regarding this loss, resulting affective and habitual shifts do not entail the final extinction of relationship. Rather, death simply relocates the substance of that connection outside the physical in technologically orchestrated memory and performed in an *after*-life. That is to say, it is a point of transition— an opening to an alternate reality where relationship is reconstituted in the form of that which is "after." Jay Electronica laments,

> The day my mama died, I scrolled her texts all day long
> The physical returns but the connection still stay strong.[19]

Furthermore, a sense of loss is amplified and chronicled as a break with the familiar in "Tha Crossroads" (1995) by Bone Thugs-N-Harmony. But this is a transition with a cosmic rationale beyond human comprehension. Such is not to suggest death is sought; it isn't. Instead, it simply consumes material life before it resets consciousness in a different realm. The reset comes with certain assurances. And this is reflected in the song's cover of Aretha Franklin's "Mary, Don't You Weep," in which life is moderated within a world teleological in nature (despite our tragic circumstances). This teleological pattern isn't negated by loss. Death comes, and so at best we mourn properly and remember the lost consistently, recognizing that death is certain as an undeniable point of transition to a different modality of life within an alternate time and space. In other words,

> Livin' in a hateful world
> Sendin' me (straight to Heaven)
> That's how we roll
> And I ask the good Lord why
> He sighed, he told me we live to die.[20]

The crossroads is important imagery extending beyond this particular song. Within the larger arena of Black cultural expression, it is a point of movement between realms of existence named and discussed frequently: for example, in the blues as a place where body and soul are connected yet distinguishable (e.g., when and where the future of one depends on the positioning of the other). A crossroads is a vibrant location of possibilities where forces battle and the future gets mapped out. As some blues tunes relay, it is a place where deals are struck that impact the spiritual and material realms of existence—determining one through a sale of one's place in the other. As Robert Johnson famously sang in 1936,

> I went to the crossroad, fell down on my knees
> I went to the crossroad, fell down on my knees
> Asked the Lord above, "Have mercy, now, save poor Bob
> if you please."[21]

For Bone Thugs-N-Harmony it is a place of gathering with a similar ability to define metaphysical circumstances beyond the framework of a particular materiality. It is a place of alternate relationality where memory is united with being:

> See you at the crossroad, crossroads, crossroads
> So you won't be lonely.[22]

Concerning melancholia, it is a place where loss is acknowledged and connection longed for. It represents, then, melancholia materialized.

A similar sense of loss as producing grief and remorse is found in Dr. Dre's "The Message" (1999). Death of a loved one breaks the persona of a gangsta—callous and hard toward the world—and in its place forges a confrontation laced with morality and existential uncertainty:

> I'm anxious to believe in real Gs don't cry
> If that's the truth, then I'm realizing I ain't no gangsta.[23]

There is a testimonial quality to the narrative as offered by Dr. Dre and Bone Thugs-N-Harmony. I say this to the degree the story of demise is rendered as an autobiographic struggle that one can't undo but can acknowledge through a pain that doesn't ultimately consume, despite its severing of life from its material moorings. For both, sadness stems from the way in which death works against life—with the reconciliation of the two, death and life, taking place in a nonmaterial framing of time and space. There is contact, to the extent those lost are remembered, but it is a connection made possible only by the loss of immediate presence. Mourning, as "Tha Crossroads" and "The Message" narrate, is personal—a consequence of enacted mutuality severed. This is also graphically portrayed in Queen Latifah's "Winki's Theme" (1993). It shares with the two others a sense of personal vulnerability or, as she sings reflecting on scripture, "There but for the grace of God do I go." With "Cross-roads" one gets a sense that death opens to a realm in which new relationships are formed through an alternate, perhaps nonmaterial, form of life. Queen Latifah acknowledges that continued engagement with the deceased—in this case, her brother—serves as a source of comfort and guidance for those marked by the inconsistencies and dilemmas of material living:

> This jam is dedicated to my brother Winki
> Who's looking down on me from Heaven
> Watching my every move as usual.[24]

The dead are disembodied but impactful, and in this sense life is radically altered in that death is followed by (or somewhat engulfed by) *after*-life, which these artists suggest can be described and performed through a familiar language and grammar of life.

After-life isn't understood using human reason—hence, there is a frequent turn to theological rhetoric of mystery and a cosmic rationality tied to an opaque teleological arrangement. Yet there is comfort expressed with this configuration of cause and effect. However, this comfort doesn't constitute contentment that subdues ultimately sadness, regret, and loss. It reduces bewilderment but doesn't short-circuit affective release even within circumstances socially numb to disregard. This is lament, melancholia, as a mode of ritualized remembering: a naming of both circumstances and those who have impacted and altered those circumstances. Something about this is unreasonable, beyond the ability of language to capture and afford comfort. It is at this point in light of such considerations (e.g., loss through death) that Queen Latifah suggests another source of vigor cosmically situated beyond the confines of the material world: "The Lord is the light of my life," she says, "and He brightens up my world."[25] Melancholia is buttressed by a contrary consideration, an alternate modality of living that does not end sorrow but rather contextualizes it.

As with the other artists mentioned here in relationship to melancholia as sorrow and mourning of loss, Queen Latifah doesn't see the "end" as *the* End. Life is followed by death, which enacts an alternate and less materially centered (but no less impactful) mode of existence. A similar sentiment is exhibited in "I'll Be Missing You" (1997), in which Sean "P. Diddy" Combs and Faith Evans express the pain and sorrow resulting from the murder of Biggie Smalls, but also acknowledge his continued impact. For Combs, death opens to another modality of living. This isn't the same as life and death being inseparable; rather, it involves a triadic structuring of existence, life–death–

after-life: "I know you still living your life, after death," is the way in which Combs expresses this metaphysical arrangement. It is a modified claim to *after*-life, a sense of connection demolished by death. The theological nature of this claim is echoed in the haunting words sung by Faith Evans—a sentiment drawn from a gospel song reimagined:

> Somebody tell me why
> One glad morning
> When this life is over
> I know I'll see your face.[26]

In Black churches, it's "Some glad morning, when this life is o'er, I'll fly away; to a home on God's celestial shore." The mechanism of transcendence is altered with removal (from material life), supplanted by reconnection with the loved one lost by a less-specified means. There is with this mode of melancholia at least a wish for this engagement, this connection.[27] Life, in a word, is normalized and amplified by means of this perspective. On the other hand, death is foreign, an intrusion into the delicate workings of existential activities and connections.

Under different circumstances—a different marker of bodied fragility and vulnerability—Common offers melancholic reflection on the claiming of life. There is a profoundly tragic quality to the narratives in "Between Me, You and Liberation" (2002)—the manner in which life is consumed by death without the possibility of remedy through technology or love. Bodies are positioned in the social world, exposed to various forms of *dis*-ease (whether biochemical disintegration, or social hostility resulting in the collapse of being) that compromise material life, rendering them weak and then gone. Pleasure fails to provide comfort, and it doesn't safeguard against the angst or the loneliness that often mark human interactions—to address it, the pain has to be performed, narrated, or spoken. Fragility and vulnerability that tie together markers of embodied meaning are quickly dispersed and preserved only in memory. For Common, melancholic memory brackets (not ends) death in a certain sense. It fosters an alternate modality of presence couched in ongoing regard voiced through performed memory. That is, as he says, reflecting on one battling cancer, "What seemed like the end was the beginning for her."[28] Life and death are disconnected—the former tames the latter through the presentation of life (e.g., material impact) after demise, or *after*-life, which conditions mourning and tempers (but doesn't end) morose dispositions.

One might describe this as a kind of theo-forensic framing of death. For those committed to this thanatological stance, only life is necessary and death is a cruel and tragic twist, or an interruption of existential interface.[29] Common expresses (manages) his depth of loss marked by disregard for difference and the presence of socially sanctioned abuse. This melancholic narrative is somewhat instructive in "Between Me, You and Liberation"—the death-dealing consequences of domestic abuse, homophobia, and so on—as the narrative laments death caused by social disregard and suggests alternate modalities of rationality that are life-affirming. Common expresses frustration over a lack of control, not being able to determine when and how one dies. This frustration heightens vulnerability and the performance of fragility to the extent death comes without any crime committed and without a comfortable rationale. There is an affective quality in this song not present in, for example, Wu-Tang Clan's "America" (1996) and its critique of sexual irresponsibility and AIDS—death brought about through willful human activity. For the latter, the narrative is pedagogical through a negative example without the same emotion or psychologically expressed sense of loss. Rather, there is some emotional distance, despite familiarity with those encountering death: "AIDS kills, word up respect this; America is dying slowly."[30] AIDS becomes a trope, a mechanism of death, forging a distinct division between embodied integrity and well-*being*, and compromised materiality.

At times memory renders the loss static as the material world continues, with the living trying to maintain connection through poetic (re)membering. The grammar and vocabulary capturing materiality are used to reflect interaction between two distinct realms. Think in terms of a sentiment from the Goodie Mob:

> The hood has changed since you left, man . . .
> Can you recall riding bicycles in the trails behind
> Krissy Collins dropping Huffys like BMXs.[31]

This isn't a poetic reconstituting of personhood. Temporality is rethought as the context for this interplay—the inevitable linkage between life and death is embodied and performed, or in other words "owned." For these artists the circumstances involve linguistic slippage between (as in to occupy simultaneously) life and death, as opposed to a full escape. Black suffering, then, in this context is an adjective, a qualifier in the naming of this framework, and it describes the nature of action, as an adverb, framing patterns of behavior within the context of this conditioning. This is not to say there is no distinction between the two—life and death—for them; but rather that the effort to differentiate doesn't make a functional difference in the long run, in that both life and death must be acknowledged and thought at the same time. That is, it changes nothing—it's a conceptual change that makes no difference to the extent it depends on ephemeral memory to ground it. Here one might even say, through a loose reference to Camus, sadness "teaches nothing."

Melancholia 2: Balancing Embodied Demise/Activity

Life and death both have significance; one might say they *matter* in that they are substantive, impinging and shaping but here without resolution. Mourning, as noted in the preceding section, pushes for one side over the other—but the sense of melancholia I now want to discuss is framed by a balance between life and death, where there is no usable distance from one (death) necessary to distinguish the other (life). Offered is vulnerability, not a splitting asunder: there is always an intimate sameness between life and death.

We become not victims, but vectors—a particular type of "organism" that through consuming (i.e., death) also presents life. In other words, in the form of a question, What if there is no distance between life and death to be mourned as loss or performed as difference? What if death isn't simply encountered but is embodied and enacted as life? The chapters in this book have provided various ways of playing out this relationship, but now for a different question: How does one express the embodied naming of this recognition?

This second type of melancholia doesn't involve a longing that disembodies through memory and that is structured by grief. It doesn't fill space and through imaginative structures deny death by projecting the one "loss" into a future free from the connotations of demise. *Melancholic* is the correct qualifier, the proper parameters, for describing this particular hip hop response to life/death/dying/demise. But by it I do not mean the more general sense of longing, or lamenting of loss—sadness generated through affective structuring(s) of in/experience noted above.[32] Instead, I want to reference an old definition of melancholia, which positions it as one of the four "humors" (fluids), or "black bile," within the body. In this way, I want to move from considering a mood or affective quality to considering the trope of melancholia as a forensic consideration that prefigures mood and has to do with "posture" as an element of balance within the social "body."[33] The old sense of melancholia as associated with black bile is also associated with earth—or what I will label a form of materiality (or grounded recognition). This melancholic "humor" is said to intensify with age—one might say it is a materiality determined in relationship to experience (rather than the lack of ongoing experience needed in order to mourn). Finally, it is one of the humors, or materials, that control the body. Bile—symbolizing the capacity to decompose, alter, or reduce—speaks a particular take that has nothing to do with loss or sadness on a fundamental level. It connotes not a state of feeling but a material alteration—an embodied reduction that pulls together and challenges the possibility of distinction needed to cast life *against* death.

In both instances, melancholia has something to do with (dis)ease. In the former case, present in relation to Common and Queen Latifah, it is a dis/ease—an altered state of mind—producing affective considerations named by sadness, discontent, and perhaps anger. With the alternative case, now under discussion, it is (dis)ease having something to do with embodied movement whereby the social body is compromised, which gives rise to a certain experience of time and space that exposes the intent of whiteness. Here is the point: melancholia in relationship to *deathlife* is the naming of the materiality of experience—the "posture"—that suggests to speak of life is to speak of death. In other words, this melancholia is a way of acknowledging and naming in an embodied fashion the "balancing"—as in *isorropia* (equilibrium), which I will take to mean existing in a state of equality, or a sameness, in that the two forces perfectly counter each other—of life and death that actually controls socially coded (both Black and white) bodies. It, by extension, serves to expose and caution against the type of harm (i.e., safeguarding of whiteness) that effort to distinguish does. In essence, it is to "speak" a warning: it names the lie of distinction so very necessary to the delusion of white life over against Black death.

One might say there is something related to moralism embedded in—or qualified by—this type of melancholia. I've written of Black moralism on various occasions, and this alternate naming comes with some modification to its structuring, though the basic impulse remains unaltered. It is—unlike with W. E. B. Du Bois, Richard Wright, and Nella Larsen—inflected with hip hop's particular encounter with absurdity. And as such it has a late twentieth-century and early twenty-first-century stylized and combated relationship to *deathlife*, which renders experience a study in thanatology cast in Black. This impulse remains rightly named moralism because it continues—and I reflect here on it in relationship to figures such as Albert Camus—a questioning serving to expose social hypocrisies or, more generally, the naming and announcing of social arrangements that are destructive despite public pronouncements and private acquiescence. It is moralistic to the extent the artist refuses to deny what is known about these circumstances: to know death as life and life as death.[34] This is a dimension of the moralist posture, naming and speaking *deathlife* accurately and without social illusion and misrepresentation.

Furthermore, this melancholia is moralistic in tone because it denies the comfort of forgetting social bad faith, which pretends the ability to distinguish life and death as an existential and metaphysical arrangement. There is no innocence, and the denial of innocence is the social lie exposed. Such is a persistence that speaks not of robust and firm living over against demise, but rather the struggle to call attention to the markings of *deathlife* without surrendering to it. And it isn't identical to becoming death alone—this is also a case of knowing limits. Put another way, what is it to know death—and to be (in) materiality presented in such a way as to make one a symbol of death despised but yet unavoidable and necessary for life? Perhaps there is related to this something of the "hunger" described by Wright or the materiality of poverty known by Camus. The moralist isn't at "ease in the world," and this stance frames the delicate balance—the materiality of embodied consumption and reconstitution, that is—of life and death together.[35] This reduction produces its own type of "nausea," or what Camus called recognition of the absurd (e.g., an effort to live within a context that is also death).

There is a matter of precision in language and action that questions the social assumption safeguarded by whiteness: to attempt to frame life and death through an illusion of distinction is faulty, and the assumption of structures of being free of this reality—that is transcendental—is a lie. As Camus reflects (and perhaps these artists and Camus are kin), "I have no wish to lie or to be lied to. I want to keep my lucidity to the last, and gaze upon my death with all the fullness of my jealousy and horror."[36] The key here is to avoid silence— that is, to deny surrender to the illusion that one is "safe." Melancholia, this second kind, speaks of balance. It is a material process for "reconstituting" in a way that holds together life and death. This is not to be dead or alive, to be one or the other—rather, to exist in/between is to be both, and these artists seek to speak that balance and in this way avoid the lie that one can be either alive or dead. Neither life nor death is a solid "something," an object or system. They are a process of interaction on which we have bestowed certain significance. In this act of granting meaning—distinctiveness—we have marked them with a particular type of independence of experience, which is only a social desire. Being the case on the metaphysical level is just one dimension of this reality; to be embodied Black is to also be both alive (e.g., an ongoing threat to whiteness and the social world) and dead (e.g., having limited value in the social world, a value that renders them objects with little agency, with little life). These artists deconstruct language—modify it and turn it against itself—in part as a means by which to expose this relational situation in which death and life are, well, the same.

Melancholia is a particular formulation and presentation of this in/betweenness. The affective response is precisely that—the sadness, depression, and so forth with which this in/betweenness is met—but here it isn't named melancholia.[37] This second mode of melancholia is not to lament the "end" but rather to acknowledge, name, and map material alteration—embodied change and the manner in which there is balance or equality that denies distinction between life and death. In this way certain artists have described becoming death as their being alive—the material alteration of the embodied being so as to degrade (not in a Bakhtinian sense) human/being. In other words, the linguistic mapping of experience as it relates to death/dying in certain expressions of rap is guided by moralistically inclined melancholia. As such, it frames the presentation of *deathlife* not along the lines of loss of metaphysical arrangements existentially presented, but rather in terms of a materiality as active and tied to a delicate balance that isn't properly mourned or lamented, but rather performed. This "balance" involves recognition of and the holding together as one the dynamics of death and life: *deathlife*. Again, it doesn't constitute a sense of loss in that such a sense is false: such distinction between life and death is a wish.

I think about moralistic melancholia in relationship to and situated within narratives such as the Orphic hustler, the Black antihero, bacchic activity, and zombies. In all these cases, language is bent and distorted to capture something of this melancholic signification of a desired bifurcation of life-death. This is a form of lucidity—tragic in its range of perception, and persistent in its refusal to modify what it uncovers. It refuses comfort and maintains balance, with the consistency of encounter as *deathlife*. It doesn't pretend loss, doesn't endorse lament but rather simply movement as a statement of balance: *deathlife*. This unwillingness to mourn stems from recognition that nothing is loss: distinction between life and death is a wish, a social fiction. The mood is different, no wistful posture toward embodiment as fragile and fleeting; instead, a signifying of circumstances through movement, through engagement. Orphic and bacchic figures share this engagement, for different reasons, without the same narrative structuring, but with a shared signification of whiteness's effort to maintain the illusion of distance and difference. The zombic figure's hunger nullifies difference, blurring in a graphic and haunting fashion distinction as it consumes both life and death, shifting perception of what might be claimed as distinction between the two. A context of misery—if this word is still applicable—is never simply a matter of life or death, but an *isorropia*-related naming of them together. To encounter one is to know the other, and rap music narrates this process and articulates particular modalities of behavior as inauthentic to the extent they are premised on what can't be. Put differently, embrace of this type of melancholia refuses to mourn because even that assumes too much concerning what is at stake—containing still a sense of loss even if it can't be healed in traditional ways.[38]

This second melancholia is more than a response to the anti-ontological positioning of Blackness with/in Black bodies as prohibiting the same affective response to the world available to those who claim the category of whiteness. Anxiety for the latter is an impulse toward what is perceived as being a viable alternative, a calm "place." Moralist melancholia is a refusal of the very language of mourning and loss and a replacement of that articulation with other alternatives that are movement related. Orphic, bacchic, zombic personae operating at a different register in the form of poetic thanatology entail a certain "posture" by means of moralistic melancholia that names a balance. This sense of melancholia grounds in the present, with no wistful concern for a romanticized past and no thought of future; rather, it is a determination to note and speak about the sameness of life and death as the shape of existence, without privileging either. This is balance; this is melancholia.

This sense of melancholia requires a balance between the mechanics of life and death together, as equal, with a deep awareness of and sensitivity to both, which is an acknowledgment of their sameness. There is here an embodied limitation—a speculation on what is obtainable and what remains beyond grasp, what is taken, and what is given in turn.[39] In this way, perhaps hip hop's narrative concerning death as presented here serves as a poetically arranged cautionary narrative: the attempt to mourn exposes the lack of a proper "subject" to consider gone. The metaphysical and existential challenge of in/betweenness is an absurd arrangement—difficult to maintain but without a real means of escape. It is more than an idea, more than an ephemerality of a graphic kind. It is an opaque materiality real to the extent that it defies departmentalization consistent with categorizations that make possible distinction between modalities of being: being alive . . . being dead. The key is to be at ease with this arrangement and, in the process, challenge living *and* dying as happening differently. This is what the artists discussed in this book portray: graphic relationships to *deathlife* exposed and played out in/through the body coded Black.

INTRODUCTION. PARADIGMS OF DEATH (OR LIFE) AND *DEATHLIFE*

Material in the section "Paradigm #1: Life and/or Death" is drawn from material first published as Pinn, "Zombies in the 'Hood"; Pinn, "When It's Over"; and Pinn, "The End." This introduction involves a redirection of some of the material in these publications so as to highlight the description of death and its relationship to hip hop as opposed to viewing hip hop as a counter to death. The aim here is different. In the articles, my intent was to present the manner in which hip hop seeks to counter social arrangements and narratives. In this introduction, I am simply interested in an analytical description of the manner in which hip hop describes and performs death.

1   Brombert, "Kafka," 642.
2   While this approach, like all the narrative strands of thought in hip hop culture in general and rap music in particular, is not gendered in a manner that totalizes a reified "masculine" sensibility, for a variety of socio-ideological reasons—the outlining of which is beyond the scope of this project—the narration of death and life within hip hop culture is most closely (but by no means exclusively) associated with the refusal by or placement of the embodied body labeled Black and male.
3   For interested, and related, discussions of whiteness with respect to notions of transcendence over against the grounding of Blackness, see Driscoll, *White Lies*; and Kline, *Racism and the Weakness of Christian Identity*.
4   I discuss this at times in relationship to Afropessimism and its understanding of Blacks as sentient beings without status as human.
5   Du Bois, *Souls of Black Folk*, 7. The concept of *technology* is borrowed from Michel Foucault. See Foucault, *Technologies of the Self*; and Foucault, *Discipline and Punish*.

6   Du Bois discusses the theme of the "Veil" in *The Souls of Black Folk*; see pages 7–15.
7   Du Bois, "Souls of White Folks," 923.
8   Du Bois, "Souls of White Folks," 933.
9   Du Bois, "Souls of White Folks," 924.
10 Du Bois, "Souls of White Folks," 926, 927.
11 Kellehear, *Social History of Dying*, 47.
12 McIlwain, *Death in Black and White*, chap. 1.
13 See Laderman, *Rest in Peace.*
14 Kellehear, *Social History of Dying*, 90–95, 136–38.
15 West, *Prophesy Deliverance!*
16 Holloway, *Passed On*, 60–61.
17 Holland, *Raising the Dead*, 15.
18 Holland, *Raising the Dead*, 23.
19 I give more attention to Trayvon Martin in Pinn, "Do Atheists Understand and Appreciate Black Bodies?"
20 Patterson, *Slavery and Social Death.*
21 See Cornel West, "Nihilism in Black America," in Dent, *Black Popular Culture*, 37–47.
22 Goffman, *Stigma*, 3.
23 Goffman, *Stigma*, 2–3.
24 Goffman, *Stigma*, 3.
25 Goffman, *Stigma*, 5.
26 Neil Small, "Death and Difference," in Field, Hockey, and Small, *Death, Gender, and Ethnicity*, 208–9.
27 Castronovo, *Necro Citizenship*, 4–5.
28 Castronovo, *Necro Citizenship*, 1.
29 Patterson, *Slavery and Social Death.*
30 Castronovo, *Necro Citizenship*, 10, 40–44.
31 Camus uses the phrase in reference to the logic behind capital punishment— the death penalty. Speaking against the usefulness of it, he argues that "capital judgment," rather than aiding, actually harms our most fundamental human solidarity, that against death. Camus, *Resistance, Rebellion, and Death*, 222.
32 Think about these aesthetic representations in relationship to Trayvon Martin and George Zimmerman. Trayvon was a "zombie" attempting to be human and to extend itself beyond the confines of death, and so it had to be resettled within its proper epistemological and ontological geography. Zimmerman's action (the killing of Martin) was an effort to restore a bizarre and damning sense of meaning—to embody death—in ways that safeguarded white Americans, through Zimmerman, with protection from death. Killing sought to confine death by protecting a particular unity of ideas around nature and meaning. On the surface this was the protection of white privilege, but on a more fundamental level it was the restoration of death's confinement by disciplining a zombie. Martin is not the first, nor will he be the last, graphic

example of how fissures in zombification are addressed. So important is the work done by the classification of zombies that the United States, among other societies, will kill (bodies, ideas, meaning) to maintain it. The strategies of "law and order" provide the justification as well as outline the most productive techniques.

33 Albert Camus, "Fourth Letter," in Camus, *Resistance, Rebellion, and Death*, 28.
34 See Alvarez and Buckley, "Zimmerman Is Acquitted."
35 Genesis 10–11. See Pinn and Callahan, *African American Religious Life*.
36 This statement could be read through the work of various rap artists, such as Ice Cube's "My Skin Is My Sin."
37 Collins, "Biggie Envy and the Gangsta Sublime," 911.
38 From Studs Terkel, "An Interview with James Baldwin," quoted in Singleton, *Cultural Melancholy*, 65.
39 See, e.g., Riley, "Rebirth of Tragedy"; Armstrong, "Rhetoric of Violence"; Smuts, "Ethics of Singing Along"; Collins, "Biggie Envy and the Gangsta Sublime"; and Hunnicutt and Andrews, "Tragic Narratives in Popular Culture." According to Gwen Hunnicutt and Kristy Humble Andrews, "about one-third of the most popular rap songs from 1989 to 2000 contained at least one reference to homicide" (618). Furthermore, they noted "that references to homicide became increasingly graphic and lurid over time" (619).
40 Warren, *Ontological Terror*, 113. For examples in Wright's work, see Wright, *Native Son*; and Wright, *The Outsider*.
41 See, e.g., Wright's *Native Son*.
42 Dr. Dre and Ice Cube, "Natural Born Killaz." See Philips, "Is America Ready for 'Natural Born Killaz'?"
43 DMX, "Bring Your Whole Crew."
44 "You're Nobody till Somebody Loves You" was first recorded by Russ Morgan in 1946.
45 This depiction of the gangsta persona and ethics is often described in relationship to literary figures. See, e.g., Malone, "Long-Lost Brothers."
46 Barrett, "Dead Men Printed," 306.
47 See, e.g., Stop the Violence Movement, "Self-Destruction"; and Goodie Mobb, "Still Standing."
48 Notorious B.I.G., "You're Nobody ('Til Somebody Kills You)." Also see Goodie Mobb, "God I Wanna Live."
49 Notorious B.I.G., "You're Nobody ('Til Somebody Kills You)."
50 Notorious B.I.G., "You're Nobody ('Til Somebody Kills You)."
51 Notorious B.I.G., "You're Nobody ('Til Somebody Kills You)."
52 Snoop Dogg, "Murder Was the Case."
53 Compare this to DMX's deal with the devil in "The Omen." With DMX, the situation is more horrific in nature. Rather than the devil safeguarding from death, DMX's deal involves a new outlet for murder—use of the demonic to bring about murder as revenge. What is gained isn't material goods and status, but rather a comfort with destruction beyond the human capacity to embrace.

54 Snoop Dogg, "Murder Was the Case."

55 Dr. Dre and Ice Cube, "Natural Born Killaz." This is also the case with Cypress Hill, "How I Could Just Kill a Man."

56 Gonsalves, "Chynna Rogers Was a Drug Addict Plagued by Demons."

57 Chynna, "Selfie." See "Chynna—Selfie (Official Video)," https://www.youtube.com/watch?v=2DPHaWiHr7g.

58 Younger, "Introducing Chynna, the Ex-model and Ex-addict Who Can Rap Her Ass Off."

59 Chynna, "seasonal depression." See "seasonal depression," https://www.youtube.com/watch?v=AUkrUduXYxM.

60 Chynna, "asmr." See "Chynna—asmr [official video]," https://www.youtube.com/watch?v=ZZtf6ibHgOw. ASMR stands for autonomous sensory meridian response. See Emma L. Barratt and Nick J. Davis, "Autonomous Sensory Meridian Response (ASMR): A Flow-Like Mental State," *PeerJ*, March 26, 2015, https://doi.org/10.7717/peerj.851.

61 For example, Chynna, "iddd." See "Chynna—iddd (official music video)," https://www.youtube.com/watch?v=PBaVrILsFzA.

62 Rapsody, "Aaliyah."

63 Lil' Kim, "Pray for Me."

64 I have not found direct source information for the 1974 article. One of the commonly referenced secondary sources is Campbell, *Talking at the Gates*, 3. I am grateful to Mayra Rivera for bringing this statement to my attention.

65 Calvin Warren, in passing, notes, "Life and death lose distinction and coherency for black being as nothing." *Ontological Terror*, 111. This is an insight we share; however, how we come to this statement and what we do with it as a conceptual framework differ. My thinking on this relationship between life and death as presented in this volume extends my earlier work in "Zombies in the 'Hood"; "When It's Over"; and "The End."

66 Warren highlights the manner in which Ronald Judy uses the language of thanatology to describe the relationship between death and Blackness: "The death that is emancipating is the negation of the materiality of Africa. Writing the slave narrative is thus a thanatology, a writing of annihilation that applies the taxonomies of death." Quoted in Warren, *Ontological Terror*, 40.

67 See Sharpe, *In the Wake*, 34–36.

68 Something of this might be accounted for in the distinction between Warren's Black nihilism and my Black moralism.

69 Warren, *Ontological Terror*, 7.

70 There is much I find compelling about Warren's critique of Black humanism, but responding to that critique isn't the purpose of this introduction, nor is it the aim of the larger book. See Warren, *Ontological Terror*.

71 J. Jackson, "A Little Black Magic," 397. I don't want to push the use of "racial Americana," in that Jackson's concern in his essay is race explicitly and not Blackness, which is my concern. Although the two are related, there's no reason to assume them identical formulations.

72 Calamur, "Ferguson Documents."

73 Quoted in Calamur, "Ferguson Documents."

74 Wilderson, *Afropessimism*, 16.

75 Luke Darby, "Florida Police Officer Arrested and Handcuffed a 6-Year-Old Black Girl for a Tantrum in Class," GQ, September 23, 2019, https://www.gq.com/story/six-year-old-black-girl-arrested-for-a-tantrum.

76 It is held at the Leopold Museum in Vienna, Austria.

77 For texts related to Afropessimism, see Frank Wilderson's *Afropessimism* and *Red, White and Black: Cinema and the Structure of U.S. Antagonisms*. Also of interest with respect to issues of Blackness, hope, and future is work in Afrofuturism. Materials in this area include Dery, "Black to the Future"; Nelson, "Afrofuturism"; Barber et al., "25 Years of Afrofuturism"; Lavender, *Afrofuturism Rising*; Womack, *Afrofuturism*; Anderson and Jones, *Afrofuturism 2.0*; Youngquest, *Pure Solar World*; and S. Jackson and Moody-Freeman, *Black Imagination*.

78 I want to thank the external reviewers for calling attention to the need for this contextual counterpoint.

79 Moten, "Case of Blackness," 177–78.

80 Moten, "Case of Blackness," 187.

81 Moten, "Case of Blackness," 214. One might also read this notion of pathology in relationship to Bruce, *How to Go Mad without Losing Your Mind*.

82 Moten, "Case of Blackness," 204.

83 Moten, "Erotics of Fugitivity," 241, 242.

84 Moten, "Erotics of Fugitivity," 253.

85 Halberstam, "Foreword," in Harney and Moten, *Undercommons*, 5.

86 Halberstam, "Foreword," 6, 7.

87 Keeling, *Queer Times, Black Futures*, 38.

88 Halberstam, "Foreword," 8–9. Calvin Warren provides a compelling discussion of this ontological emptiness, or what he references as non-ontology. See Warren, *Onticide*.

89 Moten, "Blackness and Nothingness," 738.

90 Moten, "Blackness and Nothingness," 739.

91 Moten, "Blackness and Nothingness," 740.

92 Moten, "Blackness and Nothingness," 749–50. On the para-ontological distinction between Blackness and Black people, see, e.g., Moten, "Erotics of Fugitivity."

93 Moten, "Blackness and Nothingness," 776, 778.

94 Moten, *Black and Blur*, vii.

95 Keeling, *Queer Times, Black Futures*, xiii.

96 Spillers, "Mama's Baby, Papa's Maybe."

97 Wilderson, *Afropessimism*, 168.

98 Wilderson, *Afropessimism*, 40.

99 Wilderson, *Red, White and Black*, 247.

100 Wilderson, *Afropessimism*, 92. Italics in the original.

101 Wilderson, *Red, White and Black*, 2.

102 Ta-Nehisi Coates claims Donald Trump as the first white president because he is the first to secure the office based solely on the social status of whiteness—and as a corrective (or renewing of whiteness) against the Barack Obama presidency. See Coates, "First White President."

103 I am reminded of a statement by Frank Wilderson: "Afropessimism is a looter's creed: critique without redemption or a vision of redress except 'the end of the world.'" *Afropessimism*, 174.

104 Wilderson, *Red, White and Black*, 41. Emphasis added.

105 Wilderson, *Red, White and Black*, 43.

106 Wilderson, *Afropessimism*, 12.

107 Wilderson, *Afropessimism*, 103. There is what I would describe as a "dark" hopefulness in Afropessimism to the extent that "activist" remains a viable element of its vocabulary and resistance a part of its grammar.

108 Achille Mbembe's "necropolitics" as a statement concerning the fullness of sovereignty as the ability to "kill or let live" (*Necropolitics*, 66) provides a compelling way to think about the manner in which the system of slavery and colonialism operates through the categories of life and death played out through the body. However, I sense sovereignty here involving a distinction between death *and* life played out through the bodies of those exposed to the potentiality of death (over against life) and those who determine this relationship. Mbembe references slave life as "a form of death-in-life": "Because the slave's life is like a 'thing,' possessed by another person, slave existence appears as the perfect figure of a shadow" (75). Even here, there appears to be a distinction between death and life—still life against death—that I seek to close off. See Mbembe, *Necropolitics*, chap. 3.

109 Sharpe, *In the Wake*, 7.

110 Warren, *Ontological Terror*, 111, 112–13.

111 Genesis 22:1–13.

112 I borrow this notion of Grand Unity from Albert Camus. See *Myth of Sisyphus*.

113 Wilderson, *Afropessimism*, 262.

114 Serwer, "Coronavirus Was an Emergency until Trump Found Out Who Was Dying." See also Mills, *Racial Contract*. On Arbery, see, e.g., Elliott C. McLaughlin, "What We Know about Ahmaud Arbery's Killing," CNN, May 12, 2020, https://www.cnn.com/2020/05/11/us/ahmaud-arbery-mcmichael-what -we-know/index.html; and "Ahmaud Arbery: Prosecutors under Investigation over Handling of Killing," *Guardian*, May 12, 2020, https://www.theguardian .com/us-news/2020/may/12/ahmaud-arbery-georgia-prosecutors-under -investigation.

115 See, e.g., Wilderson, *Afropessimism*.

116 Sharpe, *In the Wake*, 110.

117 Boxall, "Blind Seeing."

118 See, e.g., the manner in which death is discussed by Calvin Warren in relationship to Black being as nothingness. Warren, referencing Ronald Judy, also

speaks of thanatology as a way to describe "black being" as "the evidence of an onticidal enterprise." *Ontological Terror*, 40. Some texts regarding death are discussed in this volume. See, e.g., Holloway, *Passed On*; McIvor, *Mourning in America*; Holland, *Raising the Dead*; and Patterson, *Slavery and Social Death*.

119 Examples of melancholic-centered analysis include De Genova, "Gangster Rap"; Malone, "Long-Lost Brothers"; Ellis, *If We Must Die*; and Winters, "Contemporary Sorrow Songs."

120 I am not concerned with issues of authenticity—that is to say, with the degree to which artists "are" the stories they tell. Rather, I'm interested in the manner in which these narrations offer a language and grammar for depicting *deathlife*.

121 For an intriguing discussion of the nature and meaning of the archive, see Hartman, "Venus in Two Acts"; and Hartman, *Scenes of Subjection*.

122 Along these lines, chapters 3 and 4 project some of the logic captured in Afro-pessimism. This is particularly the case not simply in terms of the predominance of death as a way to mark out Black bodies, but also in the manner in which modes of orientation and articulation are defiled by any effort to rethink the relationship of Blackness to death.

123 Sharpe, *In the Wake*, 7–8.

1. THE ORPHIC HUSTLER

Some of the material in this chapter first appeared as "God Wears Tom Ford: Hip Hop's Re-envisioning of Divine Authority," *Media Development* 61, no. 4 (October 2014): 20–23.

1 Simone, "Sinnerman."
2 I outline much of this development in Pinn, *Writing God's Obituary*.
3 See, e.g., "Reverend Run: From Rapper to Preacher," National Public Radio, September 19, 2012, https://www.npr.org/2012/12/19/167623728/reverend-run -from-rapper-to-preacher; and "Rapper Turned Minister Kurtis Blow Is 50," National Public Radio, August 9, 2009, https://www.npr.org/templates/story /story.php?storyId=111696980.
4 UGK, "Game Belong to Me."
5 Tupac Shakur, "Blasphemy."
6 Tupac Shakur, "Blasphemy."
7 Jay-Z, *Decoded*, 24–25.
8 Jay-Z and Kanye West, "No Church in the Wild."
9 Jay-Z and Kanye West, "No Church in the Wild."
10 Jay-Z and Kanye West, "No Church in the Wild."
11 Bakhtin, *Rabelais and His World*.
12 Jay-Z, "Crown."
13 See Jay-Z, *Decoded*, 277: "Most of all, I don't think what I believe should matter to anyone else; I'm not trying to stop anyone from believing whatever they want. I believe in God, and that's really enough for me."

14 See Jay-Z, *Decoded*, 214n27.

15 See, e.g., Miller, "Real Recognize Real"; and Dyson, "God Complex."

16 Miller, "Real Recognize Real," 199.

17 Dyson, "God Complex," 55.

18 I have in mind the restriction of language found in the biblical story of Nimrod: Genesis 6.

19 See Jay-Z, "Breathe Easy": "I'm far from being God." Yet this is matched by claims to divinity in other tracks, such as "Crown." All this points to how Jay-Z highlights a certain epistemological and existential positioning that speaks to the ability to control death—that is, to confront the circumstances of death and not be tamed by them. Also see *Decoded* (158–70) for Jay-Z's take on the violent nature of urban life and public housing.

20 An even more traditional theological discussion of hip hop and God is provided in Utley, *Rap and Religion*.

21 Also related to deification of a kind, West constitutes his persona Yeezus as a morphing of the Christological event and personality in ways that highlight the roughness of Christ's encounter with the world (i.e., not the garden and prayer, but hanging with the despised); not virginal quality (tempted without sin as scripture suggests) but thoughts of Jesus "with" Mary. West, in "I Am a God," perhaps for other reasons and with a much more metallic and harsh tone, speaks his divinity in a way that pronounces a new relationship to the empirical quality of life. West's divinity is not in toto in that he is not the most high, but simply close—perhaps as close as one can get—to the ultimate source of truth, the resurrection of hip hop as the epistemology of *deathlife*.

22 Eustice, "Lil B Clarifies."

23 Martinez-Belkin, "Converting to the Church of BasedGod."

24 Jay-Z and West are not gods premised on the metaphysics, say, of the Five-Percent Nation, in that their deification has nothing to do with the ontological significance of a hidden knowledge. Their take on deification also does not entail this sect's radical individualism. The Five-Percent Nation (also known as the Nation of Gods and Earths), founded in Harlem in 1964 by Clarence 13X (aka Father Allah), believed that the Nation of Islam, from which he had split, didn't provide full knowledge of self to Black people. For example, while the Nation of Islam argued the Black man was created by God, the Five-Percent Nation proclaimed that the Black man is God, and the Black women is the Earth producing life. The Five-Percent Nation believed 85 percent of the Black population was without knowledge; 10 percent had proper knowledge but didn't share it completely; and 5 percent had proper knowledge and shared it. Hence, the name Five-Percent Nation.

25 Fear serves as a linguistic tool, a poetic device. Reflecting on his track "Beach Chair," Jay-Z says, "This is why we shouldn't be afraid. There are two possibilities: One is that there's more to life than the physical life, that our souls 'will find an even higher place to dwell' when this life is over. IF that's true, there's no reason to fear failure or death. The other possibility is that this life is all

there is. And if that's true, then we have to really live it—we have to take it for everything it has and 'die enormous' instead of 'living dormant,' as I said way back on 'Can I Live.' Either way, fear is a waste of time." *Decoded*, 285n15.

26 Jay-Z, *Decoded*, 103.

27 Jay-Z, "If I Should Die."

28 Jay-Z, "Hova Song Outro."

29 Jay-Z, "Moment of Clarity."

30 "I always felt like I kept my eyes a little bit more wide open than other people around me did—not that I was smarter, but that I saw some things very clearly." Jay-Z, *Decoded*, 303.

31 Du Bois, "Of Our Spiritual Strivings," in Du Bois, *Souls of Black Folk*, 7–15.

32 Jay-Z, *Decoded*, 93.

33 Jay-Z, verse on Kanye West, "Diamonds from Sierra Leone."

34 Spence, *Stare in the Darkness*, 166–67; quote, 3.

35 "Recall that the black parallel public is the space in which blacks come together to articulate and debate their interests, needs, and identity." Spence, *Stare in the Darkness*, 21.

36 Spence, *Stare in the Darkness*, 17.

37 Spence, *Knocking the Hustle*, xxiv–xxv.

38 Spence's personal narrative concerning this dilemma is worth considering here. See Spence, *Knocking the Hustle*, xv–xxv. His book provides rich information concerning the impact that neoliberal policies and structures have on various dimensions of Black life.

39 Spence, *Stare in the Darkness*, 24–25, 27.

40 Spence, *Stare in the Darkness*, 15. Spence outlines these two concepts more fully on pages 24–28.

41 This read involves something of a push against Spence's argument—"that hip-hop was created (like most black diasporal music forms) to affirm, to celebrate, to recognize, to journal, and to show the world that another reality is possible" (*Stare in the Darkness*, 17)—to the extent I won't assume another world is possible as anything more than the end of the world.

42 Spence, *Stare in the Darkness*, 174, 175.

43 Jay-Z, "Moment of Clarity."

44 Trachtenberg, "Hustler as Hero," 427. Another early somewhat informal examination of the "hustler" persona, including some ethnographic material, is Reynolds, "Urban Negro Toasts."

45 Trachtenberg, "Hustler as Hero," 428.

46 For a brief discussion of the academic as "hustler," see Smyth and Hattam, "Intellectual as Hustler." One valuable aspect of their article is the counterpoint it provides to the manner in which Jay-Z employs "hustler." In this way, the distinctive and layered character of the hustler as Jay-Z intends it is further amplified in comparison.

47 Jay-Z, "Kill Jay-Z."

48 Jay-Z, "Moment of Clarity."

49 Jay-Z, "Lucifer."

50 Jay-Z, "Lucifer."

51 Jay-Z, "Lucifer."

52 Jay-Z, "D'Evils."

53 Jay-Z, "D'Evils." Relate this line to "Where I'm From," in which Jay-Z says, "I'm from the place where the church is the flakiest. An' niggas been praying to God so long that they atheist."

54 See, e.g., Jay-Z, *Decoded*, 314.

55 "This Life Forever," as found in Jay-Z, *Decoded*, 206.

56 Jay-Z, "Guilty Until Proven Innocent." Also see Jay-Z, "What More Can I Say?": "There's never been a nigga this good for this long. This hood or this pop, this hot or this strong."

57 See Jay-Z, *Decoded*, 292–97. "Minor mythologies" is the way he describes the stories families tell about their members and, in this case, the stories his mother tells about him (296).

58 See Jay-Z, "Heaven."

59 Jay-Z, "Heaven."

60 This is one way to read Jay-Z's response to the killing of Biggie Smalls: Jay-Z, "The City Is Mine"; Jay-Z, "Lucifer."

61 Jay-Z, *Decoded*, 94. Also see 287n12.

62 From "History": "So long so long / So now I'm flirting with Death hustling like a G . . . Before I get killed because I can't get robbed / So before me Success and Death ménage." Jay-Z, *Decoded*, 304. Discussing "History," Jay-Z speaks to the ability to tame death, to manage and subdue it, if by no other means than to name it without fear: "Success—meaning winning on the block as a hustler—and Death and me are like three lovers" (305n13).

63 Camus, *Myth of Sisyphus*.

64 Jay-Z, *Decoded*, 206n3. See James, *Varieties of Religious Experience*, lectures V–VI; and Pinn, *Interplay of Things*, where I give more attention to the theory of the sick soul. On bleakness, see also Jay-Z, *Decoded*, 211n7: "This is a recurring image in my songs, winter as a symbol of a desolate, difficult life. . . . [I]t reinforces your sense that the universe doesn't care about you, that you're on your own in a harsh world." This points to the "sick soul" posture toward the world.

65 Jay-Z, "Hard Knock Life (Ghetto Anthem)."

66 Jay-Z, *Decoded*, 205. Readers may want to read this statement concerning the presentation of reality in light of Tricia Rose's *The Hip Hop Wars*, which offers a comparison of the critique of hip hop as violent (and degrading) and artistic apologetics, which argue for hip hop as the expression of urban reality. Also see Forman and Neal, *That's the Joint!*, 69–225.

67 See Bataille, *Visions of Excess*; and Bakhtin, *Rabelais and His World*.

68 Jay-Z, "Early This Morning."

69 Jay-Z, "Moment of Clarity."

70 Jay-Z, "Beach Chair." Also see Jay-Z, "Young Forever."

71 Jay-Z, "American Dreamin.'"

72 *The Hip Hop Waltz of Eurydice*, a play by Reza Abdoh (1990), pulls the myth into the contemporary landscape, but what I have in mind isn't captured by this reworking of Orpheus. (For more information regarding Abdoh's intent, see Féral and Abdoh, "'Theater Is Not about Theory.'" For the Los Angeles premiere, see https://vimeopro.com/adamsoch/reza-abdoh/video/156807696.

73 Wilkinson, "Mr. Subway."

74 My goal isn't a full presentation of the Orpheus story, nor am I primarily concerned with the story's place in Greek religion and mythology and the content and rationale for its continued appeal. Rather, I aim to say enough about Orpheus to provide a way of framing or thinking about the implications of relating Jay-Z as hustler to music and *deathlife*.

75 *Orfeu Negro* (Black Orpheus) was directed by Marcel Camus and written by Camus and Jacques Viot. For a brief contextual piece related to Orpheus and Brazil, see Rankine, "Orpheus and the Racialized Body." See also Perrone, "Don't Look Back."

76 See Hanchard, *Orpheus and Power*; Shepherd, *Orpheus in the Bronx*; and Jay-Z's rap corpus.

77 Sartre, "Black Orpheus" (original title, "Orphée Noir"). See Simawe, *Black Orpheus*, xix.

78 Quoted in Haddour, "Sartre and Fanon," 287, citing Senghor's *Ce que je crois* (Paris: Grasset, 1988), 137, 158.

79 Sartre, "Black Orpheus," 25. Read this, for example, in relationship to Frantz Fanon's critique (and rejection of Negritude), or in relationship to historical analysis: Banchetti-Robino, "Black Orpheus and Aesthetic Historicism"; Haddour, "Sartre and Fanon."

80 Sartre, "Black Orpheus," 18–20.

81 See Jane Olmsted's chapter, "Black Moves, White Ways, Every Body's Blues: Orphic Power in Langston Hughes's *The Ways of White Folks*" (65–89), and Maria V. Johnson's chapter, "Shange and Her Three Sisters 'Sing a Liberation Song': Variations on the Orphic Theme" (181–203), in Simawe, *Black Orpheus*. Carla Cappetti, in "Black Orpheus," places Richard Wright on the list of those who present Black life through an Orphic turn.

82 My interest isn't primarily a discussion of how and why Orpheus has appealed to peoples of African descent in general terms. Rather, I am concerned here to provide some context for my basic concern: the utility of Orpheus as an allegory of the hustler. Readers interested in information on the history of and rationale for *Black Orpheus* the journal, see Benson, *Black Orpheus*, 17–95. For readers interested in the New Negro Movement, attention should first be turned to the work of Alain Locke in Rampersad, *New Negro*.

83 See Hanchard, *Orpheus and Power*, particularly the conclusion, where Hanchard lays out the hermeneutical use of "Black Orpheus."

84 Shepherd, *Orpheus in the Bronx*, 188.

85 Shepherd, *Orpheus in the Bronx*, 189, 188.

86 Reginald Shepherd, in *Orpheus in the Bronx*, also alludes to the significance of love in relationship to death pointed out in the narrative of Orpheus. But rather than a love interest, it is the nature of love for and from his mother that he seeks to use to tame death.

87 Warden, *Orpheus*, xiii.

88 More work needs to be done on the allegorical nature of the trap house within hip hop studies. I must thank Regina Bradley, whose lecture at Rice University (August 28, 2018) provided invaluable information concerning trap culture and inspired my interest in thinking through the implications of the trap house as a dimension of Orphic hip hop.

89 Jay-Z, *Decoded*, 255. He provides a sense of the hustle as a metaphor for the tensions depicted by hip hop, its grasp of American life: "The beauty of hip-hop is that, as I said at the beginning [of the book], it found its story in the story of the hustler. But that's not its only story. At this point, it's a tool that can be used to find the truth in anything. I'm still rhyming—not about hustling in the same way I rhymed about it on my first album, but about the same underlying quest. . . . What's the meaning of life? That's the question rap was built on from the beginning and, through a million different paths, that's still its ultimate subject." *Decoded*, 256.

90 Jay-Z says this regarding his father: "When we'd go to visit my aunt and uncle and cousins my father would give me the responsibility of leading, even though I was the youngest. When I was walking with him, he always walked real fast (he said that way if someone's following you, they'll lose you) and he expected me to not only keep up with him but to remember the details of the things I was passing. . . . He was teaching me to be confident and aware of my surroundings." *Decoded*, 202.

91 See Jay-Z, "Ocean," for an example of the significance of movement as metaphor and allegory.

92 Guthrie, *Orpheus and Greek Religion*, 41.

93 Guthrie, *Orpheus and Greek Religion*; Wroe, *Orpheus*.

94 See Jay-Z, "Crown."

95 Guthrie, in *Orpheus and Greek Religion*, says: "For the present we may notice at least that Orpheus was regarded by the Greeks as the founder of a certain kind of religion, that much has been written on the Orphic religion, sometimes known more simply to-day as Orphism" (8). See also Warden, *Orpheus*, ix. The relationship, as John Warden describes it, between this sect and efforts to become divine (x) has interesting implications for Jay-Z's various claims to divinity, although the point shouldn't be pushed beyond low-level mirroring.

96 My concern isn't to sustain an argument for a direct comparison of Jay-Z and Orpheus in relation to the establishment of "movements"; rather, I am intrigued by the possibility of further understanding Jay-Z's hustler persona in relationship to Orpheus, his music, and dealings with death.

97 On Orpheus as Christ, see Vicari, "The Triumph of Art, the Triumph of Death."

98 See, for example, Robbins, "Famous Orpheus."

99 My concern isn't with these particular elements but rather the implications and range of what might be understood as shared talent, and the manner in which the application of that talent speaks to the mood and movement of death.

The adventure component of the Orpheus story is presented in Warden, *Orpheus*, 3–24, and Robbins, "Famous Orpheus," among other texts. Jay-Z's corpus certainly includes attention to the workings of relationship (especially in the context of his marriage to Beyoncé). However, the persistence and consistency of love that results in faithfulness plays out with Orpheus but not Jay-Z. For example, some writers highlight a variant of the Orpheus story that sees him reject connection with women after the final loss of his wife as she is returned to Hades—after her, he will embrace no others because "supposedly Orpheus loved Eurydice more than any mortal has ever loved." Wroe, *Orpheus*, 109. This loss takes place because he didn't abide by the rules for her safe passage, but this is due to his inability to resist looking back at her during their journey, not affection for another. One can't depict this failure as infidelity, but it could be classified as the consequence of too deep a devotion. Jay-Z, on the other hand, speaks to devotion marred by betrayal, a prime example being the narrative of his album *4:44*. In "Kill Jay-Z," for example, he chronicles his wrongdoing. However, there is introspection here that isn't present in earlier accounts of pleasure over involvement (e.g., "Big Pimpin'").

100 Guthrie, *Orpheus and Greek Religion*, 29.

101 See Du Bois, "Of Spiritual Strivings," in Du Bois, *Souls of Black Folk*, 7–15.

102 In some of my earlier work, I connected the blues legends of "bad man" characters with hip hop culture, as a way to address a lineage of rebellion and confrontation. Hip hop's relationship to death in Jay-Z's corpus entails a posture toward life/death more nuanced than one finds with these blues outlaws. See the final two chapters of Pinn, *Why, Lord?*; Pinn, "How Ya Livin'?"; and Pinn, "Gettin' Grown."

103 Guthrie, *Orpheus and Greek Religion*, 62. There are glimpses of a similar metaphysics of life-death in Jay-Z's corpus.

104 Regarding Hades, I have in mind Sisyphus. However, while Sisyphus serves death, so to speak, he does so with great punishment. Albeit, as Albert Camus notes, he was not conquered by his punishment, it did—unlike death for Orpheus or the corner for Jay-Z—curtail the full exercise of his particular talents and skills, which allowed him to initially escape death.

105 Jay-Z, "Crown."

106 Z. Smith, *Feel Free*, 65. I am grateful to Mayra Rivera for pointing out this interview, "The House That Hova Built," reproduced in Smith's collection.

107 As Baldwin reflected on his Harlem, Jay-Z might also surmise one had to belong to something in order to survive the conditions of New York City.

108 Z. Smith, *Feel Free*, 66.

109 Jay-Z, "Hard Knock Life (Ghetto Anthem)."

110 See Bataille, "Nietzsche's Laughter," in *Unfinished System of Nonknowledge*, 18–25.

111 Jay-Z, *Decoded*, 239, 240. See Bataille, *Eroticism*.

112 Jay-Z, *Decoded*, 113.

113 Although of limited applicability here (in part due to the manner in which Jay-Z speaks of addiction in broad ways that extend to a much more metaphorical take on drugs and drug use (e.g., addiction to material goods, to wealth, etc.; the potentiality of demise/death informs either context), the following is an interesting discussion of crackhead identity over against hustler identity: Copes, Hochstetler, and Williams, "'We Weren't Like No Regular Dope Fiends.'" For a discussion of Jay-Z's music in relationship to economic desire and growth, see Reeves, *Somebody Scream!*, 203–22.

Jay-Z describes this context of hearing gunfire as he encountered it during his youth. See Jay-Z, *Decoded*, 12–18.

Regarding the sense of difference, see the introduction to Bataille, *Unfinished System of Nonknowledge*. For Jay-Z, there is slippage between the concept of God and the concept of self. One gets a sense of this in an explanatory note to "Where I'm From" in which he says, "But these lines ['IF the shit is lies, god strike me / And I got a question, are you forgiving guys who live just like me? / We'll never know . . .'] aren't about God in the traditional sense, they're almost questions back to myself." *Decoded*, 214n23.

114 Jay-Z describes this context as he encountered it during his youth. See Jay-Z, *Decoded*, 18.

115 Jay-Z, "Crown."

2. THE ANTIHERO

This chapter draws on and builds on my earlier thinking about Kendrick Lamar in Pinn, "Kendrick Lamar Confronts Black Death"; and Pinn, "'Real Nigga Conditions.'"

1 Kendrick Lamar, *DAMN.*

2 Lamar was awarded the 2018 Pulitzer Prize for Music.

3 From Kendrick Lamar, "YAH.": "I got so many theories and suspicions: I'm diagnosed with real nigga conditions." I also highlight this line in Pinn, "'Real Nigga Conditions.'"

4 Zoladz, "Power of Kendrick Lamar's 'Damn.'"

5 For examples of my thinking on Black moralism, see Pinn, *Interplay of Things*; Pinn, "What Can Be Said?"; and Pinn, "Theology after 'Hope' and 'Future.'"

6 James, *Varieties of Religious Experience*.

7 Miguelito, "Praise and Questions."

8 Camus did not understand himself to be an existentialist. Rather, he understood himself to be a moralist.

9 Kendrick Lamar, "FEEL."

10 Hiatt, "Kendrick Lamar."

11 Hiatt, "Kendrick Lamar."
12 Mizruchi, "Neighbors, Strangers, Corpses," 192.
13 See Kendrick Lamar, "FEAR."
14 See Kendrick Lamar, "PRIDE."
15 See Kendrick Lamar, "FEAR."
16 Zisook, "Kendrick Lamar Responds to DJBooth Article."
17 See, for example, Douglas, *Purity and Danger*.
18 See Kendrick Lamar, "GOD."
19 See Kendrick Lamar, "DUCKWORTH."
20 See Kendrick Lamar, "FEAR."
21 This, I would argue, is the sentiment undergirding the track "LOYALTY." on *DAMN*.
22 Kendrick Lamar, "HUMBLE."
23 See Kendrick Lamar, "LUST."; Kendrick Lamar, "LOVE."
24 Kendrick Lamar, "LUST."
25 Kendrick Lamar, "LOVE."
26 Kendrick Lamar, "XXX."
27 Du Bois, "Of the Training of Black Men," in Du Bois, *Souls of Black Folk*, 81.
28 This is from Hiatt, "Kendrick Lamar."
29 Hiatt, "Kendrick Lamar."
30 See Kendrick Lamar, "DUCKWORTH."
31 Hiatt, "Kendrick Lamar."
32 Camus, *Myth of Sisyphus*, 51.
33 Camus, *Myth of Sisyphus*, 53.
34 Camus, *Myth of Sisyphus*, 54, 60–62.
35 See, for instance, Hardwick, "Eminem Dead."
36 Texts related to the nature of eulogy in hip hop include Barrett, "Dead Men Printed." My sense of eulogy is more concerned with how it functions as a trope as opposed to written texts of celebration.
37 Readers may also be interested in Eminem's memoir, *The Way I Am*.
38 It might be interesting to think about this in light of theological analysis concerned with the dangerous nature of violent memory. See, for instance, Goldstein, "Performing Redemption." Or one might view this turn to death through the work of Paul Tillich: see McLeod, "If God Got Us."
39 See Section Eighty, "Attempts to Blame Murder/Suicide on Eminem Music," for a list of fans who committed violent acts.
40 See, e.g., Garland, "Eminem's 'Stan'"; and Sule and Inkster, "Analysing Stan." Also see Sule and Inkster, "Eminem's Character, Stan."
41 Eminem, "Stan."
42 Eminem, "Stan."
43 Eminem, "Stan."
44 Eminem, "Stan."
45 See, e.g., Eminem, "The Real Slim Shady."
46 "Stan" contains a line in which Slim Shady is pleased that he serves as an inspiration to Stan. In an interview with Touré, "An In-Depth Conversation

with Kendrick Lamar," Lamar says, "I'm a human being, I'm a person, I have family, I have my own personal problems. But I have to give to the world. That's my responsibility. It's not just a job or entertainment for me; this is what I have to offer to the world."

47 Eminem, "Stan."
48 Eminem, "Stan."
49 Wang, "Kendrick Lamar's 'DAMN.'"
50 Camus, *Myth of Sisyphus.*
51 Eminem, "Bad Guy."
52 Eminem, "Bad Guy."
53 Eminem, "Bad Guy."
54 Eminem, "Bad Guy."
55 A line from Kendrick Lamar, "Alright."
56 Kendrick Lamar, "King Kunta": "Now I run the game got the whole world talkin', King Kunta / Everybody wanna cut the legs off him, Kunta."
57 Kendrick Lamar, "FEAR."
58 See Camus, *The Rebel.*
59 Kendrick Lamar, "LOYALTY."
60 Kendrick Lamar, "LOYALTY."
61 Kendrick Lamar, "FEEL."
62 Kendrick Lamar, "XXX."
63 Kendrick Lamar, "Alright": ". . . 'and we hate po-po; wanna kill us dead in the street fo sho.'" The line is also referenced at the end of "BLOOD." on *DAMN.*
64 Lamar positions a decisive answer to that question between "wickedness" and "weakness"—neither suggests a strong and transformative response to the tragic quality of life.
65 Eminem, "Bad Guy."

3. BACCHIC INTENT

1 Baker, "Two Insane Days on Tour with Tyler, the Creator."
2 I would argue that the album *Flower Boy* (2017) isn't a departure from the take on death and demise chronicled on *Goblin*, but there is movement from the erotic-transgressive realism that projects death as pleasure-joy to a type of moralism.
3 Some, like Mikko O. Koivisto, think of Tyler, the Creator's music in relationship to horrorcore rap: see Koivisto, "'I Know You Think I'm Crazy.'" I am mindful that *Goblin* has been critiqued for its brutality, its violence toward women, its aggressive masculinity, and its assumed glorification of destruction on a variety of levels. My goal here isn't to endorse the moral-ethical vision proclaimed on the album, but rather to rehearse what it tells us about hip hop's relationship to death in particular and what I am calling *deathlife* in general. See, e.g., Eate, "Scribblin' Sinnin' Sh*t."

4   Caramanica, "Angry Rhymes, Dirty Mouth, Goofy Kind." The author leaves out Tyler's line "It's a fucking fiction," but it doesn't alter the overall intent of the narrative.

5   See Eate, "Scribblin' Sinnin' Sh*t," 535. These lines are from Tyler, the Creator, "Goblin."

6   Sterbenz, "Movement, Music, Feminism," 6. Sterbenz is drawing from Long, "Listen to the Story."

7   Tyler, the Creator, "Sarah."

8   Tyler, the Creator, "Goblin."

9   As of 2015, "Yonkers" had 98 million views on YouTube. Baker, "Two Insane Days on Tour with Tyler, the Creator."

10   Eate, "Scribblin' Sinnin' Sh*t," 535.

11   Long, "Listen to the Story," 96.

12   Baker, "Two Insane Days on Tour with Tyler, the Creator."

13   Tyler, the Creator, "Goblin."

14   Tyler, the Creator, "Radicals."

15   I would also avoid assumptions of immaturity with respect to this album, which often come up when commentators compare *Goblin* to *Flower Boy*. Spencer Kornhaber reflects on this comparison in "The Classic Queer Paradox of Tyler, the Creator."

16   Tyler, the Creator, "Goblin."

17   See Bataille, *Theory of Religion*, 22.

18   Bataille, *Theory of Religion*, 28–33.

19   Bataille, *Theory of Religion*, 47.

20   Bataille, *Theory of Religion*, 48. See also Lechte, "Thinking the (Ecstatic) Essential," 38.

21   Although, as will become clear, we can think about Tyler's consumption of a roach in the video for "Yonkers" as the troubling of class (e.g., life for Blacks associated with poverty marked by the effort to escape such insects) taken out of its typical presentation. The means of production and the markers of utility are disturbed through an act of consumption as demise. Bataille provides an interesting discussion of death and thingification in relationship to slavery in *Theory of Religion*, 58–60.

22   I say this in light of Bataille's discussion of thingness as a consequence of identity restricted to work produced. See Bataille, *Eroticism*, 157–58; and Bataille, *Unfinished System of Nonknowledge*, 254. I apply a very different understanding of thing and thingness in my work *Interplay of Things*. In that text, my concern is to explore the nature of openness, the manner in which the body functions. It has little to do, in that context, with identity or ontological claims more expansively but rather works in terms of my theory of religion as a technology that exposes the interplay of "things"—which includes human bodies but without the negative connotations assumed here by Bataille.

23 I need to provide an important qualifying statement: Bataille often talks about the relationship to death as a matter of animal nature. I want to be careful here, in that the social code of race has done its work in part through an effort to render the Black body less than human. My contention is that hip hop frames something like the erotic in relationship to death, but this is not to say it does so while endorsing dehumanization of certain bodies as a necessary move. For hip hop, the erotic brings into question a range of boundaries—including how race serves as a safeguard for the status quo. On the aesthetic nature of Bataille's argument and its relationship to social codes such as race, see Stabler, "Punishment in Effigy."

24 With the "mad" characterization, I refer to the psychology of performance associated with Dionysus. See Otto, *Dionysus*, 103–19, 143. It would be interesting to read this sense of "madness" against Bruce, *How to Go Mad without Losing Your Mind*.

25 I say this having in mind Courtney Friesen's brief discussion of madness in *Reading Dionysus*, 6–10, esp. 9.

26 Friesen notes an important connection with respect to *deathlife* when reminding her readers that "a famous mid-fifth-century burial inscription from Cumae, for example, indicates a close relationship between Bacchic initiation and funerary rites: 'it is not permitted to lie here if someone is not initiated into Bacchus.'" *Reading Dionysus*, 11.

27 Tyler, the Creator, "Nightmare."

28 Bataille, *Theory of Religion*, 49.

29 Bataille, *Unfinished System of Nonknowledge*, 196.

30 Bataille, *Inner Experience*, 80.

31 Tyler, the Creator, "Tron Cat."

32 Bataille, *Visions of Excess*, 41.

33 Bataille, *Visions of Excess*, 41; Bataille, *Inner Experience*, 178–79.

34 Tyler, the Creator, "Radicals."

35 From Hartmann, "Eroticism," 183, 186.

36 Tyler, the Creator, "Yonkers." One could also think through the suicidal impulse (but without the same erotic quality) using Biggie Smalls's album *Ready to Die*. While that is an important investigation, my concern here is the relationship between the death drive and its erotic quality—a dimension of death in hip hop not so commonly explored.

37 If this chapter gives attention to the "murderer," so to speak, chapter 4 looks at death from the vantage point of the "murdered."

38 Attention to this sense of the erotic can be found in Arya, *Abjection and Representation*, 69. See Bataille, *Eroticism*, 11. Much of what Bataille describes in terms of the erotic's relationship to death has to do with sex (i.e., the "little death"). While that is useful for my argument, I am more concerned with the manner in which the erotic defines a particular moral and ethical "mood" that projects a different sense of and meaning for death.

39 Testa, "At the Expense of Life," 45, 47. Stephen Bush argues that Bataille speaks positively to the recognition of our cruel nature so as to prevent it from exploding in more detrimental ways: "Bataille wants us to acknowledge our double nature. He thinks that our impulses toward cruelty and mastery are ineradicable, and what we need to do is find proper avenues in which to express them, lest they break forth in more 'disastrous' ways, not the least of which is the 'infinite horror' of war." Bush, "Sharing in What Death Reveals," 9. This, then, would suggest there is a utility in the expression of pleasure to the extent pleasure relates to cruelty and death.

40 Tyler, the Creator, "Radicals." See Hartmann, "Eroticism," 140.

41 See Bataille, *Unfinished System of Nonknowledge*, 123. See also J. M. Lo Duca, introduction to Bataille, *Tears of Eros*: "From elimination to elimination, pain appears to him as a mediator—an intermediary and go-between—between life and death" (4).

42 Bataille, *Unfinished System of Nonknowledge*, 196.

43 Stabler, "Punishment in Effigy," 310.

44 Bataille, *Eroticism*, 16.

45 According to Bataille, "It is work that separated man from his initial animality. It is through work that the animal became human. Work was, above all else the foundation for knowledge and reason. The making of tools and weapons was the point of departure for that early faculty of reason which humanized the animal we once were." *Tears of Eros*, 41.

46 See Bataille, *Unfinished System of Nonknowledge*, 238–39.

47 Bataille, *Eroticism*, 109.

48 "Obscenity is our name for the uneasiness which upsets the physical state associated with self-possession, with the possession of a recognized and stable individuality." Bataille, *Eroticism*, 17–18.

49 Bataille, *Unfinished System of Nonknowledge*, xxiii.

50 Tyler, the Creator, "Yonkers."

51 Bataille, *Eroticism*, 18.

52 Bataille, *Unfinished System of Nonknowledge*, xxxix.

53 Bataille, *Tears of Eros*, 32.

54 Tyler, the Creator, "Transylvania."

55 Tyler, the Creator tweet, Twitter, September 13, 2012. There's also the Odd Future sketch comedy show on Adult Swim titled *Loiter Squad*.

56 Bataille, *Eroticism*, 72.

57 Tyler, the Creator, "Transylvania."

58 I explore the nature of openness in *Interplay of Things*.

59 Bataille, *Eroticism*, 21.

60 Bataille, *Eroticism*, 24.

61 The track continues with "One, two, you're the girl that I want / Three, four, five, six, seven; shit / Eight is the bullets if you say no after all this."

62 Bataille, *Eroticism*, 29.

63 Baker, "Two Insane Days on Tour with Tyler, the Creator."

64 Bataille, *Eroticism*, 44.

65 Tyler, the Creator, "Radicals."

66 Camus, *The Rebel*, 36. I recognize Camus and Bataille both speak about the political-economic arrangements of life in light of war, but their relationship to the physical dynamics of this destruction differs and, as a consequence, their conceptions of plausible moral-ethical orientations also differ. Nonetheless, it is useful for my purposes to bring them into conversation, albeit in a limited fashion. Tyler has a similar break, a similar struggle with constraint represented by social institutions (e.g., medical professionals). See Tyler, the Creator, "Golden."

67 Camus, *The Rebel*, 41.

68 Camus, *The Rebel*, 40. I have in mind Daniel W. Smith's review of *Eroticism: Death and Sensuality*, where he notes the "sacred is erotic and chaotic" (595).

69 Hegarty, "Bataille Conceiving Death," 176–77.

70 For a discussion of Bataille that seeks to trouble his concern for the Marquis de Sade's moral philosophy and does so through a Christian mysticism lens, see Bush, "Ethics of Ecstasy."

71 As Tina Arppe notes, "In the Bataillean scheme death is a profoundly ambivalent thing. By destroying the isolated (and in his isolation object-like) individual (or sacrificial animal) it opens up a fleeting breach into the (always already) 'lost' continuity of being. Thus, it is something to be celebrated." "Sacred Violence," 43.

72 In the track "Radicals," Tyler says, "Random disclaimer! Hey, don't do anything that I say in this song, okay? It's fucking fiction." Regarding Tyler, Duri Long states, "Some propose that Tyler's music is satirical—an ironic representation of hip hop culture, poking fun at the nihilistic themes often found in rap music by taking them to the extreme. They excuse his violent imagery with the fact that it is just that—imagery; he never lives out any of the fantasies he envisions." "Listen to the Story," 96. In addition, Ernest Baker states it this way: "The provocative nature of Tyler and his music is rooted in humor, not experience." Baker, "Two Insane Days on Tour with Tyler, the Creator."

73 Winkie, "20 Best Tyler, the Creator Lyrics."

74 Tyler, the Creator, "She."

75 Bataille, *Visions of Excess*, 93, 94.

76 Bataille, *Eroticism*, 167.

77 Bataille, *Eroticism*, 167; Hartmann, "Eroticism," 139.

78 Sanneh, "Where's Earl?"

79 Bataille, *Eroticism*, 168.

80 Bataille, *Eroticism*, 168–69; Marcus Coelen, "Heterology," in Hewson and Coelen, *Georges Bataille*, 88–95.

81 I say this thinking about work by Megan Moore: "Romancing Death," 402.

82 Winters, "Rac(e)ing from Death," 388.

83 Liran Razinsky says this regarding Bataille: "Survival, for Bataille, is an animal quality. Every animal is concerned with its survival. Man is willing to ap-

proach death and is thereby human. He is not a slave to his survival instinct. He gains sovereignty through his willingness to risk his life." "How to Look Death in the Eyes," 67. While something of this argument is useful in my effort to understand a particularly well-neglected mood in hip hop, it is not lost on me that Bataille's proclamation (and the Marquis de Sade's nobility) entails a certain degree of leisure—of privilege—that speaks to a depth of connection to the status quo rejected.

84 Stephen Bush gets at this point in "Sharing in What Death Reveals," 9.

85 Tyler, the Creator, "Nightmare."

86 Bataille says the following: "Erotic conduct is the opposite of normal conduct as spending is the opposite of getting. If we follow the dictates of reason we try to acquire all kinds of goods, we work in order to increase the sum of our possessions or of our knowledge, we use all means to get richer and to possess more. Our status in the social order is based on this sort of behaviour. But when the fever of sex seizes us we behave in the opposite way. We recklessly draw on our strength and sometimes in the violence of passion we squander considerable resources to no real purpose. Pleasure is so close to ruinous waste that we refer to the moment of climax as a 'little death.' Consequently anything that suggests erotic excess always implies disorder." *Eroticism*, 170.

87 Bataille, *Eroticism*, 170.

88 I say this in light of Bataille's *The Unfinished System of Nonknowledge* and the introduction to that volume by Stuart Kendall, which states, "In an attempt to understand inner experience, to bring it within the realm of consciousness, to make it possible, propositions were to be advanced, and Bataille and Blanchot had already begun the process. Their initial proposals were three: . . . rejection of all hope for salvation, indeed all hope of any kind, the acceptance of experience itself as the only value and authority, and the recognition that experience meant self-expiation, as experience occurs only in the context of self-contestation" (xxi).

89 Downing and Gillett, "Georges Bataille at the Avant-Garde of Queer Theory?," 95.

90 To the extent the language of the tragic plays out in Bataille's framework, Alexander Riley provides an interesting discussion using Nietzsche—a thinking of great importance to Bataille. However, Riley's piece is tied to the language of cultural norms when it comes to gangsta rap: it seeks only to provide an apologetic response to the language used to capture the events and moods depicted. In this way it doesn't offer a full framing of what takes place in horror rap such as Tyler, the Creator's *Goblin*. See Riley, "Rebirth of Tragedy."

91 Bataille, *Eroticism*, 174.

92 Tyler, the Creator, "Nightmare."

93 All references to "Yonkers" concern the track on *Goblin* (2011).

94 Bataille, *Eroticism*, 181–82.

95 Bataille, *Eroticism*, 183.

96 Bataille, *Unfinished System of Nonknowledge*, 197.

97 Bataille, *Eroticism*, 252; Bataille, *Unfinished System of Nonknowledge*, 197.

98 Bataille, *Unfinished System of Nonknowledge*, 123.

99 See Downing and Gillett, "Georges Bataille at the Avant-Garde of Queer Theory?," 88–90.

100 Bataille, *Unfinished System of Nonknowledge*, 207, 209, 213; Bataille, *Inner Experience*, xii–xiii.

101 Bataille, *Inner Experience*, xiii–xiv. Regarding poetry, Bataille says, "Of poetry, I will now say that it is, I believe, the sacrifice in which words are victim. Words—we use them; we make of them the instruments of useful acts. We wouldn't be human if language within us had to be entirely servile" (135).

102 Bataille, *Inner Experience*, 45.

103 Tyler, the Creator, "Sandwitches."

104 See Bataille, *Inner Experience*, 74–75; Lechte, "Thinking the (Ecstatic) Essential," 37.

105 I think this is what Bataille is getting at in *The Accursed Share: Volumes II and III* when saying, "Nothing must be concealed: what is involved, finally, is a failure of humanity. True, this failure does not concern humanity as a whole. Only servile man, who averts his eyes from that which is not useful, which serves no purpose, is implicated" (14–15).

106 I say this in light of J. M. Lo Duca's assessment of Bataille's take on death and reality, in page 5 of the introduction of *Tears of Eros*.

107 Bataille gives limited attention to Dionysus in *Tears of Eros*, 57–77. My interest in turning to Bacchus was motivated first by my effort to think through Orpheus in relationship to Jay-Z, which led me to Dionysus. Bataille, however, helps me think through the presence of death as a dimension of energetic engagement with demise marked by orgiastic practice in the Bacchus mythology.

108 In addition to Nietzsche's discussion of Dionysus in *Birth of Tragedy*, there is also his *Dionysian Vision of the World*. Attention to Nietzsche in this chapter is only indirect, as my primary theorist of concern, Bataille, employs his writings.

109 Bataille, *Inner Experience*, 175.

110 I say this, considering John F. Moffitt's work to explore descriptively and historically the way in which Bacchus appears in artistic production and thought—the manner in which it inspires thinkers and artists beyond the initial depictions of the Greek figure. See Moffitt, *Inspiration*. My effort here isn't a similar and systematic unpacking of Bacchus and the contemporary art of hip hop through direct relationship and intentional application. My acquaintance with that type of project is here only secondhand, to the extent Bataille intentionally employs Nietzsche, for instance, in framing his work. Furthermore, my concern isn't with claims to divinity or critiques of divin-

ity in hip hop. An interesting discussion of the human-divine relationality is provided by Bataille in *Theory of Religion*.

111 Richard Seaford, in chapter 6 of *Dionysos*, provides a concise discussion of Dionysus and death.

112 Bataille, *Eroticism*, 117.

113 I have in mind Friedrich Nietzsche's *The Birth of Tragedy* and the various motivations emerging through attention to his Dionysian turn.

114 For additional information on Bacchus as well as cultural uses of this mythological figure, see Seaford, *Dionysos*; Dalby, *Story of Bacchus*; Kerényi, *Dionysos*; and Moffitt, *Inspiration*.

115 I give limited attention to the appearance of Bacchus in Nella Larsen's *Quicksand* in *Interplay of Things*.

116 Detienne, *Dionysos at Large*, 2.

117 Detienne, *Dionysos at Large*, 21.

118 Marcel Detienne references Dionysus as the "Stranger who brings strangeness." See Detienne, *Dionysos at Large*, 10–18.

119 Carlevale, "Dionysian Revival," 364.

120 Schechner, "The Politics of Ecstasy," quoted in Seaford, *Dionysos*, 5.

121 For instance, as outlined by Wetmore, *Black Dionysus*.

122 See West, *Prophesy Deliverance!*

123 Larsen, *Quicksand*, 87.

124 Carlevale, "Dionysian Revival," 365. For a more substantive discussion of Dionysus's relationship to *deathlife*, see Kerényi, *Dionysos*.

125 Bailey, "Homolatent Masculinity," 186.

126 Bailey, "Homolatent Masculinity," 187.

127 Bailey, "Homolatent Masculinity," 190.

128 Bailey, "Homolatent Masculinity," 195, 196. Bailey argues, "'I don't give a fuck.' Why should someone give one? Why should one hope if 'hopes not home'? This line of reasoning demanded that I ask myself why I still care when it hurts too much. Having access to a community of people who feel similarly helps me. Through connection, I access the possible" (196).

129 Bailey connects the concept of latents, borrowed from Octavia Butler, as a way to explore the frustrations experienced by Black men in the United States. For example, she writes, "Butler's words could easily be applied to the realities of young black men in the contemporary United States. . . . The stifled powers of latents conjure the subjugated spirits of black men in a racialized United States." "Homolatent Masculinity," 188.

130 Larsen, *Quicksand*, 109.

131 Larsen, *Quicksand*, 113.

132 Koch, "Michelangelo's Bacchus," 354.

133 Koch, "Michelangelo's Bacchus," 356–58.

134 Larsen, *Quicksand*, 133.

135 Larsen, *Quicksand*, 112–14.

136 Larsen, *Quicksand*, 134.

137 Larsen, *Quicksand*, 133.

138 Tyler, the Creator, "Radicals."

139 Larsen, *Quicksand*, 135.

140 "The Religion and Political Views of Tyler, the Creator," Hollowverse, May 10, 2012, https://hollowverse.com/tyler-the-creator/. Also see Jacob Moore, "Nas and Tyler the Creator Talk God, Drugs, Bruno Mars, and Upcoming Album," Complex, October 26, 2011, https://www.complex.com/music/2011/10/nas -and-tyler-the-creator-talk-god-drugs-bruno-mars-and-nas-new-album.

141 As Walter F. Otto notes, "Dionysus, himself, is a suffering, dying god who must succumb to the violence of terrible enemies in the midst of the glory of his youthful greatness." Later he reflects that "the god himself suffers the hor- ror which he commits. That which the myth tells in words, the cultus repeats in regular sacrificial actions." *Dionysus*, 103, 107.

142 Larsen, *Quicksand*, 130.

143 Tyler, the Creator, "Goblin."

4. ZOMBIC HUNGER

The argument in this chapter builds on and serves to correct some of my thinking in "Zombies in the 'Hood." This chapter draws on Afropessimism and zombie studies to frame a response to death differently formulated than what is found in this earlier piece.

  1 While this chapter will limit itself to an understanding of the zombie within the particular framework of *deathlife*, many scholars speak in terms of two initial types of zombies: those involving control over the spirit, and those in- volving revitalization of the body of a deceased person. In addition, scholars such as Kevin Boon offer complex ways of categorizing zombies. Boon states, "The nine types, briefly defined, are as follows: (1) zombie drone: a person whose will has been taken from him or her, resulting in a slavish obedience; (2) zombie ghoul: fusion of the zombie and the ghoul, which has lost voli- tion and feeds on flesh; (3) tech zombie: people who have lost their volition through the use of some technological device; (4) bio zombie: similar to tech zombies, except some biological, natural, or chemical element is the medium that robs people of their will; (5) zombie channel: a person who has been resurrected and some other entity has possessed his or her form; (6) psy- chological zombie: a person who has lost his or her will as a result of some psychological conditioning; (7) cultural zombie: in general, refers to the type of zombie we locate within popular culture; (8) zombie ghost: not actually a zombie, rather someone who has returned from the dead with all or most of his or her faculties intact; and (9) zombie ruse: sleight of hand common in young adult novels where the 'zombies' turn out to not be zombies at all. It should be noted that these categories often overlap." Boon, "And the Dead Shall Rise: Part Introduction," in Christie and Lauro, *Better Off Dead*, 8.

  2 Evans and Giroux, *Disposable Futures*, 6.

3 Wright, *Native Son*.

4 De Genova, "Gangster Rap"; Malone, "Long-Lost Brothers"; Ellis, *If We Must Die*.

5 Collins, "Biggie Envy and the Gangsta Sublime," 911.

6 De Genova, "Gangster Rap," 106.

7 Goran Aijmer, "Introduction," in Abbink and Aijmer, *Meanings of Violence*, 1.

8 See, e.g., Flatbush Zombies, "Death 2" ("I am wicked like no other . . ."); and Dr. Dre and Ice Cube, "Natural Born Killaz," which was discussed in the introduction. The taking of life is graphic on these two tracks, but the killers are perceived as demented, troubled humans who are alive and causing death. My concern is with a different scenario—the personification or performance of death as death for death and not captured through the traditional grammar of human value, along the lines of what one might find with the Butcher Brothaz (Scum and Insane Poetry); e.g., "Death on a Meat Hook" and "Killing Spree."

9 Hunnicutt and Andrews, "Tragic Narratives in Popular Culture," 623, 625. Many hip hop tracks assume the already always presence of demise as unavoidable, but also gendered. This is not to say women don't meet a violent end in rap lyrics; they certainly do. Yet it is less common for women to be portrayed as the agent of violent death.

10 Kanye West and Jay-Z, "Monster." This is more than being mentally dead— that is, not socially conscious, or surrendering to the circumstances of social life. Gravediggaz make this type of reference during a short interview: see "Gravediggaz Interview + Live Footage from 1994." Also see [Berkeley], "Poetic of the Gravediggaz." However, what I have in mind isn't primarily an existential critique or concern but rather an ontological description. *Zombie* can also refer to those consumed by drug use (e.g., Esham's line "In Detroit, crack-head zombies still prostituting" from "In Detroit"; Lil Uzi Vert's "Yuh, servin', all of these motherfuckin' zombies," from "Run Up"; $uicideboy$'s "I be that walking zombie, bath salts, eating bodies," from "Carrollton"; or $uicideboy$'s "Dropping Adderall in alcohol and then I pop a fucking oxy; I'm a zombie, I'm a motherfucking dead man walking" from "Now I'm up to My Neck with Offers"), but that is a definition not of concern in this chapter.

11 Flatlinerz, "Flatline." This is not to say horrorcore doesn't include a multimetaphor structure whereby attention is also given to the manner in which horror reflects existential conditions, while also pointing toward a challenge to ontological frameworks. And, furthermore, horrorcore artists don't move between these two framings on a given album or even on a single track.

12 Flatlinerz, "Run."

13 This line by Frukwan lends itself to my argument, although it is followed by this from Prince Paul: "Fuck the Gravediggaz, I see zombies on the streets of Brooklyn every muthafuckin' day." It is possible they reflect first an ontological turn, while, second, Prince Paul offers an existential read. See Gravediggaz, "Ashes to Ashes."

14 See, e.g., the videos "Tech N9ne—I Caught Crazy!" and "Tech N9ne—Hard"; and Sandoval, "Behind My Face Paint." For the origin of Tech N9ne's use of face paint in 1994, see Griffin, "Tech N9ne Explains Origin of Face Paint."

15 Kubrin, "'I See Death around the Corner.'"

16 For an interesting discussion of ontology in relationship to zombies, see Cohen, "Undead."

17 Berlant and Edelman, *Sex, or the Unbearable*, vii–viii. For the way in which a similar conversation takes place in terms of mental coherence and psychic disability, see Pickens, *Black Madness::Mad Blackness*.

18 Pawlett, *Violence, Society and Radical Theory*, ix.

19 For material related to violence and subjectivity, see Evans and Giroux, *Disposable Futures*; Sarat and Shoemaker, *Who Deserves to Die*; Stone, *Anatomy of Evil*; and Kantor, *Psychopathy of Everyday Life*.

20 Fan Mason, "'The Galvanic 'Unhuman': Technology, the Living Dead and the 'Animal-Machine' in Literature and Culture," in Hubner, Leaning, and Manning, *Zombie Renaissance in Popular Culture*, 193–94.

21 This connection to religious ritual in the Americas is a primary mode of identification, but it isn't the only link to African sensibilities. "The zombie," writes Sarah Juliet Lauro, "doesn't even really belong to Vaudou. If we look further back in time than Haiti, or even Saint Dominique, we find this narrative's ancestry in colonial documents recording the people's fears of soul capture practiced by neighboring tribes in Angola." *Transatlantic Zombie*, 16. Chera Kee elucidates the Haiti connection: "Haiti's revolution deprived white Europeans and Americans of the ability to 'civilize' the black world formerly known as Saint Dominique; therefore, Haiti had to be demonized so as to create a situation where the civilizing forces of the white world could save the nation from itself. Therefore, the revolution and the nation it produced could never be seen as successful. . . . Following colonialist discourse elsewhere, many writers tended to portray Haiti as a country in ruins. Unlike other colonial holdings, however, Haiti's ruins were not evidence of a once-great empire, but rather evidence of French colonialism left to waste. Voodoo was often cited as the root cause for the devolution these authors saw at play in Haiti." "'They Are Not Men . . . They Are Dead Bodies!': From Cannibal to Zombie and Back Again," in Christie and Lauro, *Better Off Dead*, 11–12.

22 Lauro calls the zombie a "creolized and creolizing figure" as a way to capture its function as "metaphor, a symbol, an allegory, a figure, and an icon." *Transatlantic Zombie*, 3–4. Stephanie Boluk and Wylie Lenz describe the zombie as not simply being "a metaphor for the anxiety du jour, but that it is metaphor—a kind of walking meta-metaphor, and a self-reflexive metonym for the media through which it circulates." *Generation Zombie*, 10.

23 See, e.g., Guynes-Vishniac, "The Zombie and Its Metaphors."

24 See, e.g., Brooks, "Importance of Neglected Intersections"; Moreman, *Race, Oppression, and the Zombie*; Lauro, *Transatlantic Zombie*; Lanzendörfer, *Books of the Dead*; Comentale and Jaffe, *Year's Work at the Zombie Research*

Center; Platts, "Locating Zombies"; Pokornowski, "Vulnerable Life"; Crofts and Vogl, "Dehumanized and Demonized Refugees"; McAlister, "Slaves, Cannibals, and Infected Hyper-Whites"; and Peake, "He Is Dead." There is also Jean-Paul Sartre's linking of zombification and colonialism in his preface to Frantz Fanon's *The Wretched of the Earth*.

25 Patterson, *Slavery and Social Death*. As a counterpoint to how Patterson's notion of social death has been applied, see Brown, *Reaper's Garden*.

26 Wilderson et al., introduction to *Afro-Pessimism*, 8.

27 As Calvin Warren notes, in Afropessimism, this term stands for "a negative axis of being," or one might say it constitutes "ontology's necessary exclusion." See Warren, *Onticide*, 6.

28 Some in zombie studies have moved in a different direction and argue for an understanding of the zombie as posthuman. As Deborah Christie and Sarah Juliet Lauro argue, "The zombie may therefore be an apt icon for the post-human in its frustrating antipathy: Just as the post-human will always assert what the human is by that which it supposes itself to be beyond, the zombie both is, and is not, dead and alive." *Better Off Dead*, 2.

29 Two early, and opposing, viewpoints are offered in Seabrook, *The Magic Island*; and Hurston, *Tell My Horse*.

30 This line is from the film *Night of the Living Dead* (Continental Distributing, 2005).

31 Kevin Boon, "The Zombie as Other: Mortality and the Monstrous in the Post-nuclear Age," in Christie and Lauro, *Better Off Dead*, 54.

32 In references to the period of slavery, Lauro speaks of the "zombie dialectics" (i.e., the working slave and the rebellious slave—the "unity of opposites"). *Transatlantic Zombie*, 5.

33 Kee, "'They Are Not Men . . . ,'" 14.

34 Edward P. Comentale, "Zombie Race," in Comentale and Jaffe, *Year's Work at the Zombie Research Center*, 283.

35 For example, "The zombie genre can be traced to earlier critiques of capitalism, with the undead in particular appearing at a time when the shopping mall started to become a defining symbol of modernity. Zombies here would become the embodiment of a political form, one that had lost all sense of the past and had no future to speak of. . . . To become a zombie was to be devoid of any political, ethical, and social claim or responsibility . . . other than the eventual completion of the nihilistic project." Evans and Giroux, *Disposable Futures*, 17.

36 Regarding the zombie as critique of capitalism, see Giroux, *Zombie Politics*. For some attention to Romero's intent, see Crooke, "Zombies! They're Us!"; and Jen Webb and Samuel Byrnand, "Some Kind of Virus: The Zombie as Body and as Trope," in Lauro, *Zombie Theory*, 111–23.

37 Lauro, *Transatlantic Zombie*, 6.

38 David Pagano, "The Space of Apocalypse in Zombie Cinema," in McIntosh and Leverette, *Zombie Culture*, 71.

39 Tech N9ne, "Trapped."

40 Tech N9ne, "Trapped."

41 For an example from zombie studies, see Christie and Lauro, *Better Off Dead*.

42 I shape this question using a statement made in Boon, "The Zombie as Other," 54.

43 Boon, "The Zombie as Other," 54.

44 For a sense of how apocalypse functions in zombie studies, see Garrett, *Living with the Living Dead*; and David A. Reilly, "The Coming Apocalypses of Zombies and Globalization," in Castillo et al., *Zombie Talk*, 63–91.

45 Joy James and Joao Costa Vargas, "Refusing Blackness as Victimization: Trayvon Martin and the Black Cyborgs," quoted in Sharpe, *In the Wake*, 7.

46 Sharpe, *In the Wake*, 9–11, 15–16.

47 Conceived in relationship not only to Orlando Patterson's metaphor of "social death" but also to Frantz Fanon's ontological discussion: Fanon, *Wretched of the Earth*; Fanon, *Black Skin, White Masks*.

48 This turn to irrelevance over against ontological irrelevance is a modification of my argument in "Zombies in the 'Hood." Here I see the zombie's position as a much fuller disruption than I did in that article. This is my effort to refine my thinking and acknowledge the way in which the zombie short-circuits the usability of ontology as a descriptive tool with respect to Blackness/Blacks in the form of the zombie.

49 The labeling of zombies as metaphor is significant in its flexibility. As Chera Kee notes, "Imagining zombies as dehumanized things is one reason why zombies have become convenient metaphors for any number of contemporary anxieties. They are little more than empty shells, waiting for someone to project fears onto them." *Not Your Average Zombie*, 2. Kee speaks in terms of two types of zombies: "ordinary" and "extra-ordinary," with the latter entailing zombies who function at a higher state by developing "some sort of agency over their existence and defy[ing] our expectations of zombie nature" (3).

My thinking on the zombie runs contrary in a variety of ways to that of Kee, particularly as it relates to assertions of the humanity of zombies in ways that include them in the performance of personhood (e.g., dancing, drinking) in that this is to ignore the social need for the distinctiveness of the zombie. Kee is correct in noting the manner in which the trope is wrapped around populations, real and present, but I would argue she doesn't go far enough in terms of the ontological significance of this. There is, as she notes, a type of metaphysical slippage between human and nonhuman marked by her discussion of extra-ordinary zombies, yet this slippage within the social narrative is a cautionary tale concerning the presence of death. It is not a noting of anthropological commonality, but rather the pervasiveness of a biothanatological concern. To try to contain race (i.e., to read whiteness through the zombie as anything other than the non-ontological, or dead, status of Blackness) would be for me to misread the importance of irrelevance, its creation, and its configuration.

50 Boon, "And the Dead Shall Rise," 6.

51 I make this claim of existence over against ontological relevance in rela-
    tionship to Afropessimism's claims and that of Black nihilism. See Warren,
    Ontological Terror. Warren, for example, says that "blacks are the nothing of
    ontology and do not have being like those beings for whom the ontological
    question is an issue (i.e., human being)" (14).

52 As Evans and Giroux reflect, and I extend to the current discussion, "vio-
    lence seeks to curate who and what is human." Evans and Giroux, *Disposable
    Futures*, 7. For an anthropological study of zombies, see Charlier, *Zombies*.

53 Berlant and Edelman, *Sex, or the Unbearable*, vii–viii.

54 Lauro, *Transatlantic Zombie*, 25.

55 Holland, *Raising the Dead*, 6.

56 Gordon and Gordon, *Of Divine Warning*, 3.

57 Gordon and Gordon, *Of Divine Warning*, 37. Here Gordon and Gordon speak
    of the monster as "linked to the scapegoat." Also see Girard, *Scapegoat*.

58 Frank B. Wilderson III, "Blacks and the Master/Slave Relation," in Wilderson
    et al., *Afro-Pessimism*, 17–20.

59 This use of the category of "undoing" is based on a loose application of
    the idea as presented in Best, *None Like Us*. Stephen Best raises questions
    concerning the conceptual and epistemological work done by the category of
    slave/slavery within Black studies. This is beyond the concern tackled within
    this chapter. However, the idea of the "impossibility" of Blackness, noted by
    Best, offers, despite his concern with the category of "belonging," some-
    thing useful in my effort to frame the zombie as against (white) life, but of
    necessity in order to maintain human life. He speaks, for instance, of Black-
    ness's negative relationship to history over against the notion of Blackness as
    "excluded from history" (9). My argument, by extension, is that the zombie is
    such that the grammar of history as a way to gauge participation in relation-
    ship to the social world isn't possible. Zombies are outside a framework
    measurable in relationship to such categories of involvement.

60 Warren, *Onticide*, 6.

61 Frank B. Wilderson III, "The Prison Slave as Hegemony's (Silent) Scandal," in
    Wilderson et al., *Afro-Pessimism*, 74.

62 Spillers, "Mama's Baby, Papa's Maybe."

63 Spillers, "Mama's Baby, Papa's Maybe," 67.

64 Saidiya Hartman, "The Burdened Individuality of Freedom," in Wilderson
    et al., *Afro-Pessimism*, 34. Also see Hartman, *Scenes of Subjection*.

65 Brotha Lynch Hung, "D.O.A."

66 Comentale and Jaffe, *Year's Work at the Zombie Research Center*, 15.

67 Some of what I have in mind, although not with the same distinction between
    the ontological irrelevant and humans, is present in Gary Mullen's argument.
    He writes, in relationship to the television program *The Walking Dead* and
    Theodor Adorno, "The fantasy of violence against the undead is violence di-
    rected at ourselves [what I, through attention to Afropessimism, would label

'humans'], at our own vulnerability and the anonymous death that threatens all of us. The zombie genre has long served as a vehicle for the externalization of our cultural anxieties." Mullen, "Adorno, Žižek and the Zombie," 56.

68 Christina Sharpe provides an alternate way of thinking about Blacks when describing a type of subjectivity created with the modern period in relationship to slavery and postslavery terror. She defines this type of subjectivity in relationship to "monstrous intimacies" (i.e., modalities of violence out of which Black subjectivity is constituted). See Sharpe, *Monstrous Intimacies*. While I find useful framing within Sharpe's naming of the "monstrous," I move in this chapter in a different direction regarding questions of function—a shift away from intimacies, as it were, away from sexual fulfillment, social comfort, and cultural ease—to the manner in which this monstrous metaphysics serves not simply by rendering it familiar and thereby consuming, but rather as that ontological narrative that disrupts and produces a type of nausea resulting in the vomiting up of certainty and comfort. This is a different use of Black bodies, still erotic but not sexual. It is not a production of convenience through postslavery subjectivity as "fuckable" in a variety of ways—but as the trope, the cipher, the social container in which anxiety writ large can be contained. The zombie consumes this fear, eats and produces death—while posing a threat to the very structure and logic of their (read white) humanity.

69 Spillers, "Mama's Baby, Papa's Maybe," 67.

70 Wilderson, "Prison Slave," in Wilderson et al., *Afro-Pessimism*, 76–77.

71 Lanzendörfer, *Books of the Dead*, 7.

72 This is not the same predicament that Stephen Best references in regard to those "who are unfit for history," or "a people with whom we fail to identify, who appear stuck in the past beyond the reach of our historical categories; a history of people whose minds we can acknowledge but cannot know." *None Like Us*, 96.

73 Comentale and Jaffe, *Year's Work at the Zombie Research Center*, 15.

74 See, e.g., "Zombies, Run!," https://zombiesrungame.com/; "Zombie World: Park Map," https://shocktoberfest.com; and "Top Zombie Walks around the World," Travel Channel, https://www.travelchannel.com/interests/haunted/photos/top-10-zombie-walks; all accessed September 1, 2023.

75 Flatlinerz, "Good Day to Die."

76 David McNally, "Ugly Beauty: Monstrous Dreams of Utopia," in Lauro, *Zombie Theory*, 129.

77 McNally, "Ugly Beauty," 129, 130.

78 McNally, "Ugly Beauty," 130.

79 Du Bois, *Souls of Black Folk*.

80 Gangsta Boo, "Come Off Dat."

81 Esham, "The Wicketshit Will Never Die."

82 Lauro also thinks about zombies in relationship to music. For example, in her review of *The Year's Work at the Zombie Research Center*, she employs the category of "zombie jazz" in relationship to a chapter in the book dealing

with zombies and music. She writes, for instance, "The zombie's transmission is not limited to cultural appropriation but also works in a manner similar to 'sonic contagion,' by working on the listener and creating a transformative aural experience in 'the lively space of death and dissent.'" Lauro, "Asking Zombies about Zombies," 191.

83 One might think Flatbush Zombies would be a logical example of what I intend to argue regarding zombies. However, the metaphor functions in a different way for that rap group—having more to do with altered states (e.g., death of an old consciousness and rebirth of a new consciousness through psychedelic drugs) produced through certain drugs as opposed to the relationship to death I intend by using the metaphor. See the video "Flatbush Zombies Detail the Meaning behind Their Name."

84 Kangas, "History of Horrorcore Rap." Also see AllHipHop.com, "Ganxta NIP."

85 This counters the argument made by others. For example, "It is worth pointing out zombies' relation to art, which is either to ignore it or destroy it. Despite our many similarities, one thing that is distinctly different between (most) humans and zombies is their level of adroitness. Zombies are clumsy, and insensitive, with words and objects, and do not respond aesthetically or emphatically to cultural products." Webb and Byrnand, "Some Kind of Virus," in Lauro, *Zombie Theory*, 121. The difference here rests in large part on what is meant by *zombie*: I mean an embodied metaphor for death, and the authors making this claim are pointing to the material "thing" populating movies, films, and so forth.

86 Flatlinerz, "Satanic Verses."

87 Tech N9ne, "Paint a Dark Picture."

88 Tech N9ne, "Seepage."

89 Brotha Lynch Hung, "MDK."

90 Flatlinerz, "Satanic Verses."

91 This quotation entails Slavoj Žižek's perception of the zombie as recounted in Mullen, "Adorno, Žižek and the Zombie," 48.

92 Lanzendörfer, *Books of the Dead*, 18.

93 Both descriptions are from Warren, *Onticide*, 17.

94 Warren, *Onticide*, 22.

95 Zigg Zagg, "Suicidal."

96 Warren, *Ontological Terror*, 4. In this text Calvin Warren presents a critique of "black humanism," and he does so through an intriguing blend of Afropessimism and Black nihilism. And while elements of this critique—e.g., a philosophical orientation of humano-centrism as flawed (e.g., 170–71)—are compelling, there are ways in which his critique of Black humanism assumes and employs the vocabulary, grammar, and assumptions of Western humanism he seeks to challenge. I agree with Warren's presentation of Blacks as "tools," although we focus on differing dimensions of the significance of this identification. For example, Warren wants to bring back into significant discussion the assumption of "being" he believes undergirds Black humanism,

and he seeks to mark out this questioning of "being" (over against functioning) through a presentation of Black being with the word *being* crossed
out. Yet this keeps being a part of the working imaginary. As twentieth-
century artist Jean-Michel Basquiat notes in terms of crossed-out words in his
paintings, the effort to eradicate serves to highlight. It isn't clear to me that this
move on Warren's part actually captures the function of Blacks as nonhuman
devices rather than reinscribing the presentation of Blacks in relationship to
being.

97 Warren, *Ontological Terror*, 171–72.

98 Warren, *Ontological Terror*, 172.

99 Esham, "666."

100 Pokornowski, "Vulnerable Life," 19.

101 Brotha Lynch Hung, "Look It's a Dead Body." The consumption of body parts
as the practice of death isn't limited to Brotha Lynch Hung. See, for example,
the video "Flatlinerz 'Satanic Verses,'" which features the consumption of a
body. This video also features the Flatlinerz as the counterpoint to traditional
Christian imagery.

102 Lauro, *Transatlantic Zombie*, 78, 186.

103 One might think in terms of white horrorcore rap artists and what their work
says about the nature and meaning of zombification (or zombie identification) over and against the language of the social world. For example, see
Necro, *Gory Days*, and Smallz One, *Diary of a Black Widow*. Another group
within this genre, Insane Clown Posse, has a significant following—including
fans who've formed something of a horde called the Juggalos, who have been
associated with some violence. In addition to the celebration of violence and
death for the sake of violence, there is also an appeal to zombification in their
song "Zombie Slide."

Related to this, it is interesting to note that the majority of female artists
who can be clearly identified with horrorcore over gangsta rap are white
women. Much could be learned from a comparison of zombification or zombie identification with white female artists and the threat of zombification of
white women in twentieth-century zombie films. What this says about issues
of gender and social categorization in more general terms is intriguing.

104 Flavin, "The Watching Dead," 82.

105 This sentiment is similar, although the interpretative concern differs, to what
William Purcell notes when saying, "The zombie-dead have no memory of their
origins. The elevation of the cannibalistic urge is total. Memory would place
a limit upon this urge, introduce a conflicting impulse, lead to a hesitation or
perhaps even a zombie doubt. . . . The zombies embody the atavistic memory of
transgression, but they have no memory of it. There is no economy at work in
them other than the economy of hunger." "Death Drive," 4.

106 Brotha Lynch Hung, "MDK."

107 See Dawdy, "Zombies and a Decaying American Ontology."

108 Comentale and Jaffe, *Year's Work at the Zombie Research Center*, 9.

109 Zigg Zagg, "Bleeding House Mystery."

110 Gravediggaz, "6 Feet Deep."

111 It seems to be the case that this particular working through death in hip hop entails a hypermasculinity—not because there is some need for this restrictive lens but rather because even in issues of zombification as described here, the masculine is still assumed, and it is through its vectors and structuring that life and death are arranged and performed. And so, whether the grammar and vocabulary of life or of death, the male remains the assumed gendering of the metaphor.

112 Tech N9ne, "The Boogieman."

113 Gordon and Gordon, *Of Divine Warning*, 52.

114 Gordon and Gordon, *Of Divine Warning*, 50. These authors also say, "We have criticized the project of turning away from monsters and have argued for learning from them, reading the signs they signify. If our analysis is correct, then, as we gaze upon that which has fallen, which means to look upon ourselves, instead of shuddering with dread and running away, we should see our present circumstance as an opportunity to make good of what is to come. We, each generation of humanity, have been asked to save the world. We are fortunate that there may still be enough time" (120).

115 Gordon and Gordon, *Of Divine Warning*, 52.

116 This is the hook to a song by Liz Suwandi on Tech N9ne, "Cult Leader." This song is Tech N9ne's response to being compared to a cult leader.

117 Frank B. Wilderson III, "The Vengeance of Vertigo: Aphasia and Abjection in the Political Trials of Black Insurgents," in Wilderson et al., *Afro-Pessimism*, 145; italics in original. K. Aarons notes how the "anti-politics" of Afropessimism shouldn't go unquestioned but should be examined in light of other traditions of protest. See Aarons, "No Selves to Abolish."

118 Gravediggaz, "Mommy What's a Gravedigga."

119 Warren, *Onticide*, 6.

120 Comentale and Jaffe, *Year's Work at the Zombie Research Center*, 14.

121 Mathias Clasen notes that zombies trouble traditional notions of death by being "active" (e.g., moving, doing) despite "ending." See Clasen, "Anatomy of the Zombie."

122 Insane Poetry, "Faith in Chaos."

123 See Insane Poetry, "Stalkin' with the Nightbreed." In turning to what he labels "black nihilism," Warren offers a positive read of this total destruction to the extent he sees "political-philosophical death (the death of ground)," perhaps even ontological death, "as the only 'hope' for the world." More precisely, it is the only mode of hope—a spiritual hope—because it cuts against anti-Blackness by pointing toward "something" prior to the destruction of Black flesh. See Warren, "Black Nihilism," 228.

124 Gangsta Boo, "Mindstate." Thank you to Dr. Margarita Guillory for bringing Gangsta Boo to my attention.

125 Joustra and Wilkinson, *How to Survive the Apocalypse*, 138.

1   My sense of "posture" here bears some similarity to my thinking on these categories in *Interplay of Things*.

2   I reference here the ancient Greek *peri* (around) + *stellein* (to place). The use of the derivative term *peristalsis* in relationship to motion in the intestine during digestion isn't lost on me; rather, it relates to the sense of melancholia I have in mind (which connects to one of the four fundamental fluids in the body): black bile also related to digestion, balance.

3   See Tricia Rose's *Black Noise* for an early statement concerning the unique dynamics of hip hop culture.

4   Winters, "Contemporary Sorrow Songs."

5   One gets a sense of Du Bois's relationship to the spirituals in "The Sorrow Songs," in Du Bois, *Souls of Black Folk*, 180–90.

6   Du Bois, *Souls of Black Folk*, 182, 185.

7   Flatley, *Affective Mapping*, 150.

8   Flatley, *Affective Mapping*, 1.

9   M. Shawn Copeland offers an intriguing discussion of this concept of enfleshing in relationship to issues of Christology and Black suffering in *Enfleshing Freedom*.

10   Winters, "Contemporary Sorrow Songs," 14.

11   Winters, "Contemporary Sorrow Songs," 16.

12   Winters, "Contemporary Sorrow Songs," 19.

13   Tupac Shakur, "Life Goes On."

14   Flatley, *Affective Mapping*, 106–7.

15   Kristeva, *Black Sun*, 3.

16   I would argue Karla FC Holloway's insightful book *Passed On* thinks about "black death" along these lines.

17   Pete Rock & CL Smooth, "They Reminisce over You (T.R.O.Y.)."

18   Sorcinelli, "Pete Rock Cried."

19   Jay Electronica, "A.P.I.D.T.A." Jay-Z appears on this song and provides a theologized melancholic response to loss. While this is a different position than I explicate in his work elsewhere in this book, it doesn't contradict or defeat my larger argument, in that, as I've noted, there is more than one response. And one artist might generate a variety of narratives of *deathlife*. My concern is simply to highlight what I consider an underexplored and underappreciated discussion of death in hip hop.

20   Bone Thugs-N-Harmony, "Tha Crossroads."

21   Robert Johnson, "Cross Road Blues."

22   Bone Thugs-N-Harmony, "Tha Crossroads."

23   Dr. Dre, "The Message."

24   Queen Latifah, "Winki's Theme."

25   Queen Latifah, "Winki's Theme."

26   Sean "P. Diddy" Combs, "I'll Be Missing You."

27 One could easily add others to the list of artists moving in this direction. For example, see Nas, "Dance."

28 Common, "Between Me, You and Liberation."

29 The number of tracks that could be cited to make this point is substantial and would include Guru's "Eulogy."

30 Wu-Tang Clan, "America."

31 Goodie Mob, "Dead Homies."

32 Flatley provides a useful way of distinguishing affect from emotion. He writes, "Emotion suggests something that happens inside and tends toward outward expression, affect indicates something relational and transformative. One has emotions; one is affected by people or things." *Affective Mapping*, 12.

33 Alec Fraser, "A Short Look at the Etymology of 'Melancholy,'" *Lingua Frankly* 3 (2016), https://ejournals.bc.edu/index.php/lingua/article/download/9266/8574/. Also see the *Oxford English Dictionary*, "melancholia, definition 1."

34 This is a take on a line from Albert Camus's acceptance speech for the Nobel Prize. As Robert Zaretsky states it, "In his Nobel address, Camus declared that art's nobility is rooted in 'the refusal to lie about what one knows, and the resistance to oppression.'" Zaretsky, *Albert Camus*, 3.

35 Zaretsky, *Albert Camus*, 45.

36 Albert Camus, "Between Yes and No," in Camus, *Lyrical and Critical Essays*, 78.

37 Some discussions of melancholia highlight and categorize in light of this affective dimension. See, for example, Flatley, *Affective Mapping*, particularly chap. 1. Also of interest for the manner in which the affective dimension is cast in personal as well as collective terms is Holloway, *Passed On*.

38 See Bahun, *Modernism and Melancholia*, chap. 2.

39 Against this sense of limit, David McIvor speculates, in light of various murders of black bodies, on the viability and utility in practicing "a politics of mourning" by means of which it is no longer a short-term response but rather a dimension of democratic life. See McIvor, *Mourning in America*.

Big K.R.I.T. "Children of the World." *K.R.I.T. Wuz Here*. BMG Rights Management, 2010.

Bone Thugs-N-Harmony. "Tha Crossroads." *E. 1999 Eternal*. Ruthless Records, 1995.

Brotha Lynch Hung. "D.O.A." *Dinner and a Movie*. Strange Music, 2010.

Brotha Lynch Hung. "Look It's a Dead Body." *Coathanga Strangla*. Strange Music, 2011.

Brotha Lynch Hung. "Mannibalector." *Mannibalector*. Strange Music, 2013.

Brotha Lynch Hung. "MDK." *Mannibalector*. Strange Music, 2013.

Brotha Lynch Hung. "Return of Da Baby Killa." *Season of Da Siccness*. Black Market Records, 1995.

Butcher Brothaz (Scum and Insane Poetry). "Death on a Meat Hook." *M.M.M.F.D.* Lyrikal Snuff Productionz, 2018.

Butcher Brothaz (Scum and Insane Poetry). "Killing Spree." *M.M.M.F.D.* Lyrikal Snuff Productionz, 2018.

Childish Gambino. "Zombies." *Awake, My Love!* Glassnote, 2016.

Chynna. "asmr." *in case i die first*. TWIN, 2019.

Chynna. "iddd." TWIN, 2019.

Chynna. "seasonal depression." *music 2 die 2*. Honeymoon, 2017.

Chynna. "Selfie." *Chinois*. Not on label, 2013.

Common. "Between Me, You and Liberation." *Electric Circus*. MCA, 2002.

Cypress Hill. "How I Could Just Kill a Man." *Cypress Hill*. Buffhouse / Columbia, 1990.

DMX. "Bring Your Whole Crew." *Flesh of My Flesh, Blood of My Blood*. Ruff Ryders, 1998.

DMX. "The Omen." *Flesh of My Flesh, Blood of My Blood*. Ruff Riders, 1998.

Dr. Dre. "The Message." *2001*. Aftermath Entertainment, 1999.

Dr. Dre and Ice Cube. "Natural Born Killaz." *Murder Was the Case—the Soundtrack*. Death Row / Interscope, 1994.

Eminem. "Bad Guy." *The Marshall Mathers LP 2*. Effigy Studios, 2013.

Eminem. "The Real Slim Shady." *The Marshall Mathers* LP. Aftermath Entertainment / Interscope, 2000.

Eminem. "Stan." *The Marshall Mathers* LP. Aftermath Entertainment / Interscope, 2000.

Esham. "In Detroit." Psychopathic Records, 2003.

Esham. "666." *KKKill the Fetus*. Reel Life Productions, 1993.

Esham. "The Wicketshit Will Never Die." *Closed Casket*. Reel Life Productions / Warlock Records, 1994.

Flatbush Zombies. "Death 2." *BetterOffDEAD* (mixtape). ElectricKoolAde Records, 2013.

Flatlinerz. "Flatline." *U.S.A.* Def Jam / PolyGram, 1994.

Flatlinerz. "Good Day to Die." *U.S.A.* Def Jam / PolyGram, 1994.

Flatlinerz. "Run." *U.S.A.* Def Jam / PolyGram, 1994.

Flatlinerz. "Satanic Verses." *U.S.A.* Def Jam / PolyGram, 1994.

Gangsta Boo. "Come Off Dat." *Underground Cassette Tape Music*. C3Entertainment / BeatKing Made This S—t, 2014.

Gangsta Boo. "Mindstate." *Underground Vol. 3: Kings of Memphis*. Smoked Out, Street Level, 2000.

Ganksta NIP. "Horror Movie Rap." *The South Park Psycho*. Rap-A-Lot Records, 1992.

Geto Boys. "Assassins." *Geto Boys Best: Uncut Dope*. Rap-A-Lot Records, 1992.

Geto Boys. "Damn It Feels Good to Be a Gangsta." *Geto Boys Best: Uncut Dope*. Rap-A-Lot Records, 1992.

Geto Boys. "Mind of a Lunatic." *Grip It! On That Other Level*. Rap-A-Lot Records, 1989.

Geto Boys. "Mind Playing Tricks on Me." *Geto Boys Best: Uncut Dope*. Rap-A-Lot Records, 1992.

Geto Boys. "Trigga Happy Nigga." *Grip It! On That Other Level*. Rap-A-Lot Records, 1989.

Goodie Mob. "Dead Homies." *One Monkey Don't Stop No Show*. Koch Records, 2004.

Goodie Mob. "God I Wanna Live." *One Monkey Don't Stop No Show*. Koch Records, 2004.

Goodie Mob. "Still Standing." *Still Standing*. LaFace / Arista / BMG, 1998.

Grandmaster Flash and the Furious Five. "The Message." *The Message*. Sugar Hill, 1982.

Gravediggaz. "Ashes to Ashes." *The Demo Tape*. Prince Paul, 1993.

Gravediggaz. "Mommy What's a Gravedigga." *6 Feet Deep*. Gee Street, 1994.

Gravediggaz. "6 Feet Deep." *6 Feet Deep*. Gee Street, 1994.

Guru. "Eulogy." *The Ownerz*. Virgin, 2003.

Ice Cube. "My Skin Is My Sin." *Bootlegs & B-Sides*. Priority Records, 1994.

Insane Poetry. "Faith in Chaos." *Faith in Chaos (Book of Revelations)*. Grimm Reality Entertainment, 2003.

Insane Poetry. "Stalkin' with the Nightbreed." *Grim Reality*. Nastymix / Ichiban, 1992.

Jay Electronica. "A.P.I.D.T.A." *A Written Testimony*. Roc Nation, 2020.

Jay-Z. "American Dreamin'." *American Gangster.* Roc-A-Fella, 2007.

Jay-Z. "Beach Chair." *Kingdom Come.* Roc-A-Fella, 2006.

Jay-Z. "Breathe Easy (Lyrical Exercise)." *The Blueprint.* Roc-A-Fella, 2001.

Jay-Z. "The City Is Mine." *In My Lifetime, Vol. 1.* Roc-A-Fella, 1997.

Jay-Z. "Crown." *Magna Carta . . . Holy Grail.* Roc-A-Fella, 2013.

Jay-Z. "D'Evils." *Reasonable Doubt.* Priority Records, 1996.

Jay-Z. "Early This Morning." Baseline Studios, 2002.

Jay-Z. "Empire State of Mind." *The Blueprint 3.* Roc Nation, 2009.

Jay-Z. "Guilty Until Proven Innocent." *The Dynasty: Roc La Familia.* Roc-A-Fella, 2000.

Jay-Z. "Hard Knock Life (Ghetto Anthem)." *Vol. 2 . . . Hard Knock Life.* Roc-A-Fella, 1998.

Jay-Z. "Heaven." *Magna Carta . . . Holy Grail.* Roc-A-Fella, 2013.

Jay-Z. "Hova Song." *Vol. 3 . . . Life and Times of S. Carter.* Roc-A-Fella,. 1999.

Jay-Z. "Hova Song Outro." *Vol. 3 . . . Life and Times of S. Carter.* Roc-A-Fella,. 1999.

Jay-Z. "If I Should Die." *Jay-Z, Vol. 2 . . . Hard Knock Life.* Roc-A-Fella, 1998.

Jay-Z. "Kill Jay-Z." *4:44.* No I.D.'s studio, 2017.

Jay-Z. "Lucifer." *The Black Album.* Roc-A-Fella, 2003.

Jay-Z. "Moment of Clarity." *The Black Album.* Roc-A-Fella, 2003.

Jay-Z. "Ocean." *Magna Carta . . . Holy Grail.* Roc-A-Fella, 2013.

Jay-Z. "This Can't Be Life." *The Dynasty: Roc La Familia.* Roc-A-Fella, 2000.

Jay-Z. "This Life Forever." *Black Gangster.* Lightyear Entertainment, 1999.

Jay-Z. "U Don't Know." *The Blueprint.* Roc-A-Fella, 2001.

Jay-Z. "What More Can I Say?" *The Black Album.* Roc-A-Fella, 2003.

Jay-Z. "Where I'm From." *In My Lifetime, Vol. 1.* Roc-A-Fella, 1997.

Jay-Z. "Young Forever." *The Blueprint 3.* Roc Nation, 2009.

Jay-Z and Kanye West. "No Church in the Wild." *Watch the Throne.* Roc-A-Fella, 2011.

Insane Clown Posse. "Zombie Slide." *Bang! Pow! Boom!* Psychopathic Records, 2009.

Kanye West. "Diamonds from Sierra Leone." *Late Registration.* Roc-A-Fella / 2005.

Kanye West. "I Am a God." *Yeezus.* Def Jam, 2013.

Kanye West. "New Slaves." *Yeezus.* Def Jam, 2013.

Kanye West and Jay Z. "Monster." *My Beautiful Dark Twisted Fantasy.* Def Jam / Roc-A-Fella, 2010.

Kendrick Lamar. "Alright." *To Pimp a Butterfly.* Aftermath Entertainment / Interscope, 2015.

Kendrick Lamar. "BLOOD." *DAMN.* Top Dawg Entertainment, 2017.

Kendrick Lamar. *DAMN.* Top Dawg Entertainment, 2017.

Kendrick Lamar. "DNA." *DAMN.* Top Dawg Entertainment, 2017.

Kendrick Lamar. "DUCKWORTH." *DAMN.* Top Dawg Entertainment, 2017.

Kendrick Lamar. "FEAR." *DAMN.* Top Dawg Entertainment, 2017.

Kendrick Lamar. "FEEL." *DAMN.* Top Dawg Entertainment, 2017.

Kendrick Lamar. "GOD." *DAMN.* Top Dawg Entertainment, 2017.

Kendrick Lamar. "King Kunta." *To Pimp a Butterfly.* Aftermath Entertainment / Interscope, 2015.

Kendrick Lamar. "LOVE." *DAMN*. Top Dawg Entertainment, 2017.

Kendrick Lamar. "LOYALTY." *DAMN*. Top Dawg Entertainment, 2017.

Kendrick Lamar. "LUST." *DAMN*. Top Dawg Entertainment, 2017.

Kendrick Lamar. "Moral Man." *To Pimp a Butterfly*. Aftermath Entertainment / Interscope, 2015.

Kendrick Lamar. "PRIDE." *DAMN*. Top Dawg Entertainment, 2017.

Kendrick Lamar. "XXX." *DAMN*. Top Dawg Entertainment, 2017.

Kendrick Lamar. "YAH." *DAMN*. Top Dawg Entertainment, 2017.

Lil' Kim. "Pray for Me." 9. Queen Bee Entertainment / eOne, 2019.

Lil Uzi Vert. "Run Up." Label unknown, 2016.

Lord Infamous. "Anyone Out There." *Chapter 2: World Domination*. RED, Relativity Hypnotize Minds, 1997.

Nas. "Black Zombies." *The Lost Tapes*. Columbia, 2002.

Nas. "Dance." *God's Son*. Ill Will / Columbia, 2002.

Necro. *Gory Days*. Psycho+Logical-Records, 2001.

Nina Simone. "Sinnerman." *Nina at the Village Gate*. Colpix, 1962.

The Notorious B.I.G. "You're Nobody ('Til Somebody Kills You)." *Life after Death*. Bad Boy / Arista, 1997.

Pete Rock & CL Smooth. "They Reminisce over You (T.R.O.Y.)." *Mecca and the Soul Brother*. Elektra Records, 1992.

Queen Latifah. "Winki's Theme." *Black Reign*. Motown, 1993.

Rapsody. "Aaliyah." *Eve*. Roc Nation, 2019.

Robert Johnson. "Cross Road Blues." 1936. *The Complete Recordings*. Columbia, 1990.

Scarface. "Born Killer." *Mr. Scarface Is Back*. Rap-A-Lot Records, 1991.

Scarface. "Diary of a Madman." *Mr. Scarface Is Back*. Rap-A-Lot Records, 1991.

Scarface. "Game Over." *The Untouchable*. Rap-A-Lot Records, 1997.

Scarface. "Hand of the Dead Body." *Scarface*. Rap-A-Lot Records, 1994.

Scarface. "I Seen a Man Die." *The Diary*. Rap-A-Lot Records, 1994.

Scarface. "Mind Playin' Tricks on Me." *The Diary*. Rap-A-Lot Records, 1994.

Scarface. "Murder by Reason of Insanity." *Mr. Scarface Is Back*. Rap-A-Lot Records, 1991.

Scarface. "My Block." *The Fix*. Def Jam South, 2002.

Scarface. "No Tears." *The Diary*. Rap-A-Lot Records, 1994.

Scarface. "The White Sheet." *The Diary*. Rap-A-Lot Records, 1994.

Scarface and Tupac. "Smile." *The Untouchable*. Rap-A-Lot Records, 1997.

Sean "P. Diddy" Combs. "I'll Be Missing You." *No Way Out*. Bad Boy / Arista, 1997.

Smallz One. *Diary of a Black Widow*. Lyrikal Snuff Productionz, 2009.

Snoop Dogg. "Murder Was the Case." *Murder Was the Case: The Soundtrack*. Death Row / Interscope, 1994.

Snoop Dogg. "Murder Was the Case (Death after Visualizing Eternity)." *Doggy-Style*. Death Row / Interscope, 1994.

The Stop the Violence Movement. "Self-Destruction." *1000 Days, 1000 Songs*. Jive, 1989.

$uicideboy$. "Carrollton." *I Want to Die in New Orleans*. Caroline, 2018.

$uicideboy$. "Now I'm up to My Neck with Offers." KILL YOURSELF *Part XX: The Infinity Saga*. G 59 Records, 2017.

Tech N9ne. "The Boogieman." *All 6's and 7's*. Strange Music, 2011.

Tech N9ne. "Cult Leader." *All 6's and 7's*. Strange Music, 2011.

Tech N9ne. "Misery." *Misery Loves Kompany*. Strange Music, 2007.

Tech N9ne. "Paint a Dark Picture." *Killer*. Strange Music, 2008.

Tech N9ne. "Seepage." *Seepage*. Strange Music, 2010.

Tech N9ne. "Trapped." *Everready [The Religion]*. Strange Music, 2006.

Tupac Shakur. "Black Jesuz." *Still I Rise*. Death Row / Interscope, 1999.

Tupac Shakur. "Blasphemy." *The Don Killuminati: The 7 Day Theory*. Death Row / Interscope, 1996.

Tupac Shakur. "Hail Mary." *The Don Killuminati: The 7 Day Theory*. Death Row / Interscope, 1996.

Tupac Shakur. "Life Goes On." *All Eyez on Me*. Death Row, 1996.

Tupac Shakur. "Only Fear of Death." *R U Still Down?* Jive, 1997.

Tyler, the Creator. "Goblin." *Goblin*. XL. 2011.

Tyler, the Creator. "Golden." *Goblin*. XL. 2011.

Tyler, the Creator. "Nightmare." *Goblin*. XL. 2011.

Tyler, the Creator. "Radicals." *Goblin*. XL. 2011.

Tyler, the Creator. "Sandwitches." *Goblin*. XL. 2011.

Tyler, the Creator. "Sarah." *Bastard* (mixtape). Self-released, 2009.

Tyler, the Creator. "She." *Goblin*. XL. 2011.

Tyler, the Creator. "Transylvania." *Goblin*. XL. 2011.

Tyler, the Creator. "Tron Cat." *Goblin*. XL. 2011.

Tyler, the Creator. "Yonkers." *Goblin*. XL. 2011.

UGK. "Game Belong to Me." *Underground Kingz*. Jive, 2007.

Wu-Tang Clan. "America." *America Is Dying Slowly*. EastWest / Elektra, 1996.

Zigg Zagg. "Bleeding House Mystery." *Lynch by Inch*. Siccmade Music, 2003.

Zigg Zagg. "Suicidal." *Through the Eyes of She*. Siccmade Records, 2005.

Aarons, K. "No Selves to Abolish: Afropessimism, Anti-politics and the End of the World." *Mute*, February 29, 2016. https://www.metamute.org/editorial/articles /no-selves-to-abolish-afropessimism-anti-politics-and-end-world.

Abbink, J., and Göran Aijmer, eds. *Meanings of Violence: A Cross Cultural Perspective*. New York: Berg, 2000.

Abdoh, Reza. *The Hip-Hop Waltz of Eurydice*. 1990. https://vimeopro.com /adamsoch/reza-abdoh/video/156807696.

AllHipHop.com. "Ganxta NIP: The Psycho Becomes a God of Horrorcore." Accessed July 23, 2019. https://allhiphop.com/features/ganxta-nip-the-psycho -becomes-a-god-of-horrorcore-XJVDq8jP002HhTaicdI5qw.

Alvarez, Lizette, and Cara Buckley. "Zimmerman Is Acquitted in Trayvon Martin Killing." *New York Times*, July 13, 2013. https://www.nytimes.com/2013/07/14/us /george-zimmerman-verdict-trayvon-martin.html.

Anderson, Reynaldo, and Charles E. Jones, eds. *Afrofuturism 2.0: The Rise of Astro-Blackness*. Lanham, MD: Lexington, 2017.

"Andrae Crouch—Soon and Very Soon Lyrics." LyricsMania. Accessed November 21, 2013. https://www.lyricsmania.com/soon_and_very_soon_lyrics_andrae _crouch.html.

Armstrong, Edward G. "The Rhetoric of Violence in Rap and Country Music." *Sociological Inquiry* 63, no. 1 (1993): 64–78. https://doi.org/10.1111/j.1475-682X .1993.tb00202.x.

Arppe, Tina. "Sacred Violence: Girard, Bataille and the Vicissitudes of Human Desire." *Distinktion: Journal of Social Theory* 10, no. 2 (2009): 31–58. https://doi .org/10.1080/1600910X.2009.9672747.

Arya, Rina. *Abjection and Representation: An Exploration of Abjection in the Visual Arts, Film and Literature*. Houndmills, UK: Palgrave Macmillan, 2014.

Athanasopoulos Sugino, Charles. "Smashing the Icon of *Black Lives Matter*: Afropessimism and Religious Iconolatry." *Prose Studies* 40, nos. 1–2 (2018): 71–91. https://doi.org/10.1080/01440357.2019.1656400.

Bahun, Sanja. *Modernism and Melancholia: Writing as Countermourning.* Modernist Literature and Culture. New York: Oxford University Press, 2014.

Bailey, Moya. "Homolatent Masculinity and Hip Hop Culture." *Palimpsest: A Journal on Women, Gender, and the Black International* 2, no. 2 (2013): 186–99.

Baker, Ernest. "Two Insane Days on Tour with Tyler, the Creator." *Rolling Stone*, November 23, 2015. https://www.rollingstone.com/culture/culture-news/two-insane-days-on-tour-with-tyler-the-creator-233121/.

Bakhtin, Mikhail M. *Rabelais and His World.* Translated by Helene Iswolsky. Bloomington: Indiana University Press, 1984.

Banchetti-Robino, Marina Paola. "Black Orpheus and Aesthetic Historicism." *Journal of French and Francophone Philosophy* 19, no. 2 (2011): 121–35. https://doi.org/10.5195/jffp.2011.495.

Barber, Tiffany E., et al. "25 Years of Afrofuturism and Black Speculative Thought: Roundtable with Tiffany E. Barber, Reynaldo Anderson, Mark Dery, and Sheree Renee Thomas." *TOPIA: Canadian Journal of Cultural Studies*, no. 39 (Spring 2018): 136–44.

Barrett, Lindon. "Dead Men Printed: Tupac Shakur, Biggie Small, and Hip-Hop Eulogy." *Callaloo* 22, no. 2 (1999): 306–32. https://doi.org/10.1353/cal.1999.0065.

Bataille, Georges. *The Accursed Share, Vols. 2 and 3: The History of Eroticism and Sovereignty.* Translated by Robert Hurley. New York: Zone Books, 1993.

Bataille, Georges. *Eroticism: Death and Sensuality.* San Francisco: City Lights Books, 1986.

Bataille, Georges. *The Impossible.* San Francisco: City Lights Books, 1991.

Bataille, Georges. *Inner Experience.* Intersections: Philosophy and Critical Theory. Albany: State University of New York Press, 2014.

Bataille, Georges. *Story of the Eye.* Translated by Joachim Neugroschal. New York: Penguin, 2001.

Bataille, Georges. *The Tears of Eros.* San Francisco: City Lights Books, 1989.

Bataille, Georges. *Theory of Religion.* New York: Zone Books, 2012.

Bataille, Georges. *The Unfinished System of Nonknowledge.* Edited by Stuart Kendall. Minneapolis: University of Minnesota Press, 2001.

Bataille, Georges. *Visions of Excess: Selected Writings, 1927–1939.* Edited by Allan Stoekl. Theory and History of Literature 14. Minneapolis: University of Minnesota Press, 1985.

Benson, Peter. *Black Orpheus, Transition, and Modern Cultural Awakening in Africa.* Berkeley: University of California Press, 1986.

[Berkeley, Anthony Ian]. "Poetic of the Gravediggaz." Interview by Miguel D'Souza. *Bomb Hip-Hop.* Accessed July 27, 2019. http://www.bombhiphop.com/newbomb/bombpages/articles/MC/poetic.html.

Berlant, Lauren. *Cruel Optimism.* Durham, NC: Duke University Press, 2011.

Berlant, Lauren, and Lee Edelman. *Sex, or the Unbearable.* Durham, NC: Duke University Press, 2014.

Best, Stephen. *None Like Us: Blackness, Belonging, Aesthetic Life.* Durham, NC: Duke University Press, 2018.

Boluk, Stephanie, and Wylie Lenz. *Generation Zombie: Essays on the Living Dead in Modern Culture*. Jefferson, NC: McFarland, 2011.

Boxall, Peter. "Blind Seeing: Deathwriting from Dickinson to the Contemporary." *New Formations: A Journal of Culture/Theory/Politics* 89, no. 89 (2017): 192–211.

Britton, Piers. "'Mio malinchonico, o vero . . . mio pazzo': Michelangelo, Vasari, and the Problem of Artists' Melancholy in Sixteenth-Century Italy." *Sixteenth Century Journal* 34, no. 3 (2003): 653–75. https://doi.org/10.2307/20061528.

Brombert, Victor. "Kafka: The Death-Journey in the Everlasting Present." *Hudson Review* 64, no. 4 (2012): 623–42.

Brooks, Kinitra D. "The Importance of Neglected Intersections: Race and Gender in Contemporary Zombie Texts and Theories." *African American Review* 47, no. 4 (2014): 461–75. https://doi.org/10.1353/afa.2014.0062.

Brown, Vincent. *The Reaper's Garden: Death and Power in the World of Atlantic Slavery*. Cambridge, MA: Harvard University Press, 2010.

Bruce, La Marr Lurelle. *How to Go Mad without Losing Your Mind: Madness and Black Radical Creativity*. Durham, NC: Duke University Press, 2021.

Bush, Stephen S. "The Ethics of Ecstasy: Georges Bataille and Amy Hollywood on Mysticism, Morality, and Violence." *Journal of Religious Ethics* 39, no. 2 (2011): 299–320. https://doi.org/10.1111/j.1467-9795.2011.00478.x.

Bush, Stephen S. "Sharing in What Death Reveals: *Breaking the Waves* with Bataille." *Theory and Event* 18, no. 2 (2015). https://muse.jhu.edu/article/578633.

Calamur, Krishnadev. "Ferguson Documents: Officer Darren Wilson's Testimony." *The Two-Way* (blog), National Public Radio, November 25, 2014. https://www.npr.org/sections/thetwo-way/2014/11/25/366519644/ferguson-docs-officer-darren-wilsons-testimony.

Campbell, James. *Talking at the Gates: A Life of James Baldwin*. New York: Viking, 1991.

Camus, Albert. *Exile and the Kingdom*. New York: Vintage, 1991.

Camus, Albert. *Lyrical and Critical Essays*. New York: Knopf, 1968.

Camus, Albert. *The Myth of Sisyphus and Other Essays*. Translated by Justin O'Brien. New York: Vintage, 1991.

Camus, Albert. *The Plague*. New York: Vintage, 1991.

Camus, Albert. *The Rebel: An Essay on Man in Revolt*. New York: Vintage, 1991.

Camus, Albert. *Resistance, Rebellion, and Death: Essays*. New York: Vintage, 1995.

Camus, Albert. *The Stranger*. New York: Vintage, 1989.

Cappetti, Carla. "Black Orpheus: Richard Wright's 'The Man Who Lived Underground.'" *MELUS* 26, no. 4 (2001): 41–68. https://doi.org/10.2307/3185541.

Caramanica, Jon. "Angry Rhymes, Dirty Mouth, Goofy Kind." *New York Times*, May 4, 2011.

Carlevale, John. "The Dionysian Revival in American Fiction of the Sixties." *International Journal of the Classical Tradition* 12, no. 3 (2006): 364–91. https://doi.org/10.1007/s12138-006-0003-1.

Castillo, David R., David Schmid, David A. Reilly, and John Edgar Browning. *Zombie Talk: Culture, History, Politics*. Houndmills, UK: Palgrave Macmillan, 2016.

Castronovo, Russ. *Necro Citizenship: Death, Eroticism, and the Public Sphere in the Nineteenth-Century United States*. Durham, NC: Duke University Press, 2001.

Charlier, Philippe. *Zombies: An Anthropological Investigation of the Living Dead*. Gainesville: University Press of Florida, 2017.

Christie, Deborah, and Sarah Juliet Lauro, eds. *Better off Dead: The Evolution of the Zombie as Post-human*. New York: Fordham University Press, 2011.

Clark, David, ed. *The Sociology of Death: Theory, Culture, Practice*. Sociological Review Monograph Series. Cambridge, MA: Blackwell, 1993.

Clasen, Mathias. "The Anatomy of the Zombie: A Bio-psychological Look at the Undead Other." *Otherness: Essays and Studies* 1, no. 1 (2010): 1–23.

Coates, Ta-Nehisi. "The First White President." *Atlantic*, October 2017. https://www.theatlantic.com/magazine/archive/2017/10/the-first-white-president-ta-nehisi-coates/537909/.

"Code of Thug Life." Tupac.be: The Story of a Legend. Accessed December 19, 2013. https://tupac.be/en/his-world/code-of-thug-life/.

Cohen, Jeffrey Jerome. "Undead (A Zombie Oriented Ontology)." *Journal of the Fantastic in the Arts* 23, no. 3 (2012): 397–412.

Collins, Michael S. "Biggie Envy and the Gangsta Sublime." *Callaloo* 29, no. 3 (2006): 911–38.

Comentale, Edward P., and Aaron Jaffe, eds. *The Year's Work at the Zombie Research Center*. Bloomington: Indiana University Press, 2014.

Cone, James H. *A Black Theology of Liberation*. Maryknoll, NY: Orbis Books, 1986.

Connor, Marlene Kim. *What Is Cool? Understanding Black Manhood in America*. Chicago: Agate Bolden, 2003.

Copeland, M. Shawn. *Enfleshing Freedom: Body, Race, and Being in African American Theology*. Minneapolis, MN: Fortress, 2009.

Copes, Heith, Andy Hochstetler, and J. Patrick Williams. "'We Weren't Like No Regular Dope Fiends': Negotiating Hustler and Crackhead Identities." *Social Problems* 55, no. 2 (May 2008): 254–70. https://doi.org/10.1525/sp.2008.55.2.254.

Crofts, Penny, and Anthea Vogl. "Dehumanized and Demonized Refugees, Zombies and World War Z." *Law and Humanities* 13, no. 1 (June 2019): 29–51. https://doi.org/10.1080/17521483.2019.1572290.

Crooke, James R. "Zombies! 'They're Us!'" *Journal of Religion and Popular Culture* 30, no. 3 (2019): 1–15. https://doi.org/10.3138/jrpc.2017-0006.

Dalby, Andrew. *The Story of Bacchus*. London: British Museum, 2005.

Davis, Wade. *The Serpent and the Rainbow: A Harvard Scientist's Astonishing Journey into the Secret Societies of Haitian Voodoo, Zombis, and Magic*. New York: Touchstone, 1997.

Dawdy, Shannon Lee. "Zombies and a Decaying American Ontology." *Journal of Historical Sociology* 32, no. 1 (2019): 17–25. https://doi.org/10.1111/johs.12226.

De Genova, Nick. "Gangster Rap and Nihilism in Black America: Some Questions of Life and Death." *Social Text*, no. 43 (1995): 89–132. https://doi.org/10.2307/466628.

Dent, Gina, ed. *Black Popular Culture*. New York: New Press, 1998.

Dery, Mark. "Black to the Future: Interviews with Samuel R. Delaney, Greg Tate, and Tricia Rose." *South Atlantic Quarterly* 92, no. 4 (Fall 1993): 735–88.

Detienne, Marcel. *Dionysos at Large.* Translated by Arthur Goldhammer. Revealing Antiquity 1. Cambridge, MA: Harvard University Press, 1989.

Douglas, Mary. *Purity and Danger: An Analysis of Concepts of Pollution and Taboo.* New York: Routledge, 2002.

Downing, Lisa, and Robert Gillett. "Georges Bataille at the Avant-Garde of Queer Theory? Transgression, Perversion and Death Drive." *Nottingham French Studies* 50, no. 3 (2011): 88–102. https://doi.org/10.3366/nfs.2011-3.007.

Driscoll, Christopher. *White Lies: Race and Uncertainty in the Twilight of American Religion.* New York: Routledge, 2015.

Du Bois, W. E. B. *The Souls of Black Folk.* New York: Vintage Books/Library of America, 1990.

Du Bois, W. E. B. "The Souls of White Folks." In *Darkwater: Voices from within the Veil,* 29–52. New York: Harcourt, Brace, 1920.

Dyson, Michael Eric. "God Complex, Complex Gods, or God's Complex: Jay-Z, Poor Black Youth, and Making 'the Struggle' Divine." In *Religion in Hip Hop: Mapping the New Terrain in the US,* edited by Monica Miller, Anthony Pinn, and Bernard "Bun B" Freeman, 54–68. London: Bloomsbury, 2015.

Eate, Penelope. "Scribblin' Sinnin' Sh*t: Narratives of Rape as Masculine Therapeutic Performance in the Strange Case for and against Tyler, the Creator." *Journal of African American Studies* 17, no. 4 (December 2013): 529–45. https://doi.org/10.1007/s12111-012-9244-z.

Ellis, Aimé J. *If We Must Die: From Bigger Thomas to Biggie Smalls.* African American Life Series. Detroit, MI: Wayne State University Press, 2011.

Eminem. *The Way I Am.* New York: Plume, 2009.

Eustice, Kyle. "Lil B Clarifies Only the BasedGod Can Curse People." HipHopDX, May 16, 2018. https://hiphopdx.com/interviews/id.3096/title.lil-b-clarifies-only-the-basedgod-can-curse-people.

Evans, Brad, and Henry A. Giroux. *Disposable Futures: The Seduction of Violence in the Age of Spectacle.* Open Media Series. San Francisco: City Lights Books, 2015.

Fanon, Frantz. *Black Skin, White Masks.* New York: Grove, 1967.

Fanon, Frantz. *The Wretched of the Earth.* New York: Grove, 1963.

Féral, Josette, and Reza Abdoh. "'Theater Is Not about Theory': An Interview with Reza Abdoh." *TDR (1988–)* 39, no. 4 (1995): 86–96. https://doi.org/10.2307/1146485.

Field, David, Jennifer Lorna Hockey, and Neil Small, eds. *Death, Gender, and Ethnicity.* London: Routledge, 1997.

"Flatbush Zombies Detail the Meaning behind Their Name." August 22, 2012. https://www.youtube.com/watch?v=6Hj4LmV5WY0.

Flatley, Jonathan. *Affective Mapping: Melancholia and the Politics of Modernism.* Cambridge, MA: Harvard University Press, 2008.

"Flatlinerz 'Satanic Verses' [HD]." October 22, 2009. https://www.youtube.com/watch?v=SS-1xBIKw2M.

Flavin, Christopher M. "The Watching Dead: The Panoptic Gaze and Ideologic Zombies." *Journal of Cultural and Religious Theory* 13, no. 2 (2014): 82–95.

Fontana, Andrea. *Death and Dying in America.* Cambridge, UK: Polity, 2009.

Forman, Murray, and Mark Anthony Neal, eds. *That's the Joint! The Hip-Hop Reader.* 2nd ed. New York: Routledge, 2012.

Foucault, Michel. *Discipline and Punish.* New York: Vintage, 1995.

Foucault, Michel. *Technologies of the Self: A Seminar.* Amherst: University of Massachusetts Press, 1988.

Friesen, Courtney J. P. *Reading Dionysus: Euripides' Bacchae and the Cultural Contestations of Greeks, Jews, Romans, and Christians.* Studien und Texte zu Antike und Christentum 95. Tübingen: Mohr Siebeck, 2015.

Garland, Emma. "Eminem's 'Stan' Gave a Face and Name to Fandom." *Vice,* September 29, 2017. https://www.vice.com/en_ca/article/a3kj5j/eminem-stan -fandom-obsession-deep-dive.

Garnes, Lamar. "'Hustler Masculinity' as Catalyst to Self-Affirming Black Masculinity and Community in Claude Brown's 'Manchild in the Promised Land.'" *CLA Journal* 59, no. 1 (2015): 4–19.

Garrett, Greg. *Living with the Living Dead: The Wisdom of the Zombie Apocalypse.* New York: Oxford University Press, 2017.

Girard, René. *The Scapegoat.* Translated by Yvonne Freccero. Baltimore: Johns Hopkins University Press, 1989.

Giroux, Henry A. *Zombie Politics and Culture in the Age of Casino Capitalism.* Popular Culture and Everyday Life. New York: Peter Lang, 2011.

Goffman, Erving. *Stigma: Notes on the Management of Spoiled Identity.* New York: Touchstone, 1963.

Goldstein, Evan. "Performing Redemption: Metzian Theology in the Art of Kendrick Lamar." *Elements* 11, no. 2 (2015). https://doi.org/10.6017/eurj.v11i2.9066.

Gonsalves, Jenifer. "Chynna Rogers Was a Drug Addict Plagued by Demons That Haunted Her Till the Tragic End." *MEAWW,* April 9, 2020. https://meaww.com /chynna-rogers-drug-addiction-death-overdose-asap-mob-yams-mac-miller -addict-opiate-rapper.

Gordon, Jane Anna, and Lewis R. Gordon. *Of Divine Warning: Reading Disaster in the Modern Age.* Boulder, CO: Paradigm, 2009.

Gordon, Lewis R., ed. *Existence in Black: An Anthology of Black Existential Philosophy.* New York: Routledge, 1997.

"Gravediggaz Interview + Live Footage from 1994." November 10, 2010. https:// www.youtube.com/watch?v=-BCCiIREFzc.

Griffin, Greg. "Tech N9ne Explains Origin of Face Paint." Strange Music, June 7, 2016. https://www.strangemusicinc.com/2016/06/tech-n9ne/watch-tech-n9ne -explains-origin-facepaint/.

Guthrie, W. K. C. *Orpheus and Greek Religion: A Study of the Orphic Movement.* Princeton, NJ: Princeton University Press, 1993.

Guynes-Vishniac, Sean. "The Zombie and Its Metaphors." *American Quarterly* 70, no. 4 (2018): 903–12. https://doi.org/10.1353/aq.2018.0072.

Haddour, Azzedine. "Sartre and Fanon: On Negritude and Political Participation." *Sartre Studies International* 11, nos. 1/2 (2005): 286–301. https://doi.org/10.3167/135715505780282515.

Hallam, Elizabeth. *Beyond the Body: Death and Social Identity.* New York: Routledge, 1999.

Hanchard, Michael George. *Orpheus and Power: The "Movimento Negro" of Rio de Janeiro and Sao Paulo, Brazil, 1945–1988.* Princeton, NJ: Princeton University Press, 1994.

Hardwick, Jack. "Eminem Dead: Is This Proof Rapper Died Years Ago?" *Daily Star*, February 8, 2017. https://www.dailystar.co.uk/showbiz/eminem-dead-fan-theory-eminem-16982688.

Harney, Stefano, and Fred Moten. *The Undercommons: Fugitive Planning and Black Study.* New York: Minor Compositions, 2013.

Hartman, Saidiya V. *Scenes of Subjection: Terror, Slavery, and Self-Making in Nineteenth-Century America.* New York: Oxford University Press, 1997.

Hartman, Saidiya. "Venus in Two Acts." *Small Axe* 12, no. 2 (2008): 1–14.

Hegarty, Paul. "Bataille, Conceiving Death." *Paragraph* 23, no. 2 (2000): 173–90. https://doi.org/10.3366/para.2000.23.2.173.

Hewson, Mark, and Marcus Coelen, eds. *Georges Bataille: Key Concepts.* New York: Routledge, 2016.

Hiatt, Brian. "Kendrick Lamar: The *Rolling Stone* Interview." *Rolling Stone*, August 9, 2017. https://www.rollingstone.com/music/music-features/kendrick-lamar-the-rolling-stone-interview-199817/.

Holland, Sharon Patricia. *Raising the Dead: Readings of Death and (Black) Subjectivity.* New Americanists. Durham, NC: Duke University Press, 2000.

Holloway, Karla FC. *Passed On: African American Mourning Stories, A Memorial.* Durham, NC: Duke University Press, 2002.

Hubner, Laura, Marcus Leaning, and Paul Manning, eds. *The Zombie Renaissance in Popular Culture.* New York: Palgrave Macmillan, 2014.

Hunnicutt, Gwen, and Kristy Humble Andrews. "Tragic Narratives in Popular Culture: Depictions of Homicide in Rap Music." *Sociological Forum* 24, no. 3 (2009): 611–30.

Hurston, Zora Neale. *Tell My Horse.* Philadelphia: J. B. Lippincott, 1938.

Jackson, John L., Jr. "A Little Black Magic." *South Atlantic Quarterly* 104, no. 3 (Summer 2005): 393–402.

Jackson, Sandra, and Julie E. Moody-Freeman, eds. *The Black Imagination: Science Fiction, Futurism and the Speculative.* New York: Peter Lang, 2011.

James, William. *The Varieties of Religious Experience: A Study in Human Nature.* Enlarged edition, with appendices and introduction by Joseph Ratner. Gifford Lectures on Natural Religion, 1901–2. New York: Penguin Classics, 1982.

JanMohamed, Abdul R. *The Death-Bound-Subject: Richard Wright's Archaeology of Death.* Post-Contemporary Interventions. Durham, NC: Duke University Press, 2005.

Jay-Z. *Decoded.* New York: Spiegel and Grau, 2010.

Joustra, Robert, and Alissa Wilkinson. *How to Survive the Apocalypse: Zombies, Cylons, Faith, and Politics at the End of the World.* Grand Rapids, MI: William B. Eerdmans, 2016.

Kangas, Chaz. "The History of Horrorcore Rap." *LA Weekly*, November 5, 2013. https://www.laweekly.com/the-history-of-horrorcore-rap/.

Kantor, Martin. *The Psychopathy of Everyday Life: How Antisocial Personality Disorder Affects All of Us.* Westport, CT: Praeger, 2006.

Kee, Chera. *Not Your Average Zombie: Rehumanizing the Undead from Voodoo to Zombie Walks.* Austin: University of Texas Press, 2017.

Keeling, Kara. *Queer Times, Black Futures.* New York: New York University Press, 2019.

Kellehear, Allan. *A Social History of Dying.* New York: Cambridge University Press, 2007.

Kellogg, Jean. *Dark Prophets of Hope: Dostoevsky, Sartre, Camus, Faulkner.* Chicago: Loyola University Press, 1975.

Kerényi, Karl. *Dionysos: Archetypal Image of Indestructible Life.* Mythos. Princeton, NJ: Princeton University Press, 1976.

Kline, David. *Racism and the Weakness of Christian Identity: Religious Autoimmunity.* New York: Routledge, 2020.

Koch, Linda A. "Michelangelo's Bacchus and the Art of Self-Formation." *Art History* 29, no. 3 (2006): 345–86. https://doi.org/10.1111/j.1467-8365.2006.00506.x.

Koivisto, Mikko O. "'I Know You Think I'm Crazy': Post-horrorcore Rap Approaches to Disability, Violence, and Psychotherapy." *Disability Studies Quarterly* 38, no. 2 (2018). https://doi.org/10.18061/dsq.v38i2.6231.

Kornhaber, Spencer. "The Classic Queer Paradox of Tyler, the Creator." *Atlantic*, July 21, 2017. https://www.theatlantic.com/entertainment/archive/2017/07/tyler-the-creator-flower-boy-coming-out-queerness/534486/.

Kristeva, Julia. *Black Sun: Depression and Melancholia.* European Perspectives. New York: Columbia University Press, 1989.

Kubrin, Charis E. "'I See Death around the Corner': Nihilism in Rap Music." *Sociological Perspectives* 48, no. 4 (2005): 433–59. https://doi.org/10.1525/sop.2005.48.4.433.

Laderman, Gary. *Rest in Peace: A Cultural History of Death and the Funeral Home in Twentieth-Century America.* New York: Oxford University Press, 2003.

Lanzendörfer, Tim. *Books of the Dead: Reading the Zombie in Contemporary Literature.* Jackson: University Press of Mississippi, 2018.

Larsen, Nella. *Quicksand.* Edited by Deborah McDowell. American Women Writers Series. New Brunswick, NJ: Rutgers University Press, 1986.

Lauro, Sarah Juliet. "Asking Zombies about Zombies." *Journal of Modern Literature* 40, no. 2 (2016): 189–92. https://doi.org/10.2979/jmodelite.40.2.12.

Lauro, Sarah Juliet. *The Transatlantic Zombie: Slavery, Rebellion, and Living Death.* American Literatures Initiative. New Brunswick, NJ: Rutgers University Press, 2015.

Lauro, Sarah Juliet, ed. *Zombie Theory: A Reader.* Minneapolis: University of Minnesota Press, 2017.

Lavender, Isiah, III. *Afrofuturism Rising: The Literary Prehistory of a Movement.* Columbus: Ohio State University Press, 2019.

Lechte, John. "Thinking the (Ecstatic) Essential: Heidegger after Bataille." *Thesis Eleven* 52, no. 1 (1998): 35–52. https://doi.org/10.1177/0725513698052000004.

Long, Duri. "Listen to the Story: Banksy, Tyler the Creator, and the Growing Nihilistic Mindset." *Journal of Hip Hop Studies* 1, no. 1 (2014): 81–120.

Longstaffe, Moya. "A Happy Life and a Happy Death: The Quest of Camus's Etranger." *French Review* 64, no. 1 (1990): 54–68.

Majors, Richard. *Cool Pose: The Dilemmas of Black Manhood in America.* New York: Lexington, 1992.

Malone, Eddie. "Long-Lost Brothers: How Nihilism Provides Bigger Thomas and Biggie Smalls with a Soul." *Journal of Black Studies* 46, no. 3 (2015): 297–315. https://doi.org/10.1177/0021934714568893.

Martinez-Belkin, Neil. "Converting to the Church of BasedGod: Lil B's MIT Lecture Won Me Over." *Vice*, November 23, 2014. https://www.vice.com/en_us/article/68wy3r/lil-b-mit-lecture.

Mbembe, Achille. *Necropolitics.* Durham, NC: Duke University Press, 2019.

McAlister, Elizabeth. "Slaves, Cannibals, and Infected Hyper-Whites: The Race and Religion of Zombies." *Anthropological Quarterly* 85, no. 2 (2012): 457–86. https://doi.org/10.1353/anq.2012.0021.

McIlwain, Charlton D. *Death in Black and White: Death, Ritual and Family Ecology.* Cresskill, NJ: Hampton, 2003.

McIntosh, Shawn, and Marc Leverette, eds. *Zombie Culture: Autopsies of the Living Dead.* Lanham, MD: Scarecrow, 2008.

McIvor, David Wallace. *Mourning in America: Race and the Politics of Loss.* Ithaca, NY: Cornell University Press, 2016.

McLeod, James D. "If God Got Us: Kendrick Lamar, Paul Tillich, and the Advent of Existentialist Hip Hop." *Toronto Journal of Theology* 33, no. 1 (June 2017): 123–35. https://doi.org/10.3138/tjt.2017-0006.

Miguelito. "Praise and Questions: How Kendrick and Chance Talk to God in Different Ways." DJBOOTH, April 21, 2017. https://djbooth.net/features/2017-04-21-kendrick-chance-talking-to-god.

Miller, Monica R. "Real Recognize Real: Aporetic Flows and the Presence of New Black Godz in Hip Hop." In *Religion in Hip Hop: Mapping the New Terrain in the US*, edited by Monica R. Miller, Anthony B. Pinn, and Bernard "Bun B" Freeman, 198–213. London: Bloomsbury, 2015.

Miller, Monica R., Anthony B. Pinn, and Bernard "Bun B" Freeman, eds. *Religion in Hip Hop: Mapping the New Terrain in the US.* Bloomsbury Studies in Religion and Popular Music. London: Bloomsbury, 2015.

Mills, Charles. *The Racial Contract.* Ithaca, NY: Cornell University Press, 1999.

Mizruchi, Susan. "Neighbors, Strangers, Corpses: Death and Sympathy in the Early Writings of W. E. B. Du Bois." In *The Souls of Black Folk: W. E. B. Du Bois*, edited by Henry L. Gates Jr. and Terri Hume Oliver, 123–95. New York: W. W. Norton, 1999.

Moffitt, John F. *Inspiration: Bacchus and the Cultural History of a Creation Myth.* Philosophy of History and Culture. London: Brill, 2005.

Moore, Megan. "Romancing Death: The Erotics of Grief in the Old French Philomena." *Literature Compass* 13, no. 6 (2016): 400–411. https://doi.org/10.1111/lic3.12321.

Moreman, Christopher M. *Race, Oppression and the Zombie: Essays on Cross-Cultural Appropriations of the Caribbean Tradition.* Jefferson, NC: McFarland, 2011.

Morrison, Toni. *Beloved.* New York: Vintage, 2004.

Moten, Fred. *Black and Blur.* Durham, NC: Duke University Press, 2017.

Moten, Fred. "Blackness and Nothingness." *South Atlantic Quarterly* 112, no. 4 (Fall 2013): 737–80.

Moten, Fred. "The Case of Blackness." *Criticism* 50, no. 2 (Spring 2008): 177–218.

Moten, Fred. "Erotics of Fugitivity." In *Stolen Life*, 241–67. Durham, NC: Duke University Press, 2018.

Muhammad, Elijah. *Message to the Blackman in America.* Chicago: Secretarius Memps Publications, 1997.

Mullen, Gary A. "Adorno, Žižek and the Zombie: Representing Mortality in an Age of Mass Killing." *Journal for Cultural and Religious Theory* 13, no. 2 (Summer 2014): 48–57.

Murray, Albert. *From the Briarpatch File: On Context, Procedure, and American Identity.* New York: Pantheon, 2001.

"Nas—Black Zombie Lyrics." AZLyrics. Accessed June 5, 2023. https://www.azlyrics.com/lyrics/nas/blackzombie.html.

Nelson, Alondra, ed. "Afrofuturism." Special issue, *Social Text* 20, no. 2 (June 2002).

Nietzsche, Friedrich Wilhelm. *The Birth of Tragedy.* Oxford World's Classics. Oxford: Oxford University Press, 2000.

Nietzsche, Friedrich Wilhelm. *The Dionysian Vision of the World.* Translated by Ira J. Allen. Minneapolis, MN: Univocal, 2013.

Otto, Walter Friedrich. *Dionysus: Myth and Cult.* Dunquin Series 14. Dallas, TX: Spring, 1965.

Patterson, Orlando. *Slavery and Social Death: A Comparative Study.* Cambridge, MA: Harvard University Press, 1982.

Pawlett, William. *Violence, Society and Radical Theory: Bataille, Baudrillard, and Contemporary Society.* Classical and Contemporary Social Theory. Burlington, VT: Ashgate, 2013.

Peake, Bryce. "He Is Dead, and He Is Continuing to Die: A Feminist Psycho-Semiotic Reflection on Men's Embodiment of Metaphor in a Toronto Zombie Walk." *Journal of Contemporary Anthropology* 1, no. 1 (2010): 49–71.

Perrone, Charles A. "Don't Look Back: Myths, Conceptions, and Receptions of *Black Orpheus.*" *Studies in Latin American Popular Culture* 17 (January 1998): 155–77.

Philips, Chuck. "Is America Ready for 'Natural Born Killaz'?" *Los Angeles Times*, October 20, 1994. https://www.latimes.com/archives/la-xpm-1994-10-20-ca-52583-story.html.

Pickens, Therí A. *Black Madness::Mad Blackness*. Durham, NC: Duke University Press, 2019.

Pinn, Anthony B. "Do Atheists Understand and Appreciate Black Bodies?" Richard Dawkins Foundation, May 4, 2012. http://old.richarddawkins.net/articles /645837-do-atheists-understand-and-appreciate-black-bodies.

Pinn, Anthony B. "The End: Thoughts on Humanism and Death." In "Secular Theologies and Theologies of the Secular," edited by Whitney Bauman. Special issue, *Dialog* 54, no. 4 (December 2015): 347–54. https://doi.org/10.1111/dial.12207.

Pinn, Anthony B. *The End of God-Talk: An African American Humanist Theology*. New York: Oxford University Press, 2012.

Pinn, Anthony B. "End of the 'End': Humanism, Hip-Hop, and Death." In *Humanism: Essays on Race, Religion, and Cultural Production*, 127–35. London: Bloomsbury, 2015.

Pinn, Anthony B. "'Gettin' Grown': Notes on Gangsta Rap Music and Notions of Manhood." *Journal of African American Men* 1, no. 4 (1996): 61–73.

Pinn, Anthony B. "God Wears Tom Ford: Hip Hop's Re-envisioning of Divine Authority." *Media Development* 61, no. 4 (October 2014): 20–23.

Pinn, Anthony B. "'How Ya Livin'?' Notes on Rap Music and Social Transformation." *Western Journal of Black Studies* 23, no. 1 (1999): 10–21.

Pinn, Anthony B. *Humanism: Essays on Race, Religion and Cultural Production*. London: Bloomsbury, 2015.

Pinn, Anthony B. *Interplay of Things: Religion, Art, and Presence Together*. Durham, NC: Duke University Press, 2021.

Pinn, Anthony B. "Kendrick Lamar Confronts Black Death." *Houston Chronicle*, May 2, 2018. https://www.houstonchronicle.com/opinion/outlook/article /Kendrick-Lamar-confronts-black-death-Opinion-12878601.php.

Pinn, Anthony B. "'Real Nigga Conditions': Kendrick Lamar, Grotesque Realism, and the Open Body." In *Kendrick Lamar and the Making of Black Meaning*, edited by Christopher M. Driscoll, Anthony B. Pinn, and Monica R. Miller, 231–44. New York: Routledge, 2020.

Pinn, Anthony B. *Terror and Triumph: The Nature of Black Religion*. Minneapolis, MN: Fortress, 2003.

Pinn, Anthony B. "Theology after 'Hope' and 'Future.'" *American Journal of Theology and Philosophy* 40, no. 2 (May 2019): 24–47.

Pinn, Anthony B. "What Can Be Said? African American Religious Thought, Afro-Pessimism and the Viability of Hope." *Black Theology: An International Journal* 18, no. 2 (2020): 144–57.

Pinn, Anthony B. *Why, Lord? Suffering and Evil in Black Theology*. New York: Continuum, 1995.

Pinn, Anthony B. *Writing God's Obituary: How a Good Methodist Became a Better Atheist*. Amherst, NY: Prometheus Books, 2014.

Pinn, Anthony B. "Zombies in the 'Hood: Rap Music, Camusian Absurdity, and the Structuring of Death." In *Religion in Hip Hop: Mapping the New Terrain in the US*, edited by Monica R. Miller, Anthony B. Pinn, and Bernard "Bun B" Freeman, 183–97. London: Bloomsbury, 2015.

Pinn, Anthony B., and Allen Dwight Callahan, eds. *African American Religious Life and the Story of Nimrod*. New York: Palgrave Macmillan, 2008.

Platts, Todd K. "Locating Zombies in the Sociology of Popular Culture." *Sociology Compass* 7, no. 7 (2013): 547–60. https://doi.org/10.1111/soc4.12053.

Pokornowski, Steven. "Vulnerable Life: Zombies, Global Biopolitics, and the Reproduction of Structural Violence." *Humanities* 5, no. 71 (2016): 1–22. https://doi.org/10.3390/h5030071.

Purcell, William. "The Death Drive, Zombies, and Zombie Capitalism." *International Journal of Žižek Studies* 10, no. 3 (2016): 1–14.

Rampersad, Arnold. *The New Negro: Voices of the Harlem Renaissance*. Edited by Alain Locke. New York: Touchstone, 1999.

Rankine, Patrice. "Orpheus and the Racialized Body in Brazilian Film and Literature of the Twentieth Century." *Forum for World Literature Studies* 3, no. 3 (2011): 420–33.

Razinsky, Liran. "How to Look Death in the Eyes: Freud and Bataille." *SubStance* 38, no. 2 (2009): 63–88. https://doi.org/10.1353/sub.0.0046.

Reeves, Marcus. *Somebody Scream! Rap Music's Rise to Prominence in the Aftershock of Black Power*. New York: Faber and Faber, 2008.

Reynolds, Anthony M. "Urban Negro Toasts: A Hustler's View from L.A." *Western Folklore* 33, no. 4 (1974): 267–300. https://doi.org/10.2307/1498547.

Riley, Alexander. "The Rebirth of Tragedy out of the Spirit of Hip Hop: A Cultural Sociology of Gangsta Rap Music." *Journal of Youth Studies* 8, no. 3 (September 2005): 297–311. https://doi.org/10.1080/13676260500261892.

Robbins, Emmet. "Famous Orpheus." In *Orpheus: The Metamorphoses of a Myth*, edited by John Warden, 2–21. Toronto: University of Toronto Press, 1982.

Robinson, Lisa. "The Gospel According to Kendrick Lamar." *Vanity Fair*, June 28, 2018. https://www.vanityfair.com/style/2018/06/kendrick-lamar-cover-story.

Rose, Tricia. *Black Noise: Rap Music and Black Culture in Contemporary America*. Middletown, CT: Wesleyan University Press, 1994.

Rose, Tricia. *The Hip Hop Wars: What We Talk about When We Talk about Hip Hop—and Why It Matters*. New York: Civitas, 2008.

Sandoval, Victor. "Behind My Face Paint: Tech N9ne's Top 10 Face Paint Designs." *Strange Music*, October 28, 2011. https://www.strangemusicinc.com/2011/10/tech-n9ne/face-paint-tech-n9nes-top-10-designs/.

Sanneh, Kelefa. "Where's Earl? Word from the Missing Prodigy of a Hip-Hop Group on the Rise." *New Yorker*, May 23, 2011. https://www.newyorker.com/magazine/2011/05/23/wheres-earl.

Sarat, Austin, and Karl Shoemaker, eds. *Who Deserves to Die: Constructing the Executable Subject*. Amherst: University of Massachusetts Press, 2011.

Sartre, Jean-Paul. "Black Orpheus." Translated by John MacCombie. *Massachusetts Review* 6, no. 1 (Autumn–Winter 1964–65): 13–52.

Seabrook, William. *The Magic Island*. New York: Blue Ribbon Books, 1929.

Seaford, Richard. *Dionysos*. Gods and Heroes of the Ancient World. New York: Routledge, 2006.

Seale, Clive. *Constructing Death: The Sociology of Dying and Bereavement*. New York: Cambridge University Press, 1998.

Section Eighty. "Attempts to Blame Murder/Suicide on Eminem Music." Accessed July 2, 2020. https://forum.sectioneighty.com/attempts-to-blame-murder -suicide-on-eminem-music.t35887.

Serwer, Adam. "The Coronavirus Was an Emergency until Trump Found Out Who Was Dying." *Atlantic*, May 8, 2020.

Sharpe, Christina. *In the Wake: On Blackness and Being*. Durham, NC: Duke University Press, 2016.

Sharpe, Christina Elizabeth. *Monstrous Intimacies: Making Post-Slavery Subjects*. Durham, NC: Duke University Press, 2010.

Shepherd, Reginald. *Orpheus in the Bronx: Essays on Identity, Politics, and the Freedom of Poetry*. Poets on Poetry. Ann Arbor: University of Michigan Press, 2007.

Sigurdson, Ola. "Slavoj Žižek, the Death Drive, and Zombies: A Theological Account." *Modern Theology* 29, no. 3 (July 2013): 361–80.

Simawe, Saadi, ed. *Black Orpheus: Music in African American Fiction from the Harlem Renaissance to Toni Morrison*. Garland Reference Library of the Humanities 2097; Border Crossings 9. New York: Garland, 2000.

Singleton, Jermaine. *Cultural Melancholy: Readings of Race, Impossible Mourning, and African American Ritual*. Urbana: University of Illinois Press, 2015.

Smith, Daniel W. Review of *Erotism: Death and Sensuality*, by Georges Bataille and Mary Dalwood. *Journal of Religion* 67, no. 4 (1987): 595–96.

Smith, Suzanne E. *To Serve the Living: Funeral Directors and the African American Way of Death*. Cambridge, MA: Belknap Press of Harvard University Press, 2010.

Smith, Zadie. *Feel Free: Essays*. New York: Penguin, 2018.

Smuts, Aaron. "The Ethics of Singing Along: The Case of 'Mind of a Lunatic.'" *Journal of Aesthetics and Art Criticism* 71, no. 1 (2013): 121–29.

Smyth, John, and Robert Hattam. "Intellectual as Hustler: Researching against the Grain of the Market." *British Educational Research Journal* 26, no. 2 (2000): 157–75. https://doi.org/10.1080/01411920050000926.

Sorcinelli, Gino. "Pete Rock Cried When He First Heard the 'T.R.O.Y.' Sample." *Medium*, May 27, 2019. https://medium.com/micro-chop/pete-rock-cried-when -he-first-heard-the-t-r-o-y-sample-4a23b656bd45.

Spence, Lester K. *Knocking the Hustle: Against the Neoliberal Turn in Black Politics*. Brooklyn, NY: Punctum Books, 2015.

Spence, Lester K. *Stare in the Darkness: The Limits of Hip-Hop and Black Politics*. Minneapolis: University of Minnesota Press, 2011.

Spillers, Hortense J. "Mama's Baby, Papa's Maybe: An American Grammar Book." *Diacritics* 17, no. 2 (1987): 64–81. https://doi.org/10.2307/464747.

Stabler, Albert. "Punishment in Effigy: An Aesthetics of Torment versus a Pedagogy of Pain in Georges Bataille and Eric Garner." *Photographies* 9, no. 3 (September 2016): 307–26. https://doi.org/10.1080/17540763.2016.1202131.

Sterbenz, Maeve. "Movement, Music, Feminism: An Analysis of Movement-Music Interactions and the Articulation of Masculinity in Tyler, the Creator's 'Yonkers' Music Video." *Music Theory Online* 23, no. 2 (2017): 1–16. https://doi.org/10.30535/mto.23.2.6.

Stone, Michael H. *The Anatomy of Evil*. Amherst, NY: Prometheus Books, 2009.

Sule, Akeem, and Becky Inkster. "Analysing Stan: What Eminem's Ill-Fated Fictional Superfan Can Tell Us about the Brain and Mental Health." *The Conversation*, March 5, 2018. http://theconversation.com/analysing-stan-what-eminems-ill-fated-fictional-superfan-can-tell-us-about-the-brain-and-mental-health-88968.

Sule, Akeem, and Becky Inkster. "Eminem's Character, Stan: A Bio-Psycho-Social Autopsy." *Journal of Hip Hop Studies* 4, no. 1 (2017): 43–49.

"Tech N9ne—Hard (Ft. MURS)." May 21, 2014. https://www.youtube.com/watch?v=7WoWRX7076c.

"Tech N9ne—I Caught Crazy! (4EVER)." May 29, 2019. https://www.youtube.com/watch?v=uzMMfRjRdAk.

Testa, Carlo. "At the Expense of Life: Death by Desire in Balzac, Bataille, and Goethe's 'Faust.'" *Comparatist* 14 (1990): 44–61.

Touré. "An In-Depth Conversation with Kendrick Lamar." *I-D*, October 16, 2017. https://i-d.vice.com/en_us/article/j5gwk7/an-in-depth-converation-with-kendrick-lamar.

Trachtenberg, Stanley. "The Hustler as Hero." *Antioch Review* 22, no. 4 (1962): 427–34. https://doi.org/10.2307/4610464.

Utley, Ebony A. *Rap and Religion: Understanding the Gangsta's God*. Santa Barbara, CA: Praeger, 2012.

Van Deburg, William L. *Hoodlums: Black Villains and Social Bandits in American Life*. Chicago: University of Chicago Press, 2004.

Vicari, Patricia. "The Triumph of Art, the Triumph of Death: Orpheus in Spenser and Milton." In *Orpheus: The Metamorphoses of a Myth*, edited by John Warden, 207–30. Toronto: University of Toronto Press, 1982.

Wang, Oliver. "Kendrick Lamar's 'DAMN.' Is Introspective and Unforgiving." National Public Radio, April 17, 2017. https://www.npr.org/2017/04/17/524351436/kendrick-lamars-damn-is-introspective-and-unforgiving.

Warden, John, ed. *Orpheus, the Metamorphoses of a Myth*. Toronto: University of Toronto Press, 1982.

Warren, Calvin L. "Black Nihilism and the Politics of Hope." *CR: The New Centennial Review* 15, no. 1 (2015): 215–48. https://doi.org/10.14321/crnewcentrevi.15.1.0215.

Warren, Calvin L. *Onticide: Afropessimism, Queer Theory and Ethics*. Ill Will Editions, 2015. https://illwilleditions.noblogs.org/files/2015/09/Warren-Onticide-Afropessimism-Queer-Theory-and-Ethics-READ.pdf.

Warren, Calvin L. *Ontological Terror: Blackness, Nihilism, and Emancipation*. Durham, NC: Duke University Press, 2018.

West, Cornel. *Prophesy Deliverance! An Afro-American Revolutionary Christianity.* Philadelphia: Westminster John Knox Press, 1982.

Wetmore, Kevin J. *Black Dionysus: Greek Tragedy and African American Theatre.* Jefferson, NC: McFarland, 2003.

Wilde, Oscar. *The Picture of Dorian Gray.* Franklin Park, IL: World Library, 2009.

Wilderson, Frank B., III. *Afropessimism.* New York: Liveright, 2020.

Wilderson, Frank B., III. *Red, White and Black: Cinema and the Structure of U.S. Antagonisms.* Durham, NC: Duke University Press, 2010.

Wilderson, Frank B., III, Saidiya Hartman, Steve Martinot, Jared Sexton, and Hortense B. Spillers, eds. *Afro-Pessimism: An Introduction.* Minneapolis, MN: racked & dispatched, 2017.

Wilkinson, Alec. "Mr. Subway." *New Yorker*, January 11, 2009. https://www .newyorker.com/magazine/2009/01/19/mr-subway.

Wilmore, Gayraud S. *Black Religion and Black Radicalism.* Garden City, NY: Anchor, 1973.

Winkie, Luke. "20 Best Tyler, the Creator Lyrics." Red Bull, July 24, 2017. https:// www.redbull.com/us-en/top-20-best-tyler-the-creator-lyrics.

Winters, Joseph. "Contemporary Sorrow Songs: Traces of Mourning, Lament, and Vulnerability in Hip Hop." *African American Review* 46, no. 1 (2013): 9–20. https://doi.org/10.1353/afa.2013.0012.

Winters, Joseph. "Rac(e)ing from Death." *Journal of Religious Ethics* 45, no. 2 (2017): 380–405. https://doi.org/10.1111/jore.12182.

Womack, Ytasha L. *Afrofuturism: The World of Black Sci-Fi and Fantasy Culture.* Chicago: Lawrence Hill Books, 2013.

Wright, Richard. *Native Son.* New York: Harper Perennial Modern Classics, 2008.

Wright, Richard. *The Outsider.* New York: Harper Perennial Modern Classics, 2008.

Wright, Richard, and Paul Gilroy. *Eight Men: Short Stories.* 3rd ed. New York: Harper Perennial Modern Classics, 2008.

Wroe, Ann. *Orpheus: The Song of Life.* New York: Overlook, 2011.

Younger, Briana. "Introducing Chynna, the Ex-model and Ex-addict Who Can Rap Her Ass Off." *Pitchfork*, January 19, 2018. https://pitchfork.com/features/rising /introducing-chynna-the-ex-model-and-ex-addict-who-can-rap-her-ass-off/.

Youngquiest, Paul. *A Pure Solar World: Sun Ra and the Birth of Afrofuturism.* Austin: University of Texas Press, 2016.

Zaretsky, Robert. *Albert Camus, Elements of a Life.* Ithaca, NY: Cornell University Press, 2010.

Zisook, Brian "Z." "Kendrick Lamar Responds to DJBooth Article about 'DAMN' Album." DJBOOTH, April 28, 2017. https://djbooth.net/features/2017-04-28 -kendrick-lamar-god-response.

Zoladz, Lindsay. "The Power of Kendrick Lamar's 'Damn.' from Back to Front." *Ringer*, December 21, 2017. https://www.theringer.com/2017/12/21/16803970 /kendrick-lamar-damn-deluxe-reverse-order.

music and, 10–18, 46–48; social status
    and, 14; in sorrow songs tradition, 152;
    US preoccupation with, 125–26; zombies
    and, 126–28
deathlife: Afropessimism and, 29, 31–34;
    defined, 2–3; divine hustle and, 56–64;
    joy and, 97–98; in Lamar's *DAMN.*,
    74–83; melancholia and, 149–63; nar-
    rations of, 38–41; Orphic hustler and,
    66–69; paradigm of, 18–37; in Tyler,
    the Creator's work, 100–108; whiteness
    and, 4; zombies in framework of, 131–37,
    188n1
debt, slavery and colonialism and, 57
decay, Blackness and, 2
Decoded (Jay-Z album), 50
De Genova, Nick, 126
deification: in hip hop, 52–56, 172n21,
    172n24; in rap music, 48–56
demonic: Blackness as, 23; in rap music,
    167n53
Detienne, Marcel, 116
Diary of a Black Widow (Smallz One
    album), 196n103
Dionysus, 115–18, 182n24, 189n141
dis/ease, melancholia and, 160–63
divinity, hip hop and, 56–64, 172n19
Dixon, Troy, 153–54
DMX (rap group), 12, 39, 167n53
"DNA." (Lamar), 81
Douglas, Mary, 79
Dr. Dre, 12, 155, 189n8
Du Bois, W. E. B., 3, 39, 56–57, 75, 78,
    151, 160
"DUCKWORTH." (Lamar), 79–80
Dyson, Michael Eric, 52–53

Eate, Penelope, 99
economics of whiteness, 57–64
Edelman, Lee, 127, 134
elegaic response, *deathlife* and, 18
Eminem, 40, 83–89, 91–93
eroticism and death, 99, 102–15; bacchic
    framing of, 116–18
Esham (rap artist), 139, 141
Eshu (African deity), 63–64
Evans, Brad, 125–26
Evans, Faith, 156–57

evil, Lamar's perception of, 77–78
existentialism, in rap music, 75–76, 152–59

Fanon, Frantz, 27, 175n79, 192n47
"FEAR." (Lamar), 77, 79, 81–82
film, zombies in, 143–47
Five-Percent Nation, 172n24
Flatbush Zombies (rap group), 195n83
Flatley, Jonathan, 151–52, 199n32
"Flatline" (Flatlinerz), 126–27, 189n11
Flatlinerz (rap group), 127, 138–40
Flavin, Christopher, 143
Flower Boy (Tyler, the Creator album),
    180n2, 181n15
Floyd, George, 7
4:44 (Jay-Z album), 60
Franklin, Aretha, 154
Friesen, Courtney, 182n26
fugitivity, Blackness and, 28

Gangsta Boo (rap artist), 138–39, 147
gangsta rap: death in, 11, 126; zombies in,
    126–28
Ganksta NIP (rap artist), 144
gender: bacchic impulse and, 115; in
    hip hop culture, 118–20, 165n2,
    189n9; horrorcore rap and, 196n103,
    197n111
Geto Boys (rap group), 49
Giroux, Henry, 125–26
"Goblin" (Tyler, the Creator), 99–100
Goblin (Tyler, the Creator album), 98–108,
    112, 180nn2–3, 181n15
"GOD." (Lamar), 81
Goffman, Erving, 7–8
Good Friday, biblical story of, 74
Goodie Mob (rap group), 39, 158
Good Kid, M.A.A.D. City (Lamar
    album), 82
Gordon, Jane Anna, 134, 145, 197n114
Gordon, Lewis, 134, 145, 197n114
Gory Days (Necro album), 196n103
gospel music, 46–48
Grandmaster Flash and the Furious Five
    (rap group), 151–52
Gravediggaz (rap group), 127, 144, 146,
    189n10, 189n13
Gravedigger (rap artist), 126–27

.